Leave it to Me

Don Murfet

AN ANVIL PUBLICATIONS
PAPERBACK

© Copyright 2004

Don Murfet

First published in 2004

A CIP catalogue record for this title is
available from the British Library

ISBN 0-9547280-0-9

Anvil Publications
www.anvilpublications.co.uk

Printed and Bound in India by Gopsons Papers Ltd.

Contents

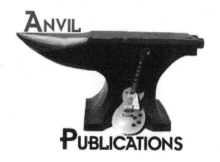

CHAPTER ONE

1963 – 1994

LED ZEPPELIN

'Bonzo's dead,' said a shaky voice on the phone. It was Ray Washbourne – the PA to Peter Grant, Led Zeppelin's manager.

The enormity of his words took a few moments to sink in. And then that cold fact took its grip on my guts. I was sickened. John Bonham was such a lovely bloke; I'd been through so much with him...It was a shock. But there was no time for grief – not yet. But maybe I'm starting at the end? Before going into John's tragic death, I'll explain how I came to be involved with Led Zeppelin and how I had come to be so close to that legendary band's members.

*   *   *

They say first impressions last – and that's certainly true of my first encounter with Peter Grant. The name Peter means 'rock', and no-one ever epitomised 'rock' – in both senses of the word – like Peter. He was physically huge; an enormous hulk of a man, a former wrestler who, on that fateful night in 1964, had landed the job of Road Manager for the evening's show at Edmonton's Regal Theatre. With wild American Blues legend Bo Diddley and the latest teen sensations, a louche and motley bunch of kids called The Rolling Stones, on the bill it wasn't going to be an easy ride. But old Peter was a rock in the face of any crowd, no matter how unruly. And, as I was to find out later, he was 'rock' personified in other ways too – notably in his unrelenting passion for what became known as 'rock 'n' roll habits'. But more of that later...

I wasn't exactly uninitiated in the esoteric ways of the music business behind the scenes and I'd turned up to take care of someone else on the bill: Tommy Roe, who'd just scored a big hit with *Sheila* and who was represented in the UK and US by G.A.C., the massive American agency into which my mentor Vic Lewis had tied his own London firm. Used to breezing my way unquestioned past Security to the backstage area, I strolled through the front-of-house and made my way easily to the pass door (the door at the side of the stage leading into the auditorium that was a feature of all the old theatres). There I was accosted by this towering giant with piercing eyes and a Mandarin-style moustache and beard who growled, 'Who are you and where do you think you're going?'
I gave him my name and humbly explained that I there was there to look after Tommy Roe and after a painfully long and, on my part at least, very tense pause, the future legend shrugged and let me pass with a gruff, 'OK.'

Sad to say, the strikingly vibrant Regal Theatre's days as a Rank cinema, concert hall and focus of local social life are long gone. Like so much that we took for granted as part of the rock 'n' roll life's rich fabric, it's been torn apart and now, where guitars and drums rang out almost nightly, you only hear the ring of cash registers. No longer Regal – it's now a lowly local supermarket. Thinking back on it, I and associates like Peter Grant, Don Arden, Mickey Most and countless others were incredibly lucky to have been starting out in the music business in the mid-sixties – a time now acknowledged as one of the most creative, vibrant and innovative that British rock 'n' roll has ever seen. At the time, though, like the people who saw no heritage of great import in the old Regal Theatre, we just saw every epoch-

6

making event as another 'day at the office'. If only we'd known the significance of the times we were living in – and our impact on them!

It may not have seemed the most auspicious of introductions, but increasingly my life was to become intertwined with Peter's – and those of the bands with whom we both became associated. Within a year or so I found myself sharing the same London business address – 35 Curzon Street – with Peter and a whole gang of blokes whose names now read like a Who's Who of major music business figures: Don Arden, Vic Lewis, Micky Most, Pat Meehan, Barry Clayman, Ken Pitt, Alan Blackburn, Don Black, Barry Dickens, Irene Korf, Colin Berlin and Richard Cowley.

I was still working for Vic – and Peter was the road management supremo for another soon-to-become-legendary rock figure: Don Arden. Don was one of the new and seminal breed of band promoters that the Sixties sired – dynamic, charismatic, creative and often even more outrageously flamboyant than the artists they looked after. With a fast growing stable of the hottest, brightest stars, including The Small Faces and Black Sabbath, Ozzie Osbourne's Birmingham rockers, who were to become the definitive 'Heavy Metal' act, Don was something of a star himself. Incidentally, his daughter Sharon later managed and married Ozzie. And the more he shone, the more trouble gravitated towards him, wherever in the world he showed his face. Which, of course, was why he needed to be surrounded by brick shithouses of men like Peter and his equally imposing colleague, Pat Meehan. No matter what he got up to, you simply didn't cross Don Arden – and over the years there were many who rued the day they'd tried. One hapless accountant springs to mind. He made the (almost literally) fatal mistake of mismanaging Arden's financial affairs in the early 70s. Don and his son David weren't the types to call the cops. They called the shots.

I don't recall exactly what that poor accountant's fate was, other than that he was held prisoner for a while – but I'm sure their vengeance was swift and terrible. It was certainly illegal, because David ending up doing time for it and Don fled to the States, just out of reach of the long arm of British law. As Arden's right hand man, and a force to be reckoned with in his own right, Peter was a formidable character – and one you definitely wanted on your side. Although I never had any business dealings with him, I always got on well with Don Arden and found him great company.

Another nascent manager/producer star saw the value of having a man of Peter's magnitude in his orbit – and soon Peter was installed at the Oxford Street offices of one Mickey Most (now sadly departed) and Ron Madison. Mickey was riding his first wave of success – and it was a big one. Not only was his record label, RAK, immensely successful with hits by the likes of Donovan and Herman's Hermits but he was also handling seminal acts such as The New Vaudeville Band and, crucially, The Yardbirds – a group whose success at this stage was to lead to undreamable prosperity in the future for Peter.

Things were taking off for everyone around me – and by late '65 I thought it was time I struck out on my own. I knew all about the hassles the most popular acts faced – and the three most important of them were security, privacy and transport. With my new venture I was going to solve all three at a stroke, fill what I saw as a gaping hole in the market – and, with a bit of luck, fill my pockets at the same time!

I was right. Artistes Car Services, as I christened my new enterprise, was an immediate success. The core of the idea was to offer performers a genuinely luxurious ride to and from their concerts with a minimum of fuss and total, uncompromised security and discretion. This proved to be exactly what the new breed of pop stars needed as their fans' adulation began to feel like persecution. That year some very big people rode in our sumptuously appointed limos, including The Beatles and Donovan among many others in an increasingly galactic list that began to read like a Who's Who of British rock 'n' roll. But undoubtedly the biggest arse to grace the seats of my fleet of cars was that of Peter Grant! From 1966 onwards he relied on us to get his fledgling acts from A to B (and often via C and D and all the way to Z!) and back again without incident or embarrassment. Of course, that meant we saw each other on a regular basis and, with so much in common, it was almost inevitable that we became close friends. What it really all boiled down to was trust. A simple thing, you might think – but a rare and valuable commodity in that exciting, yet frightening dog-eat-dog time and place. Ultimately, Peter knew that he could rely absolutely on me – and, by association, on the team of level-headed, broad-minded, strong but utterly discreet men I employed. The old-school rule books had gone out of the window and he knew we could cope with any of the bizarre problems this new untamed form of showbiz could throw up. More importantly, he knew we could make them go away.

Nevertheless, it soon became apparent that many of these problems were actually of Peter's own making – certainly he increasingly involved us in circumstances that had little to do with our original remit: chauffeuring the artists to the gig and back again and protecting them all the way. Drawn into all sorts of disputes from run-ins with the authorities to 'withdrawing' illegal bootleg albums from record shops, I found myself in the dubious role of Peter's personal 'troubleshooter'. I suppose it was a compliment really. It showed his utter faith in my integrity – a faith that was, though I say it myself, completely justified. However, over the following years, it embroiled me in difficult personal, even intimate, situations that, often, I could have done without - even if Peter had convinced himself that he was merely acting in his artists' best interests. For example, if a band member lost interest in a particular girlfriend, it was our job to make her *persona non grata* and ensure that she was no longer on the scene. Cast-off groupies were 'cleansed' from the band's entourage with ruthless efficiency - the unfortunate girl concerned would suddenly find that the backstage doors and party venues that had once magically opened for her were now firmly closed - and often slammed - in her face. But it wasn't only people who were intimate with the band who we had to remove. Sometimes Peter simply took an instant dislike to a face in the crowd for no apparent reason. Ours was not, as they say, to question why, and it was down to me to get the unfortunate owner of the face he'd taken exception to removed. Of course I tried to elicit some sort of rationale from the great man as to what constituted a 'threat to security' – but in the end it was a lot easier to just 'do it' than to try and reason with him.

All the hassle and heartaches paid off handsomely though when Peter asked me to take on the Road Management duties for the forthcoming US tour of his new management signings – The Jeff Beck Group. It was quite an honour. Probably the first 'supergroup', the band comprised four established faces (two quite literally!) who were destined for a place among the greatest in the history of rock 'n' roll: former Yardbirds guitar hero Jeff Beck, of course, future Faces and Rolling Stones strummer Ronnie Wood on bass, new boy Tony Newman on drums and a fresh-faced former grave-digger with a voice that sounded like it was made from the gravel he dug – one Rod Stewart. Like everything else in the music business in those days (and right up to this day I suspect) the job description of Road Manager was an elastic one. I imagine even the uninitiated would expect it to involve overseeing the hotel bookings, flights, shipping, trucking, setting up, soundchecking and breaking down the PA, lighting and staging at each venue. In fact most of that would be handled by the Roadies themselves – and the Road Manager would only get 'hands on' when there were problems to sort out, such as equipment going astray. Less obvious are what you might call 'ancillary' duties – and they were often the least predictable, most onerous and prone to disaster. There were disputes and fights to settle, bills to pay, concert promoters to harangue and haggle with over percentages of gross and 'dead wood' to keep an eye on ('dead wood' was the unsold tickets, which had to be meticulously checked because they were our only means of verifying the number of tickets sold – and therefore the percentage owed to the band). And then there were services of a more personal and often illicit nature that are always in demand with a rampant rock group pumped full of adrenalin and testosterone after a great gig. I'm sure I don't need to spell out the exact nature of such missions! Suffice to say I jumped at the job and threw myself into it wholeheartedly as always!

I'd already met Jeff Beck some years before – he'd turned up at the office in his pre-Yardbirds days several times while Vic Lewis was courting him for a management deal. Jeff had recorded a single called 'That Noise' and CBS were keen to sign him but he hesitated before signing just long enough to get another offer. As you can imagine, Vic was gutted when 'the one that got away' joined the Yardbirds and began his meteoric rise to stellar status. That single never saw the light of day – and nor did Vic's hopes of managing Jeff Beck. It turned out that Vic's loss was Peter Grant's very lucrative gain – and it was my baptism of fire in the sheer madness and barely contained anarchy that was life on the road in the

States with one of the original hair-raisingly hedonistic rock supergroups.

I didn't meet the rest of Jeff's boys until our rendezvous at Heathrow. Like a dog urinating to mark out its territory, I knew I had make my mark immediately – stamp my authority on the lot of them. If I didn't I might as well not get on the plane. I should explain that some of the Road Manager's more banal duties are also the biggest nightmares. Like coaxing a hideously hung-over musician from his hotel bed and getting him onto the plane/tour bus/stage on time. They don't thank you for it and a lot of the time you had to be the 'bad guy'. In fact at times I felt like some kind of satanic scoutmaster!

The high jinks started almost the second that the plane levelled out at cruising altitude and the seat belt lights went out. The boys were in a particularly playful mood, like a bunch of schoolboys on an outing with teacher – although considerably less innocent. They seemed set on testing me; goading me to see just how far they could push me and at times it was hard to tell the playing up and play-acting from whatever would pass as normal behaviour in the unique world of a successful rock musician, which is, as far as I can tell, one gigantic amusement park. I took the wind-ups and pissing about with good humour until suddenly the atmosphere of levity dropped like a.... well like a Led Zeppelin...Young Rod was squirming in his seat, clearly overcome with nausea. As he clutched his stomach in agony and gagged and heaved those dry retches that make everyone around feel sick too, a couple of concerned fellow passengers got out of their seats and rushed to his aid. Right on cue he shuddered, convulsed and spewed forth a torrent of evil-looking grey vomit all over his would-be Good Samaritans. Bet that was the last time they rushed to the assistance of an unruly rocker! It turned out that the disgusting globby mess that splattered out of Rod the Mod's mouth wasn't vomit at all – just an unpleasant papier maché of superstar spittle and the paper he'd been chewing up since take-off. Not, I imagine, that this was much consolation to the people whose clothes were soaked in it!

Unfortunately that was just the start. They got down to some serious drinking and some bright spark suggested a game of 'Kelly's Eye.' What that involves you really don't want to know. OK, maybe you do! Here's how it worked. One of the group, sitting in the window seat (which is important) would call out weakly for a stewardess (and they were generally female in those days. Somehow the game wouldn't have the same appeal these days with as many males as females in the flight crew). When the stewardess arrived and asked what was wrong, the occupier of the window seat would mumble incoherently in reply. So she'd lean forward, cocking an ear to hear what he was trying to say. He'd groan something equally unintelligible under his breath. Keen to do her duty and help an ostensibly sick passenger, she'd lean further forward, now almost prone across the aisle seat. He'd gasp helplessly. And what the hapless stewardess took to be the whimper of a seriously ill man was actually the strain of stifled laughter – because the further she stretched over, the higher up her thighs her skirt would ride and the better the view for the rest of the group, ogling enthusiastically from behind. I don't think the name of the game needs any further explanation! And from there things went downhill fast. Halfway into the flight the band were considerably higher than the plane that carried them. Their raucous laughter, shouting – screaming even – was getting out of control. And it was out of order. It was time, I decided, to draw the line. Not the kind of line usually associated with rock stars – but it certainly got right up their noses! Ironically, the relative newcomer to rock, Tony Newman, was by far the most obnoxious of the four. So I decided to single him out – make an example of him; lay my cards on the table and see if he'd call my bluff (and it really, really was not a bluff!).

I lunged across the aisle and loomed over the back of his seat – and my face was right in his face, livid with pent-up fury. The hearty guffawing instantly shrivelled to the sheepish titter of chastised schoolboys (or boy scouts).
'Listen you!' I roared at the top of my voice, 'Two of us can play this game – and I don't mean Kelly's bleedin' Eye! We can do this tour two ways. I could make it hard for you – really hard – or...we could learn to work together!'

It worked. I suppose that when my words sunk in they thought about just how unpleasant I could make their life on the road – how their post-gig sexual and chemical proclivities could be curtailed by a martinet of a Road Manager bent on laying down the law to the letter of their contracts. They had little option but to toe the line for a while. I'd made my point – and made my mark. Temporarily at least, I'd tamed the wildest of party animals and for the rest of the tour The Jeff Beck Group were, if not exactly model citizens, admirably civilised. They'd learnt a valuable lesson from that little *contretemps* – and more importantly, so had I.

That Jeff Beck tour set the tone for my future life on the road. The hassles, the chaos and the loose cannons would be the same despite that fact that in my career I've worked with a diverse range of artists that includes Led Zep, David Cassidy, Adam and the Ants and The Sex Pistols among many others. In the end, as I learnt, the musical trends may come and go but that quintessential rock 'n' roll attitude, like the song, remains the same. And long may it stay that way! Frankly, it wouldn't have been much of a challenge if I'd been in charge of a bunch of choirboys – and nor would it have been as lucrative!

14

The attitude was a constant – and so were the hassles. They might be different in their precise nature, but I learned to anticipate the unexpected so that in the end there wasn't much that could shock or faze me. I became an accomplished 'firefighter'. When things got heated I cooled the situation. When tempers blazed I extinguished them and when bands' self-destructive urges looked like making them crash and burn I usually managed to control the fire without losing the vital spark that made these guys legendary. I think it was Neil Young who said it's better to burn out than fade away – well I'm not so sure, but I certainly got the impression that most of Zep (with whom I was to work later on) and the Jeff Beck Group would have gone along with that philosophy! Sadly, there were to be times when I couldn't prevent a great talent from falling prey to his own volatility and unquenchable lust for excess, more of which later...

A perennial problem that always rankled with the acts was when greedy agents booked them into venues that were entirely unsuitable – in terms of size, access, acoustics or even sheer mortal danger for fans and performers alike. One of Jeff and the lads' gigs was a perfect example of the bookers' total lack concern for their performers' image and style of music. To their horror they found that they'd been booked to perform at a kids' summer camp – one of those places where American parents dump their stroppy teenagers for the school holidays. Playing to an audience of thirteen and fourteen-year-olds was not a job for scrious rock musicians – that was for children's entertainers and cutesy pop performers. To say the band were unhappy would be an understatement – and, when the inevitable on-stage shenanigans started and they began to treat the gig as little more than a private party, the organisers and their charges were unhappier still. Always the wild card, Tony Newman abandoned his drum kit and kept up the percussion as he staggered from table top to table top by banging his sticks on anything that would make a noise – bottles, pipes, chairs, you name it. At least he stopped short of banging out a paradiddle on a teenage head – well, at least I think he did! And then Jeff and Woodie joined in. Not to be outdone by their drummer's antics, they picked up a fire extinguisher and liberally doused the first few rows of the audience with foam. Talk about dampening the audience's spirits - sheer bloody pandemonium broke out! The organisers were evidently not amused. As they picked up the phone to call the police I realised that it was time for action. The ability to think on your feet is one of the first attributes anyone should look for in a prospective Road Manager – and I pride myself on the number of scrapes and brushes with the law I got my bands out of over the years. On this occasion a quick getaway was called for – my speciality!

I bundled the band out of the hall and into the waiting Limousine as quickly as I could and the sleek stretched motor screeched out of the compound in a mad dash for the state line and immunity from arrest. We made it in the nick of time – but that wasn't much consolation to my assistant, Henry (the Horse) Smith, who'd had to stay behind with the truck and all the band's gear. When the cops arrived they didn't see the funny side. Quite the contrary, in fact, because they were determined to confiscate anything they could lay their hands on in an attempt to force the band to come back and face the music. And when you consider the vast value of a major band's touring technology, we probably would have had no alternative but to turn ourselves in and cough up the fines and/or backhanders, if not face jail sentences, to get it all back. But the appropriately named Henry had horse sense. He claimed that all the equipment belonged to him and that he'd simply lent it to the group for the performance and didn't expect to ever see them again. Unbelievably the police swallowed the story and let him – and the band's equipment – go free. All we lost was Ronnie's bass guitar and a few

16

odds and sods – not that that stopped the boys sulking about it for a day or two! I've had better times – but few of them were entirely without some kind of incident...

...Like the Jeff Beck Group's gig at Schenectady Hall in upstate New York, for example. It seemed that things were really looking up when we heard that Peter Grant's latest managerial signing – Led Zeppelin – were also on the American east coast at the time on their inaugural US tour and arrangements were quickly made for the two bands to hook up for some serious partying. Led Zep and the Jeff Beck Group – talk about an explosive combination!

Those two now legendary bands may have been volatile – but their signing was a major coup for Peter. The downside, for Peter and for me was that great talents are notoriously 'too hard to handle', as the song goes. In Beck, he had one of the world's greatest guitarists and a proven record seller – temperamental, often stroppy but always ready to pull a rabbit out of the hat. In the end, though, it was Zeppelin that was to be Peter's great cash cow – and one he'd take to rich new pastures and milk for all it was worth.

Right from the off, everyone knew that Led Zeppelin was a cut above the rest of the rockers – a true supergroup in the making. Formed by Jimmy Page, one of the key songwriter/producers of his generation, from the ashes of The Yardbirds, Zep blended vintage blues and heavy rock with consummate musicianship and made all those elements add up to something far greater than the sum of their parts. Added to Page's prodigious talents was lead singer Robert Plant. And what a find he was! An imposing handsome blond Viking of a man whose sex appeal was as powerful as his thunderous, yet soulful and vulnerable voice. John Paul Jones on bass was no less gifted – both at laying down the deep, throbbing basslines that melded the Zep sound together and at laying the countless women that fell willingly at his feet. And then there was Bonzo on drums. I would grow to love John Bonham (that was his real name) dearly. He was a good - even great - man; a funny man and a great friend. He was also one of the wildest I've ever known – and I've known some very wild men in my time, as you can tell from other chapters in this book! I'd describe him as a playboy – but the term has too many suave and pretentious associations to sum up an irrepressible character like Bonzo. He was a walking bag of contradictions: a gentle soul who was nevertheless the epitome of the 'wild man of rock' with an iron constitution capable of withstanding his prodigious and insatiable appetite for booze and drugs. His formidable drumming was the kingpin of Zep's musical direction and rightly made him a rock legend – but his offstage antics were equally hardhitting and were to become equally famous.

Given their origins, it was almost inevitable that media interest in the band verged on the rabid – even before the release of their first album. And if the critics were a little sniffy about them at first, the live audiences fell in love with Zep at first sight and sound! America was similarly smitten, thanks largely to the heavy radio promotion of *Whole Lotta Love*, (later the Top of the Tops theme for many years – and recently revived in that role!).

Anyway, Zep were coming along on The Jeff Beck Group's tour bus to the Schenectady Hall gig – but it soon became clear that they weren't just there to appreciate the performance. Richard Cole, their notorious Road Manager, lost no time at all in getting up to mischief with the rest of Zep following his lead. While Jeff, Rod, Ronnie and Tony were grooving away on stage the majestic Zep boys held court in the dressing room with numerous excited females in attendance. Knowing their reputation, you'd have thought it would be John Paul, Jimmy or Bonzo who'd make the first lecherous leap on the compliant assembly of girls – but no, it was Richard Cole. When a pleasantly plump, rather innocent-looking girl walked shyly through the dressing room door in search of her rock gods, Richard lunged at her and literally swept her off her feet, spinning her upside down and rubbing his face lasciviously in her crotch. And that was just for starters. For all I know she enjoyed it – but I'm pretty sure the victims of the next little prank weren't at all happy.

One of the boys, unnoticed in a corner of the dressing room, decided to urinate into a big jug of Coca Cola – and, as you've probably guessed, he offered this foul tainted chalice to every hapless girl who stepped tentatively into the room in the hope of having some contact with her heroes. Poor girls, I thought. It wasn't funny. Just crude. And cruel. But it wasn't the worst abuse of these innocents who threw themselves at the rock 'n' roll animals they lionised. I'd just about had enough of that kind of behaviour and had stepped outside with Peter for a breath of fresh air – both literal and metaphorical – only to walk straight into a distraught young girl as she emerged from the toilets in floods of tears. Clearly grateful to find two potential knights in shining armour, she turned to us and wailed, 'There's a guy in there who's just been groping me!'
Fired up with righteous indignation, Peter and I stormed into the toilets (or should I say 'Rest Rooms' since we were in America!) and immediately confronted the groper – who was about to regret the sexual assault bitterly because he, and I, were introduced to Peter's celebrated 'kicking trick'. This involved taking the terrified bloke by the scruff of the neck and kicking him in the shins, again and again. And then again and again. And again. And again - boot cracking against bone with a rhythmic precision that Bonzo would have been proud of. This treatment was followed up with Peter's other mode of administering punishment – namely a stiff four fingers shoved into and under the ribcage, which really takes your

breath away! As I've mentioned, Peter was a whale of a man, about six foot two and weighing in at something over 300lbs. A kicking from Peter was like one from a carthorse – and one that the groupie groper wasn't going to erase from his memory or his shins for a helluva long time! After a minute or so, that must have seemed like a lifetime to the groper, Peter finally laid off, dragged the guy's limp and crippled form to the door and hurled him through it like the sack of shit he clearly was. Unlike a sack of shit, however, he actually bounced off the floor before hauling himself painfully to his feet and wobbling off, dazed and confused, in the immortal, and accurate, words of the Led Zep song. The message came over loud and clear: urinating in a bottle was one thing, but nobody messed with Zep's fans when Peter was around, whether they were male or female.

The two bands' paths were to cross several times over the next few days as their respective tours wended their way across the States – but it was at the Singer Bowl, a massive sports complex doubling as a concert venue just outside New York's Flushing Meadows that things really came to a head. Jeff and the boys were supporting America's flavour of the month, Vanilla Fudge. More significantly, as it turned out, Alvin Lee's new band, Ten Years After, were opening the star-studded bill. The Zep boys and their entourage said they'd be there to lend Jeff a bit of moral support. I thought that was quite touching to begin with – such selfless solidarity between two of the UK's best bands while they were touring on foreign turf. But of course it wasn't as simple – or as innocent as that. Nothing ever was! Hindsight being 20:20, maybe I should have sussed that there was more to their eagerness to attend than geeing their mates along. In fact that had nothing to do with it. The Zep boys were there to get their own back on Lee for some pretty nasty remarks he'd once made about Jimmy Page – and Jeff Beck's roadies seemed happy to help them wreak their revenge, egged on, inevitably, by Bonzo and Richard Cole. Chick Churchill – one of Ten Years After's associates – was unlucky enough to be caught without backup in a locker room by a vengeful rabble of roadies who scared the crap out of him before ruthlessly stripping him of his clothes. Then they stripped him of his dignity by dumping him naked and trussed like a lamb to the slaughter in the starkly lit corridor outside.

Next it was Ten Years After's turn for the revenge of Zeppelin. Hidden in the anonymity of the shadows in a corner in front of the stage, the Zeppelin crew pelted Alvin Lee mercilessly from the moment he took the stage with anything that came to hand – including hot dogs, burgers, orange juice and probably much messier and more painful missiles. It was glorious! Lee and his band had no idea who the mysterious assailants in the shadows could be. The shower of debris stole their thunder, undermining the storming performance they'd had their hearts set on and, understandably enough, mediocrity was all they could muster.

In retrospect, Peter and Jimmy – the two partners in crime – had to be behind this. It was their way of saying, 'Don't ever mess with the Zeppelin!'

If that had been the sum total of their retribution for an off-colour comment, I guess it would have been 'fair dos'. But they'd already planned a masterstroke that would add insult to injury. Of course, as far as the audience was concerned, Led Zep's joining The Jeff Beck Group on stage was an impromptu jamming session. I knew different! Having ruined Alvin Lee's set, a band that hadn't even been booked to play was about to steal the show. And steal the show they did. But even the Led Zep boys hadn't planned the finale that was to be the highlight of the night!

21

Bonzo had been at the backstage booze. Nothing unusual about that – or about the fact that, drunk as a lord, his drumming on the fast blues the galaxy of rock stars was playing was as blisteringly bang on the nail as ever. What was a bit unusual was the fact that he'd suddenly decided to do a 'Full Monty' while he was at it, still hitting that kick drum with mechanical, maniacal precision and venom despite the strides and underpants tangled round his ankles. For most of the audience, the sight of his private pubics made public was just a bit of a Bonzo bonus to the already exciting event.

But, among the ogling crowd, some punters were less impressed at the sight of Bonzo's manhood flapping about on the drum stool. I clocked one humourless woman talking animatedly to one of the fairly heavy local police presence. Like a chill wind, the prudish outrage swept through the crowd and it was clear to see that the cops were not amused. Now I'm not saying I'd normally think Bonzo getting his kit off was going too far. On the contrary, high spirits and outrageous behaviour like that are the all part of the sheer joy of rock 'n' roll – and long may it stay that way. A few people will always be upset by it - but when the police are among the ones with the hump, that's when the fun stops and the trouble starts. Of course, it was my job to make sure it didn't.

I could see the cops rallying together, conferring and calling for backup. I had to get Bonzo off the stage before they could arrest him. Suddenly I had a plan. I took Henry the Horse aside and told him to kill all the lights the moment the performers finished their song. He did so, plunging the stage into darkness for about ten seconds – just long enough for Richard Cole and I to grab Bonzo by the arms, pull his pants up and drag him full pelt backstage. Obviously we couldn't hide him in the band's dressing area – that was the first place the cops would look for him. So we lugged him into another locker room nearby which, since it was fully equipped with shower facilities and suchlike and plastered with sporting paraphernalia, I assumed was an American Football players' changing room. Somewhere out there, the police were stumbling about in the darkness, their mood turning as black as the blackout we'd plunged them into.

I kicked the door shut and locked it. Hearts banging as loud as Bonzo's drumming and holding our breath in case we were heard, Richard and I set about tidying up the legless sticksman. We waited. Bonzo, by now, was unconscious, draped lifelessly over a chair, marooned helplessly in the empty tiled expanse of the backstage changing room. The distant rumble of angry men echoed along the corridors outside – then suddenly loomed uncomfortably close. And then there was an explosion of outraged voices. At first it was an incomprehensible babble. Then it was way too close and way too clear.
'Where is the dirty motherfucker?' one loud American voice kept roaring with an authority that cut through the general furore. At least, I thought, we were safely locked in this room. No one could hear us. Bonzo was temporarily out of the game. Keep schtum and we'd be in the clear.

But then there was a thunderous banging at the door - the kind of banging that won't take no for an answer. The door burst open to reveal five or six huge cops with waists as wide as their minds were narrow. Some traitor must have given them the master key. We were outnumbered, out muscled, outweighed and, most importantly, outlawed.

Richard and I stood in front of Bonzo in a forlorn attempt at solidarity – as if we could hide him; protect him. Two of the police posse strode forward – too close for comfort, intimidating, demanding to know if this was the drummer who'd just given his public a pubic performance (not that they put it that delicately!).

'Look, he's just drunk – he's harmless,' I spluttered. 'Look at him – he didn't mean any harm...'

The cops looked with distaste over my shoulder at the inert figure sprawled over a chair in the middle of the bleakly lit and Spartan room. Neither was impressed. Their collective sense of humour bypass was obviously complete. I suppose it wasn't much of an excuse. It can't have been - because then they whipped out their batons threateningly, making it utterly clear that they meant business.

To be honest, at that point, Richard and I had given up the ghost. We were all going to get nicked and that was that. But neither we nor the cops had reckoned on a far superior authority. I'd thought the police had made a fairly impressive entrance just minutes ago. But the door through which they'd marched with such self-righteous import suddenly exploded open to admit the furious and fighting mad figure of Peter Grant. He was always almost ludicrously huge – but fluffed up, furious and bristling with rage like a giant Mother Hen hell bent on protecting her chicks he almost took the door off its hinges. The door wasn't the only thing almost unhinged by his entrance: the cops clucked in panic – overshadowed and overawed and chickening out completely.

'I'm the manager of the band,' Grant boomed imperiously. 'Who's in charge here?'

The gobsmacked police officers silently pointed out their Captain, whose eyes met Peter's and were fixed in his glare.

'You and me need to talk – alone.' Peter said quietly. 'Get your men out of here.'

With a wave of his arm the Captain dismissed his troops and Richard and I followed suit – we didn't need telling. Closing the door carefully behind us, we left Bonzo, Peter and the Captain in the room and waited. And waited. And waited.

Finally, after about ten minutes that seemed a lot longer, the Captain emerged, all that anger drained from his fat face, and

24

beckoned his men to follow. Bemused, we gingerly stepped back into the locker room, where Peter greeted us with a smile.

'Well done!' he beamed. 'Now, let's get Bonzo on the bus.'

I didn't need to be told twice. I grabbed the still-prone Bonzo and hauled him bus-wards and within minutes Peter and Led Zep, complete with their semi-conscious drummer, were speeding out of town. No charges. No arrest. In fact, it was as if the incident had never happened. I was in awe of Peter's unique brand of diplomacy that had somehow convinced the outraged cop Captain to let the matter drop. It was amazing the authority that guy commanded. Maybe it was his sheer size and physical presence...Well, that and the sheer size and physical presence of his wallet – as I found out when I asked Peter later on the bus.

'That was a cheap get-out, Don!' he laughed heartily. 'It only cost me $300!'

So now I knew how Led Zeppelin did business – and how the big man made problems just disappear. It was a lesson I'd take to heart – and which would take me to the very heart of the stellar supernova that Zeppelin were about to become.

The irony was that the quiet, understated style of getting things done that I'd developed for myself was sometimes at odds with Peter's methods. The further their balloon went up, the more money there was sloshing around – and Peter's preferred way of dealing with problems was to throw money at them. And that may have taken the edge off tricky situations – but it also brought a whole new range of complications. Despite – or maybe because of – his unquestioned authority within the rock 'n' roll sphere, Peter was drawn to people who had power of other kinds. He seemed to be influenced by anyone who was 'connected' – whether in government circles or in the underworld. One gentleman – although I'm not sure the term is accurate in this case – seemed to hold particular sway over Peter. Herb

Elliott. That was his name. Ex CIA or ex-Agency, he appeared on the scene after a huge US tour that Zep had just completed and he soon became instrumental in smoothing the band's way through the States. The powers that be move in mysterious ways and this Herb guy was clearly connected. As if by magic the band had police escorts on demand and incidents such as that Singer Bowl debacle were ironed out and wiped away without the need for negotiation.

One time outside Peter's favourite London hotel – the Montcalm at Marble Arch – I spotted three dodgy looking men in a car, who were definitely staking out the hotel. Naturally, I mentioned it to Peter and Herb.
'What make of car? Registration?' Herb asked in a flash.
I told him – having made a mental note of the licence plate just in case. Herb left the room purposefully and was back in ten minutes.
'It's OK. They're police – but they're looking for someone else,' he said with an air of confidence that could only come from a man with some serious contacts at the highest level...

*   *   *

Maybe here's the right place for me to go back to the beginning, where, you may remember, I opened with the tragic end of John Bonham.
'Get down to Jimmy's and take care of things,' Ray had said in that awful phone call to tell me Bonzo was dead.
'OK, leave it to me, I'd replied. And I knew from long experience that Ray and Peter Grant wouldn't have called if the shit wasn't about to hit the fan. I had to get down to Jimmy Page's place sharpish. It was down to me to contain the situation, limit the damage – and that probably meant keeping the police and the press at bay.

I put the phone down, grabbed my keys and in minutes I was out of my office in the NOMIS complex in Sinclair Road, W14 and gunning my BMW onto the A4 and speeding west for Windsor, where Jimmy, the prince of rock's royal family, had a palatial mansion, the Old Mill House in Mill Lane, Baggott (incidentally, formerly owned by Michael Caine) - a stone's throw from another royal household: Windsor Castle.

My mind raced faster than the car's screaming engine. John's dead. How? Was it accidental? Did he suffer? What about Pat...And Jason, his wife and son? That frantic half-hour's drive was on auto-pilot as a cascade of John's larger than life exploits flashed through my mind - fleeting recollections that made me smile despite the Bonzo-sized hole deep in the pit of my stomach. This tragedy was the latest in a run of bitterly bad luck for the band. Whether by sad coincidence or something more sinister, the Grim Reaper had been knocking at Zeppelin's door much too often for comfort of late – as I was reminded when I stumbled breathless into the guest room at Jimmy's mansion to find Bonzo's body, lifeless on its side where Benjy le Fevre, his personal roadie, had put him to bed after his drinking session, having taken care to prop his back with a bolster to ensure that he couldn't roll over and choke on his own vomit. The central heating had been left on but later someone had opened the windows – and it was the fresh air, I was told, that had caused the strange discoloration of his face. It was as if John's life and soul went out of the window as the fresh air blew in.

Arriving at around noon, I'd beaten the police and press to the scene. Professionals to the end, the roadies - Benjy and Rex King - and, Jimmy's manservant Rick Hobbs had already 'cleaned up', by which they meant that they'd got rid of anything potentially incriminating or embarrassing to the band or John's family. The one thing even they couldn't conceal or control, though, was his blood – and whatever that contained would be revealed in the post mortem. To the uninitiated that might sound impressively level-headed and professional; but to a seasoned roadie it's pretty much standard procedure; as routine as tuning a guitar and placing the monitors correctly – especially if your man indulged heavily in all the usual extracurricular rock 'n' roll habits! And there's no denying that John Bonham indulged – in fact he was the epitome of the wild man of rock, modelling himself on his boyhood hero, the late, great Keith Moon. It transpired that the boys had been rehearsing that day and Bonzo, characteristically, had been hitting the vodka hard – at least four quadruples, by all accounts as well as who knows how many speedballs, the last of which was to be John's final hit. But, ironically, it wasn't that heady mix of coke and smack that killed him. Tragically, despite Benjy's diligent precautions, it was later found that John had vomited and inhaled at the same time in his deep drunken sleep, setting up a fatal siphon effect whereby the contents of his stomach were pumped into his lungs.

Shaking off my initial shock, I took charge of my emotions – and then I took charge of the situation.

You have to be pragmatic at times like that. It was too late to do anything for John – and I could take care of his family later. Right now, damage limitation was the name of the game – and the first threat was the police. I briefed everyone in the house: keep your mouths shut and make sure the cops confine their investigation to the guest room. They must not be allowed to nose around the rest of the house! I didn't know what they might find – but whatever they turned up, I was sure it wouldn't do the band any good. And once the press got wind of it they'd have a field day - especially since Bonzo was the second visitor to have died in one of Jimmy Page's guest rooms in just over a year. In fact that earlier incident served as a sort of rehearsal for this latest tragedy...

On October 24th 1979 Paul McCartney's company, MPL Communications, hired us to provide men to check the guest list and handle the overall security at a very prestigious award ceremony that The Guinness Book of Records was holding at Les Ambassadeurs nightclub just off London's Park Lane. Everybody who was anybody was there, including the press, paparazzi, liggers and jibbers (jibbers are people who blag their way into gigs, receptions or backstage without a pass or invitation), largely because Paul was being presented with a medallion cast in rhodium (which is a very hard, silvery platinum-like metal element) by a government minister. I was just checking out the members of Pink Floyd when one of my men said that there was a call for me upstairs (obviously this was a long time before the advent of mobile phones!). At the reception desk I found the call was from Ray Washbourne – and it wasn't the best of news! They'd just found one of Jimmy's guests dead at his home at Plumpton Place, Sussex. Predictably, he wanted me to get down there and take care of things.

'I think someone may have phoned for an ambulance,' he said, 'but that's all I know.'

'Leave it to me,' I said before telling Gerry Slater, my business partner, what had happened and taking off like a scalded cat.

I arrived at the same time as the police. Obviously that was because they'd been called out by the ambulance crew – which is standard procedure. Their presence meant that I couldn't 'clear up' the way I'd have liked to. All I could do was confine their investigations to the guest room where the guy, whose name I later found out was Richard Churchill-Hale, had popped his clogs. And that annoyed the cops intensely! If I'd arrived ten minutes later they'd have been all over the house like a rash – so I was very lucky, timing-wise. I didn't get a chance to 'clear up' completely so they did find 'substances' by his bedside. It transpired that the poor bloke had overdosed – but because he was a guest, staying in a guest room, the room he slept in was where the police's snooping stopped...

Anyway, going back to Bonzo, I knew that the press would hound his family pitilessly – and that simply wasn't an option. I had to keep a lid on it for as long as I possibly could, at least until Peter turned up and started throwing his weight around – and, as demonstrated that time at the Singer Bowl, that was a lot of weight to throw!

The police weren't happy about being stymied at every turn. But what could they do? It was apparently an accidental death – nothing suspicious about it. A drunken man had seemingly inhaled his own vomit - period. There was no good reason for them to snoop around, no matter how much they'd have liked to. Anyway, it was the law – they knew it and so did I. Funny how rock 'n' roll makes lawyers out of everyone involved – just like crime!

Sure enough, by the time Peter and Ray arrived and John Bonham had 'left the building' for the last time in the ambulance, the road had filled with reporters and the mob was growing by the minute as the circling vultures homed in on the smell of death. The three of us discussed all the angles, analysed the kinds of problems that might ensue, made contingency plans and decided how we would box for the next few days. That resolved, Peter and Ray went off to console the boys in the band. It was only after his unusually subdued departure that it dawned on me that Peter hadn't been in his normal control-freak manager mode. Far from it – he was obviously deeply shocked by the event and, after our preliminary talk, left the whole affair to me to deal with.

At least I didn't have to worry about the rest of the band – they'd made a hasty departure minutes after John's body had been discovered and I'd arranged for more of my men to go and look after them until they were safely ensconced in secure retreats where there would be no intrusions. That may sound callous. It wasn't. It was, again, standard procedure. When there was a 'death in the family' unwritten rule number one was to make sure that the band were as far away from the action as possible. It meant fewer questions for them to answer. But more importantly it allowed them to grieve in private, protected from the press (which in such situations might as well be an abbreviation of pressure!).

The platoons of press and police set up camp at The Old Mill House for days. So I did too. I hardly left Jimmy's place for the following few days. Keeping the hounds at bay was a full time job and a hard one, with the more dogged photographers climbing over the walls – and driving me and my men up the wall in the process. There were a few little incidents – but nothing I couldn't handle – and I managed to contain the situation as effectively as anyone could. Maybe I shouldn't have bothered. They'd caught the whiff of a story that was a tabloid hack's wet dream: rock star, booze, drugs and death – and if there wasn't any sex they'd find a way to work some in. So, if they couldn't get the story from the horse's mouth they'd let their imaginations – and Led Zep cuttings archives – run riot. Predictably, they added that Ol' Black Magic to the lurid mix, concocting ludicrous fantasies involving Jimmy Page and his admittedly strong interest in the occult in general and Aleister Crowley in particular. For example, he owned a house that had formerly belonged to Crowley and in which there had allegedly been a terrifying catalogue of murders and suicides. The place was also apparently haunted by the spirit of a man who'd been decapitated there some three hundred years earlier – all lurid grist to the newspaper mill!

31

Having been so close to so many famous people whose lives had been blighted and hacked to pieces by the lies and sensationalism of the gutter press hacks, I knew exactly what they'd do to John's memory, given the chance. They didn't care whose feelings they hurt as long as they could drag up enough dirt to muddy the issue – because they know mud sticks. Any little association, any name, any snippet of gossip or unsubstantiated innuendo would do if they could cook it up into a tasty dish for their hungry public. I wouldn't mind so much if what they printed were true – but in my experience they get it wrong most of the time and hurt people more than they'll ever know. But they never, ever apologise. Worse still, they never, ever, seem to care. Luckily enough, because John was so well-liked by his friends, there were very few new revelations about him. In fact, it's a tribute to his friends' loyalty and integrity that all the press could do was dig up and rehash old stories.

Despite the press, I at least partially succeeded in controlling the way the whole tragic affair was perceived by the public by keeping a lid on everyone involved and ensuring that they didn't disclose anything. And now I faced another, far more unsettling, task: to make sure John looked his best for his swansong show for all the family and friends who wanted to pay him their last respects. To do him justice, the mortician needed to know what this vacant frame had been like in life – larger than life was what Bonzo had been. I found a photo that captured that free spirit we'd lost and made an appointment at Kenyon Morticians in Kensington – at which I duly arrived, full of trepidation.

After polite introductions in the office, I was ushered into the area where the bodies were stored, silently awaiting their burial or cremation. It was cool like...well, like a morgue really. I, on the other hand, wasn't cool at all. I was chilled to the bone when the mortician reverently drew John out of what looked like an oversized filing cabinet – the one where they file your life when it's no longer current. Desecrated by the autopsy and horribly discoloured, this wasn't the Bonzo I'd known and loved. John's wasn't the first dead body I'd seen and wouldn't be the last, but that didn't make that 'death mask' any less mortifying. I was calmed, though, by the mortician – a kind, congenial and fascinating man – who soothingly discussed the whole mysterious process of his profession with me. It's a tribute to his professionalism and integrity that when he looked at John's body, having talked about John with me and examined the photo I'd brought along, he saw him through my eyes. He explained the way he would use make-up and style his hair and assured me that by the time he began his quiet sojourn in the Chapel of Rest, John would look peaceful and serene – and no-one would see any sign of the autopsy or the discoloration that had so disturbed me. Bonzo, peaceful and serene. That's a first, I thought.

A consummate professional in the art of sending people gracefully to their final rest, he was just as skilled in bringing peace to the living – and, having put my mind at ease, he shared some of the intimate and touching aspects of his craft. In another 'file' was another body – that of a sixty-year-old Greek or Cypriot woman. She was fully clothed and looked as if she'd just fallen asleep. But it had been a very long snooze because, amazingly, she'd been dead for nearly two years. Evidently her husband had requested that they kept her there, perfectly peaceful and preserved, until he died – which apparently would be soon – so that they could make their final journey together; go home to be buried in their own country. And this wasn't a one-off – he told me he'd once kept the body of an exiled African head of state for more than six years because his family was waiting until their country's political climate changed before they could take him home and bury him in his native soil. I found myself moved by the reverence with which this gentle man accommodated people's last wishes in God's departure lounge. There couldn't have been anyone better to administer this art to John: a great and talented artist performing his art for another great and talented artist.

A few days later I returned to see his handiwork and my faith was fully justified – John had been transformed. He looked lifelike – perhaps better than he'd looked for several years. All his confusion and conflict was resolved; the stress and strain relieved. He just looked bloody handsome and, finally, the wild man of rock was completely at peace.

I phoned Peter to tell him that the funeral arrangements could go ahead and also that people could now go and pay their last respects. John was to be buried near his home at Rushock in Worcestershire, where he had lived with his wife, Pat, and Jason, his son.

My involvement in John's demise had been a tragedy in three acts. Act One: the death scene at Jimmy's house. Act Two: the Chapel of Rest. Act Three was the funeral – and again my own grief had to be put on hold because my team and I had been employed to ensure that it would be a dignified and respectful occasion, unsullied by intrusive press or fans. It was the last meaningful thing I could do for John – and I was determined to do that sad duty well, despite the irony that 'quiet and dignified' were hardly what the wild man would have wanted. What he definitely would have wanted, though, was for Pat, his beloved wife, to be spared any more stress and strain than she was already suffering. And that, I'd make sure of – for Pat, for Jason and for John. My lads and I met, appropriately, at John's favourite watering hole just opposite the graveyard where he was to rest, to toast him the way he'd have wanted us to. In fact Pat made a remark that June (my wife) and I will never forget.

'From his grave, John can see this pub, so he can see us celebrating his life as he would have wanted us to.'

With that deeply moving thought in mind, I reluctantly left John's close family and many other friends – many of whom were my friends too – to say their final goodbyes while we prepared to fortify the church against the inevitable onslaught.

Security was just one aspect of the operation. There were more sensitive duties to deal with too and I'm proud to say that the busload of my men I brought in did an admirably discreet and respectful job and behaved impeccably. You'd never have known that their background was in the rather less formal world of rock 'n' roll – but it was clear that their solemnity and dedication to the job was inspired by the fact that most of them had worked with Zeppelin at one time or another. They acted as ushers for the collected family and friends and were invaluable in helping to receive and lay out with due solemnity the innumerable floral tributes that poured in. Of course I made sure that the men were strategically placed and blended in – the last thing we wanted was for them to look oppressive, like a bunch of bouncers. And to their credit they blended with considerable diplomacy and aplomb. In the pub, then before, during and after the service, they kept the hordes of press, autograph collectors and souvenir hunters at a respectful distance with nothing more dramatic than a wagging of fingers, a meaningful look and a shake of the head that said 'that's a no no!'. The respect with which the onlookers treated the proceedings was impressive – particularly the national press boys, who aren't renowned for their sensitivity. Mind you, they weren't behaving themselves out of any sense of decency! Just to make sure they behaved, we had quietly pointed out that if they took any liberties on that day they'd pay dearly for them in future. They knew we were the boys in charge of most major rock 'n' roll happenings they'd want to cover and took the warning to heart – as well they might – and were on their best behaviour.

That day a cornerstone of one of the world's greatest bands was lowered into the ground – and the lack of Bonzo's unbeatable beats undermined Page, Plant and Jones. Soon they announced that they felt they couldn't go on without him. It was the end of an era. Yet another rock legend had succumbed to the lethal cocktail of self-doubt, temptation and adulation that only the great stars ever sample. Because when you're very, very high there's a very long way to go down. John was history – and so was the band. History in the real sense of the word.

CHAPTER TWO

1980 – 2003

ADAM ANT

Her eyes wide as saucers, her face flushed with excitement, she half-screamed two words at me that were going to change my life for the next three years: 'ADAM ANT!!!'

As my thirteen-year-old daughter shouted out the name, I looked closely at her with new interest – because in her eyes I suddenly recognised a look that I'd seen thousands of times before while I'd been looking after David Cassidy, The Monkees, the Bay City Rollers and the Osmonds among many other teen pop idols. It was that familiar doe-eyed look of utter adulation, hero worship, infatuation...Call it what you will, it told me one crucial piece of information: there was serious money in this! When teenage girls go all gooey at the mere mention of a pop star's name you're talking about a phenomenon that's bound to be big – very big indeed. And the great thing was that I had a chance to get in on the ground floor with an act that was about to set the world on fire – the chance, with no exaggeration, of a lifetime. Adam Ant and his musical partner, co-writer and lead guitarist, Marco Pirroni, had just asked me to become the new manager of Adam and The Ants, the band that had emerged from the creative white heat of punk rock and managed to remain red hot with an utterly fresh new blend of punk's raw energy with the theatrical glitz and drama of glam rock. Adam's flamboyant sense of style had caught the imaginations of the post-punk 'New Romantics' (otherwise known as 'The cult with no name') but, more importantly, he'd caught the eye of the kids – and that's what really made Adam and The Ants almost certainly the hottest act in the UK at the time.

Despite the fact that I'd been working with some of the greatest artists and acts in rock and pop for over twenty years – work that had necessitated close collaboration with their management – it was something of a leap into the unknown for me. For all my broad and often bizarre experience, I'd never actually been an artist's manager before. Of course I knew what was involved – and probably far more than many other newcomers to the role would be likely to have gleaned. Trusted by some of the sharpest in the business, I'd been privileged to sit in on countless meetings, shared confidences and spent considerable periods alone with them – often in the midst of the most trying times a music business manager has to face. I'd even been privy to a fair bit of high level wheeling and dealing and ducking and diving – including some of the more colourful ways in which some of these guys get their business done!

So not only did I have a pretty good head start in the management stakes – I also knew that I could call in many favours if I needed them. Only that morning, almost immediately after an auspicious chat with Adam and Marco, I'd got straight on the phone to two good friends of mine, both of whom were premier division managers of world class acts. The first was Peter Grant (about whom you will already have read in this book – and of whom you'll be reading more, I assure you!). As manager of Bad Company, Stone the Crows and Maggie Bell and another little outfit by the name of Led Zeppelin, of whom I imagine you'll have heard, Peter knew everything there was to know about managing a successful act - and a bit more besides. I said to Peter that I'd been considering passing on the opportunity. After all, I knew that it was a job that every Tom, Dick and Harry thought they could do but that few could really handle with

38

much success – a bit like managing the England football team really! I even suggested that Peter might like to add Adam and The Ants to his already impressive roster of artists. He declined, saying that he was already over-committed. But he knew all about Adam – and he was convinced that they were going to be very big indeed.

'Go for it Don,' he urged. 'You know how the business works – and if you need any help or advice, any time, you know you just have to call me!'

I was now pretty well convinced that I had to take up Adam and Marco's offer. Just one more call though...And Colin Johnson, who managed Status Quo at the time, more or less repeated Peter's words of encouragement – so I had the blessing of two of the best managers in the business. But there remained some greater powers with whom I needed to consult over a dinner meeting before making the final decision: June, my wife, my two sons Bradley (17) and Gregg (15) and, of course, the girl whose lit-up eyes had told me everything I needed to know – my daughter Lyndsey. There wasn't much to discuss – and the next morning I phoned Adam and told him I'd be happy to become his manager.

Why, you might ask, did an up and coming star like Adam ask me to manage him when he had the pick of the music business elite? Well, there's a story to that! Like so many success stories in the music business the Ants management offer had a lot to do with me being in the right place at the right time – but I firmly believe in making your own luck. I always try and give people a bit of a leg-up in the business if I can and more often than not the people you help will be happy to return the favour if they make it up that greasy pole – even if only by giving you a chance to quote for some work.

'Why choose me?' I asked Adam.

'Well I had the likes of Harvey Goldsmith onto me asking to manage me,' he replied. 'But I'm not relaxed about working with them. They've all got their big flash houses and Rolls Royces and everything... But they don't know anything about me. Whereas I can talk to you; you're more down to earth. And you've already been helping me out in all sorts of ways for nothing so I know I can trust you – and you've got a really successful company and you've been in the business for a long time so I know you know what's what. I just think you'd make a good manager – that's all.'

That was good enough for me!

Our relationship started when Adam and The Ants and I had the misfortune to cross paths (and later swords) with a small time promoter, band manager of sorts and all round thug called Jock McDonald. Early in 1980 Adam and the Ants had been booked for a gig at the Rainbow Theatre in Finsbury Park, North London – one of the UK's largest and busiest venues, holding around 3,500 punters almost nightly. The venue's management, Laurence and Jamie Bloom and Alan Schaverein, appointed my company, Artistes Services, to handle the venue's security at all events promoted there. When the promoter – yes, you've guessed it, it was Jock McDonald – failed to stump up the contractually agreed deposit to cover the vast expenses involved just in opening the place, the Blooms threatened to pull the show. They weren't unreasonable – they gave him as much time as was humanly possible but the final deadline had to be four hours before the concert was due to start. That deadline came and went and no money was forthcoming – so they pulled the plug. Our job was to face the (lack of) music with the punters and the promoter's crew. The Blooms were concerned that a horde of disappointed punk rockers meant big trouble. Actually, they were wrong – Adam's fans may have been fierce-looking but on the whole they were perfectly reasonable and well-behaved (just goes to show you really can't judge a book by its cover!). Contrary to expectations, we didn't get any grief from McDonald's boys either – although in the light of later experiences with them I'm dead sure that it was only because they were outweighed, outnumbered and outclassed by my guys!

Maybe it was that incident that prompted the Ants to call me some time later. They asked me to go down and meet them at John Henry's rehearsal studios in Market Road, London N.7, just off the Caledonian Road, where they were rehearsing for their first national tour. From the off, I could see who were the main men: Adam and Marco did all the talking.

Their problem, basically, was that they'd outgrown the scene they'd emerged from. The punk phenomenon was, at first, a very small one in which everyone knew everyone else and the idea of a punk band acting like 'stars' went against everything punk rock was about. With bands like The Clash actively sneaking their fans into their gigs and hotel rooms on tours it just wasn't done to exclude anyone. That was all very well – and great fun for all concerned when the bands were playing small clubs – but now that Adam and the Ants were playing major venues the backstage liggers were no longer friends – they were fans. And that's a very different thing. It was getting them down. Adam, in particular, as I was to learn, always put 200% into every performance and when he finished the gig he simply couldn't handle hordes of hangers-on hogging his dressing room. At the same time, it went against the all-for-one, one-for-all grain of punk to alienate the fans whose loyalty had got them where they were. Could I help? We talked. The big problem was that the tour was already over budget - so hiring Artistes Services lock stock and barrel was out of the question. So I helped them out with an affordable but effective solution – the first of a couple of favours through which I unknowingly proved myself to Adam. My suggestion was that I sent Dave Moulder, one of my best men, along on the tour with them to sort things out. Adam would pay Dave a modest weekly wage and cover his food, accommodation and travel costs. Of course I was foregoing any profit for myself – but much more inconvenient was losing a top bloke for seven long weeks. At the back of my mind there was also a fair chance that I'd lose him for good if the Ants offered him a permanent job – something that had happened more than once. I needn't have worried – they were an honourable lot and they looked after Dave very well without trying to lure him away. As I knew he would, Dave solved all their backstage security problems at a stroke and made life easier and safer for them in ways they hadn't even thought of. As well as setting up tight security procedures on stage, backstage and at all access points, he ensured that they got in and out of venues without incident. Sometimes, on the road, the fans are the least of your worries – such as when a bunch of spiky haired punks in make-up and bondage gear turn up in a greasy spoon, the jealously protected domain of hairy-arsed truckers. Funny enough, the Ants got a much warmer welcome at the roadside cafes once they had an ex-Para who'd been on secondment to the SAS backing them up!

The tour ended in October or November 1980 and Dave came back into the Artistes Services fold, leaving the Ants to their own devices. Looking back, it's a shame I couldn't have spared him to stay with them because Jock McDonald reared his ugly head again. He was managing one of the second wave of punk bands who had all the attitude of the original punks with none of the wit and irony. The Four by Twos were thick as the 4" x 2" lumps of wood their name referred to (among other nastier references) and it seemed that Jock McDonald's idea of creating controversy, and by extension notoriety, was simply to cause as many fights as possible – like attacking Adam and the Ants at Top of the Pops, on which they were trying to promote their new single 'Ant

Music', which reached number two in the charts on January 17th '81 (the album 'Kings of the Wild Frontier' went to number one in the album charts on the 24th) They assaulted Adam and a couple of the guys in the band and seriously frightened everyone else present, including Amanda Donohoe, Adam's girlfriend at the time. And of course, since it all kicked off at the studios of the UK's ultimate pop show, the tabloids had a field day with it.

That wasn't all. Not content with a punch-up, McDonald's thugs left with some not very subtly implied threats. And that was the second time Adam and Marco were to turn to me for help – which I readily agreed to provide.

I got hold of McDonald.
'If you or your group go anywhere near Adam and his band – or his girlfriend Mandy,' I said, 'I'll deal with you personally because the Ants are now under my protection – got it? You see Adam or the group in the street, you cross the road and steer well clear. And if you can't avoid them – you apologise properly for that little ruck at Top of the Pops. In fact I'm not going to let you ever do anything like this again to anyone in the business. I'm protecting the business from the likes of you...I won't stand for any of more your crap! Understand?'

As far as Adam and the Ants were concerned it seemed that Mr McDonald had understood me loud and clear. But evidently, he didn't think the warning applied to anyone else because shortly afterwards my very good friend, the successful promoter, Ian Wright, and his partner and co-promoter John Giddings, fell foul of McDonald and the Four by Twos. I don't know what his argument with those two was – presumably something to do with another disastrous gig since they were promoters – but he and his group stormed into their offices, knocked them about and completely trashed the place. Soon afterwards I had a call from Ian asking for help – the poor bloke was most unhappy. So, again, I got a message to Jock McDonald to say that Ian and John were under my protection and 'out of bounds' to him and his thugs.

It wasn't only Adam, Ian and John that had got the rough end of the Four by Twos. They were throwing their weight around all over the place – or to be more accurate, anywhere and at anyone that ensured they'd get some press coverage. Their favourite arena seemed to be Mortons in Berkeley Square, Mayfair, which really was the 'in place' for the in crowd at the time – all the stars and showbiz people went there. And it was at Mortons that Denny Laine of Wings had the bad luck to have a run-in with Jock McDonald and his thugs. I wasn't there at the time but apparently they laid into Denny and a big mêlée broke out as a fellow called Steve, the manager of the famous World's End pub in the Kings Road, and John Miller piled in to back up the Wings guitarist. Now Miller was not a bloke you'd want to mess with. Ex-Black Watch (or one of those other elite army regiments), he fancied himself as a ladies' man and as a major hard man. Remember the time when someone illegally kidnapped the escaped Great Train Robber Ronnie Biggs in Brazil? They held him on a boat offshore in an attempt to get him back to the UK and claim the reward... Well that was John Miller. He lost a lot of friends in that escapade, including me (I'd employed him briefly, but hadn't been very impressed with his attitude). One thing he wasn't short of was nerve, I'll say that for him. He made himself very busy that night but, despite his formidable reputation, he wasn't that much help to poor old Denny because one of the Four by Twos bottled him and knocked John out cold – at least that's what I was told. Inevitably the police arrived and, rather unfairly I thought, Denny was arrested – I think they let him off with a caution though. As you'd expect, bearing in mind how huge Paul McCartney and Wings were at the time, there was a huge furore about the whole incident in the press – so I suppose McDonald got what he wanted: more pointless and worthless fame for his pointless and worthless band.

Then I got an anxious call from MPL (McCartney Productions Limited).
'Don...Look, about this thing with Denny...This guy's a lunatic...We've got to have this stopped Don...We want him taken care of...we can't have him going round beating up bands...'
We were doing a lot of work for MPL at the time – but that wasn't why I agreed to sort McDonald out. The music business had been good to me – and so had many of the people this guy was hurting. Making things safe for the whole business was just an extension of what I and my boys did all the time really – protecting people had become second nature to me.
'Don't worry,' I said immediately. 'Leave it to me.'
McDonald might have thought he and his band were a force to be reckoned with - and I'd heard that he always carried a blade strapped to his wrist - but when I send men out to protect people they're properly trained to deal with nasty little gangsters like that. He wouldn't give us much trouble.

Once more I got hold of Mc Donald.
'Right that's it – as far as I'm concerned you and your group are finished in this business,' I told him. 'Understand?'
He understood all right – especially when I stretched the point just a little bit by mentioning that I'd been offered a contract to do him some very serious damage – but that I'd turned it down and was letting him off with a warning.... This time.

And, as if by magic all the trouble stopped and the punters down at Mortons could stop looking over their shoulders for the Four by Twos. Not that McDonald was letting on that

45

he'd been intimidated. A few weeks later, after I'd become Adam's manager, I was walking down Conduit Street in London's West End when a van pulled up beside me and there at the wheel, bold as brass, was Jock bloody McDonald!

'Hi,' he said, cockily as always. I nodded in acknowledgement but with obvious displeasure.

'You owe me,' he said.

'Owe you? I don't owe you anything. How do you make that out?' I snapped back, outraged by the sheer bloody gall of the man.

'It was because of me beating up Adam Ant that you got to be his manager...So you owe me!' he stated as if it were a perfectly obvious and reasonable suggestion.

'Wrong,' I grated. 'You owe me!'

'Why...What for?' he questioned in feigned innocence.

'You owe me your life, sonny,' I spat back with venom, 'because after you and your mates beat up Denny Laine, John Miller, Ian Wright and John Giddings there was a contract out on you. You picked on the wrong people mate – and it's only thanks to me that you're still walking the streets. I told them I'd put a stop to you and your mates' shenanigans for good – and for nothing. So think yourself lucky!'

He drove off. Strangely, he suddenly had nothing more to say to me!

I suppose in some small way he was right – it was at least partially due to my protecting Adam from the likes of McDonald that he knew he could trust me.

Anyway, as soon as I'd said 'yes' to Adam, almost before I had time to draw breath, I was riding a wave; caught up in a whirl of meetings and introductions with lawyers and accountants, members of the band, road crew, publishers, office staff...And it wasn't just people on the inside – there was a massive groundswell of interest from excited record labels, music publishers and radio and TV people. Fine-tuned by years of experience with other high rollers that were about to break, their radar had spotted Adam's boat coming in – and they were all anxious to put their oar in and drive it along with self-interested advice, demands and requests about the new course his career should take.

Of course I also had to make sure that Artistes Services, my own existing business, wasn't affected by the politics surrounding my new appointment. There were a lot of resentful people about when I put a stop to them taking liberties in the way they spent Adam's money for him – among them Falcon Stuart, Adam's previous manager. On top of that can of worms there was the business of deciding on an agent for the band, which was not a particularly tricky process in itself, but I could only pick one of them, which could mean upsetting the rest – and as a security provider I worked closely with all of them! In the end I went with a familiar name: Ian Wright, who now had his own agency, which was called Excel Talent.

It was sink or swim time – and fortunately for me I'd swum with too many sharks over the preceding twenty years to be put off my stroke by the feeding frenzy. But I knew I couldn't afford to get carried away by this surge of enthusiasm. My instincts told me to withdraw a little – not to make myself too available, without alienating or snubbing any of these people who were so keen to promote Adam and make him the highest roller to come out of the 'New Wave'. By holding back, I gave myself some time to get my priorities straight and get a proper understanding of what it was I had to do. I realised that although I was the focal point for all these crucial contacts I also had to act as the buffer between my artist and all these pressures. I made my mind up not to be bullied by the giant corporations that were vying for as much control as they could get over all the minutiae of a pop artist's work: album and single delivery dates, shows, personal appearances, tours and TVs and so on. To them, Adam and his band weren't musicians or artists – they were simply 'their product' – and as such to be exploited and manipulated ruthlessly to maximise sales. I thought my artists deserved better – and I was determined to make sure they got it.

Adding to the wise counsel of Peter Grant and Colin Johnson, I sought advice wherever I could find it – and that wasn't always at the top. On the contrary, it was the younger staffers at the big organisations – the junior A&R executives and press officers, as yet untainted by cynicism – who gave the frankest, most useful advice and threw their total commitment behind Adam (A&R means Artistes and Repertoire – the department responsible for finding, signing and developing acts). And it was in no small part thanks to their input that I came up with what was a fairly radical PR strategy. The established wisdom was that you courted the music press and perhaps the mainstream quality press to gain 'credibility' and critical acclaim. 'Sod that!' I thought. Some of the snootier, 'hipper than thou' elements of the music press had already begun their 'set 'em up and knock 'em down' backlash with some spiteful comments describing Adam and The Ants as the 'Fag end of Rock'.
'Who needs 'em!' I thought. Instead of being used by the music press, I used the tabloids, who were more than happy to be used if it gave them good copy. Newsworthiness, I decided, was the name of the new game, and if nothing else, Adam has always been that! And since any one of the tabloids had a circulation many times greater than that of all the music press combined, we got a lot more fame with a lot less pain – initially at least. But more of that later...

All these challenges aside, my official appointment as Manager of Adam of the Ants was an event worth celebrating so I took Adam to Rags, the private club and restaurant in Chesterfield Street, which was sister club to the world famous Tramp in Jermyn Street, owned by Johnny Gold.

While Adam and I were enjoying our meal a waiter appeared and ceremoniously deposited a bottle of extremely expensive Champagne on our table, explaining that it had been sent with the compliments of a well-known record company executive at a nearby table. It was a very generous gesture – especially at Rags' prices – and more so since he didn't even work for CBS, with whom the Ants were signed. Adam and I were bemused at first – until we were informed that the gift was in celebration of a very exciting piece of news that he'd heard first: the Ants' album, 'Kings of the Wild Frontier', had just reached number one in the UK charts! (Now we were well and truly on our way! Adam was undeniably the biggest pop star in Britain – and I was his manager!

Just as I was about to open the Champagne and get stuck in like a triumphant Formula One driver on the winners' podium I noticed that Adam looked distinctly uncomfortable about the whole thing.
'What's the problem Adam?' I said. And almost before he replied I realised what the problem was. You will, no doubt, remember the refrain from the hit single Puss in Boots, in which Adam has a pop at the cynicism of the press about his clean-living lifestyle: *Don't drink, don't smoke, what do you do?* Well it's absolutely true. In all the time I worked with him Adam never smoked, took drugs or touched a drop of alcohol – not even a beer would pass his lips. In fact he abhorred the idea of putting anything harmful in his body – and it's well documented that his only vice, if you can call it that, was sex. Even chocolate was a no no with Adam in case it brought him out in spots! I think his aversion to alcohol stemmed from the fact that his father was an alcoholic whose sleazy activities and eventual imprisonment caused Adam

49

much heartache and embarrassment – but I'm sad to add that I've just heard, at the time of writing in July 2003, that these days Adam is smoking and drinking, among his other problems, more of which later.

'What am I going to do Don?' he pleaded. 'I can't drink it – but it was such a kind gesture. I can't send it back...What would he think of me?'

Of course I had no such inhibitions about necking a bottle of the finest Champagne you can get but, in solidarity with Adam's sensibilities, I suggested a diplomatic solution – something I'd find myself doing more and more in my new management role.

'Don't worry about it Adam,' I reassured him. 'We'll just open the bottle, I'll have a drop or two and you can just pretend to take a sip now and then. We'll raise our glasses to the guy, he'll be happy and then, when he leaves, we can give the rest of the bottle to the waiter!'

And that's what we did – although Adam worried the whole time about being sussed and appearing ungrateful. The same sort of thing happened many times after that. On one occasion we were at Stringfellows. After I'd had a word with Peter Stringfellow, any such generous gestures were automatically converted to a free meal on the house to save Adam any further embarrassment.

The celebrations, such as they were, over with, it was time to stamp my mark on Adam's increasingly global business arrangements and make sure all concerned knew that I was now in charge. To cover myself against any previous claims on the Ants, I checked with Adam's lawyers that all previous management contracts had been terminated. Malcolm McClaren, the Sex Pistols' manager had been managing Adam and the Ants for a while and then had handed the reins to one Falcon Stuart, whom I'd never met. As I mentioned earlier, it was becoming increasingly clear to me that various

50

people had had their hands in the till and I was going to find out who was doing what and put a stop to it. A particularly flagrant example came up on our first trip to America. I was at the CBS offices in Manhattan, NYC on a bit of a 'meet and greet' – again making my presence felt as Adam's new manager – when it seemed that there was some confusion.

'Oh, well we just talked to Falcon Stuart about the band,' one of the financial staff said offhandedly to me.

'Well he's got nothing to do with Adam any more,' I said.

'Yes he has – he's Adam's manager,' came the reply. 'He was here asking for money for a promotional tour for Adam and the Ants.'

I was flabbergasted.

'No he isn't. Let me tell you, he's got no right to do that. He's got nothing whatsoever to do with Adam – he's just taking liberties. I'm the manager now.'

Now I'd never met Falcon Stuart and I had no idea whether he was under the impression that he was still involved (although the lawyers had assured me that no contract between him and Adam existed, either because there hadn't been one or because it had been terminated) or was simply chancing his arm. Either way I couldn't have him undermining my authority – or mining the increasingly rich mother lode of money owing to Adam.

Two nights later I had my chance to set the bloke straight. The music business is quite a small one really and you're bound to bump into everyone else at one time or another – especially if you're staying at one of the rock 'n' rollers' favourite hotels, in this case The Gramercy Park Hotel, in the pleasantly leafy downtown end of Manhattan's Lexington Avenue in easy walking distance of the delights of Greenwich Village. Perfect for famous people who don't want to be found by fans, The Gramercy was (and still is) popular with bands because it has a unique old-fashioned elegance and style of its own, yet it is completely discreet. Gramercy Park itself is actually the hotel's own private fenced-off and locked garden, to which only residents have keys, and the casual passer by could walk past the hotel entrance without thinking for a moment that some of the world's most famous and sought-after stars were knocking them back in the Gramercy's dark and sumptuous bar!

So it wasn't all that surprising when, as we strolled out of the lobby, Adam said, 'Look, there's Falcon!'
I saw my chance.
'Wait here a minute,' I said, and caught up with Adam's erstwhile Svengali.
'Look Falcon,' I said, after introducing myself, 'you're nothing to do with Adam or the Ants any more. If I ever, ever, hear again that you've been going round purporting to be Adam's manager and trying to rip off money I'll come after you myself. Ask anyone in the business about me. They'll tell you I'm true to my word and that I don't make empty threats.'
He didn't have a lot to say to that. I went on.
'Have I made myself clear? You have nothing – repeat nothing – to do with Adam now. And you've got no rights over anything – none of it. And if you do anything like that again I'll stop you for good. I won't take the legal route - that's not my game. I'll do it in person.'
That was the first and last time I ever saw Falcon Stuart. I did find out that it wasn't only CBS that he'd tried to touch for some money; he'd done the rounds in New York without, I might add, any luck. I can't say for sure that he was on the blag – I don't know what he was up to. For all I know he was after money that he was owed in the past – but even if that was the case he still shouldn't have been misrepresenting himself as Adam's current manager!

Falcon Stuart was just one of several figures from Adam's past who would keep coming back to haunt him. Another was his wife, Eve (her real name is Carol Ann Mills, by the way. She'd changed it so that the happy couple could be known as Adam and Eve!). Since he was so happily coupled with Amanda Donohoe, it came as quite a surprise when Adam mentioned in passing that he was married.

'Oh,' I said. 'This isn't very good for a young pop star that all the girls are in love with.'

Adam assured me that it had all been over with Eve for a long time and that she was living with Kevin Mooney from the Ants. Nevertheless, I decided that a nice quiet divorce was called for and, with Adam's blessing, started making the arrangements. But once someone had a word in Eve's ear about the money she could make out of the situation, the 'nice quiet divorce' went right out of the window. I'm sure Eve didn't mean to do Adam any harm, but the press did - and we were faced with some very nasty revelations in the papers, raking up Adam's half-hearted suicide bid some years before and accusing me of being a gangster. We did get our own back on the press on that occasion though! They made the mistake of printing a couple of the caricatures Adam had done at art college and which Eve had kept – and they were very good! One was of Margaret Thatcher in a very compromising bondage scenario and the other was a fantastic caricature of Lord Longford scrawling graffiti on the wall while urinating in a public toilet. They were Adam's copyright and they had no right to print them – so we sued the Express and won about ten grand! It wasn't the money that mattered – it was the revenge that was sweet. And it was also tax-free!

That wasn't the only time we got our own back on the press. One afternoon, a certain photographer from The Sun followed Adam as he left some West End establishment in a cab with a young girl DJ called Mo who worked at

Stringfellows and scared the life out of him. He could have been a stalker or an assassin for all Adam knew, so he asked the cab driver to lose the car that was tailing them. He tried but failed and, when they stopped, this guy leapt out, ran up to Adam's cab and took a snap of Adam and Mo. Adam jumped out and demanded that he stop taking pictures. The photographer's answer was unprintable – unlike his pictures of the two of them in the taxi, which appeared all over the press the next morning.

Adam was furious when he phoned me and asked me to sort this bloke out.

'I want this guy seen to!' he raged.

'Well who is he,' I asked.

'Dave Hogan – he works for The Sun.'

'OK, leave it with me,' I said, in my usual style.

I got hold of someone on the phone at The Sun, found out that Hogan was a freelancer, got his home number and dialled it straight away.

'I understand that you've been terrorising my artist,' I said, and he answered along the lines that it went with the territory and that he'd take pictures of who he bloody well liked. I pointed out that he'd scared the hell out of Adam; that he could have been an attacker...But he wasn't having any of it. He wouldn't even apologise – and that got my goat!

'OK Dave, I'm gonna teach you a lesson. I'm gonna hurt you,' I informed him in a matter of fact way.

'What do you mean?' he said, panicking.

'You'll find out!' I said and hung up leaving him, no doubt, picturing acts of terrible violence.

As a paparazzo, he used to hang around at places like Stringfellows, The Embassy and Legends – anywhere, in fact, where he thought he'd spot some famous faces to photograph. And guess who controlled the doors at all those top London clubs? And guess who worked with the guys who controlled the doors at virtually every other decent nightspot in London? Yes – it was me.

Next time Dave Hogan turned up at Stringfellows he was unceremoniously turned away. The same thing happened at Legends – and then at every other venue he tried. I'd hurt him all right! He couldn't work at all without my say-so! In the end I received a letter from Kelvin McKenzie, editor of The Sun, threatening me with all kinds of things. I phoned him up.

'I won't have you threatening my staff...You told him you were going to hurt him...' he shouted.

'Yes I did,' I interrupted. 'And I have hurt him because he can't work! You may be the top man on your paper but on the streets, I'm the top man mate and Dave Hogan doesn't work till I decide he can. Look, he took a liberty. He wasn't apologetic and to tell you the truth I knew what he'd think when I said I'd hurt him – but all I intended to do was stop him working. He's had his lesson now – so you tell him from me he can go back to work now!'

With that I hung up. Funny enough, I'd never even met Dave Hogan. And when someone pointed him out to me at the Montreux pop festival, it was a bit of a shock – the guy was bloody massive!!! Anyway, we were introduced and, mentioning that the Montreux show's organisers were giving all the photographers the runaround, he asked me nicely if I could help and whether he could get a shot of Adam. So I obliged and had a few words in a few ears, notably Adam's, and he got his shot. Simple as that. He only ever had to ask me nicely!

The longer I worked with Adam and the closer we became, the more I realised what a complex, and in some ways deeply troubled, character he was – but also that he was, and is, equally decent, honest and consummately professional. I'm in no position to form or offer an opinion on his psychological state but I can't help wondering whether the staggeringly dramatic difference between Adam's personality as a 'real person' and that as 'Adam Ant' holds any clue to the psychiatric problems he's endured over the years.

I know for a fact that his father's unsavoury antics didn't help. An alcoholic and solitary figure after the death of Adam's stepmother, Les Goddard was often to be seen around the Victoria Station area boasting that he was Adam Ant's dad. This didn't go unnoticed by the pimps running the rent boys that haunt the station area – it was the perfect bait with which to lure young runaway boys and seduce them into prostitution. Drunk and very lonely, Adam's father would do anything for a bit of company – so it was a simple matter to get him to let them use his nearby flat. Then all they had to do was approach any kid that looked lost and invite him round to see Adam Ant's gold discs. A few drinks and joints later the punters they invited to the flat could easily have their way with the new recruits. Soon the place was little short of a gay brothel – as we realised when Adam's dad was arrested for 'propositioning a minor'.

It turned out that Les, who was an ex-army guy with a real interest in military paraphernalia, used to have young local lads round to do some Airfix modelling. Pretty innocent in itself, until one of the lads, via his mother, accused Les of propositioning him. Well, by now all the locals knew that Les was Adam Ant's dad, which may have added fuel to the fire of the scandal. Anyway, the police didn't waste any time arresting him and charging him with propositioning a minor.

Of course Adam was upset – and he was also worried about the almost inevitable scandal the press would make of it – somehow managing, no doubt, to smear Adam's name in the process. I had to limit the damage this could do to my artist and friend, emotionally as well as professionally, so I rang Ralph Heamms, a very famous top lawyer who acted for all

56

sorts of big names, the Krays among them, as well as for little old me!

'Adam's dad's been nicked for propositioning a minor. I need you to sort it,' I said and gave him the names of the relevant police station and of the copper in charge.

'Leave it with me,' he said.

I don't know what he did – or how he did it but, incredibly, he rang back in half an hour.

'Hi Don. It's done. Don't worry. You won't hear any more about it.'

Just like that! Extremely impressed and very relieved, I asked him what we owed him. And the price of one of the top legal brains in the country for this priceless service was this: 'Just get Adam to give me a call and have a chat with my daughter!'

Talk about a bargain! But typically, Adam did more than was asked of him and he went round to Ralph's for dinner one evening, to his young daughter's utter delight, I'm sure! Imagine Adam's relief when I announced that the whole incident was done and dusted – at least from an official point of view.

Unfortunately that wasn't the end of it. Adam was off to America for a few days and, thinking the trouble was over, he'd gone round to visit his father to say goodbye and found that Les was no longer living alone. He rang me, outraged.

'Don, you've got to do something. There's some drag queen living with my dad!'

'Mmmm,' I thought. 'Here we go again.'

He left it to me and off I went to sort it. After all, Adam paid the rent for his father's flat so he had every right to object to someone else living there. Of course I got rid of said transvestite sharpish and without much trouble - but now I suspected that the goings-on in that flat were even more sordid than they already appeared. Feeling a bit out of my depth in that seamy gay underworld, I asked one of my best security guys, Michael Jackson, who happened to be gay, to go with me to the flat and have a look round (I should mention that Michael's a white man in case of confusion with Micky Jackson – a good mate of mine and my families and one of my Security Managers who was black and most definitely not gay!). I took him down there and left him there with Adam's dad, making some excuse, and waited in the car until Michael emerged about half an hour later.

'What do you think Mick?' I asked.

'Well he's gay,' he said.

'No!' I blurted in amazement.

'Yep. I can't tell you why I know – but I just know. 100 percent,' Mick said.

Adam was just off to America on tour – but I caught him before he left and broke the news that his father was gay. He was absolutely pig sick (ironically for a guy who almost made it acceptable for blokes to wear make-up, Adam was repelled by homosexuality). He was sicker still when I shared my suspicions about what was going on at the flat.

'They're using your dad down there, and he's letting these kids turn tricks in his place,' I said.

'Can you put a stop to it,' he asked.

'I'll do what I can – but I warn you it might mean getting him sectioned for a bit,' I said.

But about a week later, while we were getting our own ideas of sorting things out together, and Adam was in the US, the police raided the flat. They weren't after Adam's dad – they'd just followed some of the kids there in their search for an evil paedophile serial killer whose crimes were all over the papers at the time. They found Les Goddard in bed with a young boy and he was eventually sentenced to eighteen months. Adam saw very little of his father after that, although, through me, he constantly supplied him with money and clothes and all his material needs. When he came out of prison Goddard senior went to live with his mother in the country and slowly drank himself to death.

58

Of course the headlines didn't mention the name 'Goddard'. It was much more lucrative for them to say 'Adam Ant's Father!!!' More pressure and depression for Adam!

When he put on that elaborate and carefully conceived make-up he wasn't just putting on an image; he was literally transforming himself from the gentle unassuming soul that was Stuart Goddard into the sassy, sexy superstar that was Adam Ant! And perhaps he was also escaping the horrors that haunted his past and present. The ideas and designs for that ever-evolving image didn't come out of nowhere – they were drawn from his childhood fascination with romantic heroes. Blackbeard, the pirate, for example, inspired the little black bows in his hair that caused such a stir at one point and the Prince Charming look (as well as much of the decor of the Berkamsted house) was drawn from Napoleonic imagery that Adam had found in a French museum.

When we were on tour he'd go back to whatever hotel we were using to get ready (unless it was too far away, in which case he'd have to make do with the usually limited facilities in the venue's dressing room). And although that famous make-up looked bold and striking it took a very, very long time to get right – and once he'd got that mask on he became a totally different character to the diffident 'one of the lads' he'd been a couple of hours earlier. He'd emerge from his room in all his glory. And from that instant Adam was something else - the absolute master of all he surveyed. The transformation was unbelievable. He'd be totally keyed up; on a knife edge – and he was ruthless! God forbid anyone played a bum note or the lighting man missed a cue by a millisecond...He wouldn't tolerate any mistakes of any kind – and that attitude wasn't just confined to the performers. It included everyone involved in the tour. The on-stage performance had to be 100% as far as he was concerned –

whatever your job was you had to give 100% of yourself, whether you were the guitarist or the Tour Manager or the bus driver. He wouldn't accept anything less – and he wasn't averse to shouting at me either. And if there'd been the slightest cock-up in the show he was inconsolable, irate. He tore strips off anyone and everyone. From the moment he put that uniform on he became this martinet; this fascist dictator of a perfectionist. But then, when it was time to get out the cotton wool and mop it all away it was as if he was wiping away every trace of the larger than life character of Adam Ant; stripping himself of that personality and resuming the utterly opposite, humbler, gentler one of the Stuart Goddard that all of us came to know and love so well.

It was that utterly perfectionist side of Adam that led to the sacking of bassist Kevin Mooney from the Ants in February 1981 – and quite rightly so.

It was the 'Twenty-Five Years of British Pop' segment of the Royal Variety Performance at the London Palladium – one of those events an invitation to which tells you that you really are among the most famous of the famous. Not a gig you'd want to screw up – especially if you're the Prince Charming of the pop aristocracy!

All the boys did their own make-up – and even if theirs wasn't quite as detailed and elaborate as Adam's, it took just as long to apply if they wanted to get it right. Kevin turned up with Jordan – the celebrated punk icon, that is, as opposed to the Page Three girl – and he was wearing something quite outrageous. Trouble was, it just wasn't the kind of thing one of the Ants should be wearing at all - in fact he looked disastrous. If you've ever seen the Greek soldiers' traditional uniform you'll have some idea of what I'm talking about: white tights and a little frilly pearly white dress-type arrangement that certainly looked weird, but not remotely in

60

the way that Adam had of making outlandish costumes look cool, glam and larger than life. He just looked like a bloke in a skirt really – not the same thing at all! Worse still, his face make-up was completely at odds with the Ants' look. All the rest of the band and the assembled crew looked at him in amazement.

'What's going on?' I said to Adam. 'Tell him to get back there and get changed pronto!'

'We can't,' Adam replied quietly. 'It's too late.'

Adam was in full costume – which meant he would not take this lightly. It was clearly an affront to his authority, undermining the carefully created image of the group. They'd done the dress rehearsal hours before and Kevin had given no indication that he intended to make this sudden change. You could feel the tension in the air – but Adam was right. There was no time to make Mooney change – and even if there had been, changing his attitude would have taken a lot longer!

Incidentally, the dress rehearsal for a show like a Royal Command Performance isn't like a soundcheck and run-through at a rock 'n' roll gig. It's all planned down to the last detail (OK, maybe not so different from one of Adam's gigs!). You go through the whole thing, with every little move preordained in intricate detail: where you come on from and precisely when; where you make your exit from the stage – not forgetting to bow to the Queen and her team! Another fundamental difference is that the whole thing's lip-synched. In other words, all the acts mime to a tape – primarily because there's no time to set up the sound for bands and, probably, secondarily so that no-one gets the chance to introduce any nasty surprises!

I stood in the wings to watch my boys perform. And to my horror, Kevin Mooney was not doing what he was supposed to at all. I knew what his problem was. The band had grown out of punk and that was where I realised Kevin's heart still was. I suppose I can't blame him for that – but I can blame him for letting Adam and the others down out of his own egotistical obsessions. Basically he wanted to be the next Sid Vicious and that was the direction in which he wanted to steer the band – which was all very well, but the fact was that Adam and the Ants were no longer a punk band and hadn't been for quite some time. The new breed of 'kids' had discovered them – and although Adam was more creative, powerful and downright thrilling than today's more middle of the road offerings, the Ants were a pop group now – with a capital P!

In the middle of their one song, Kevin's guitar strap broke – or maybe he pulled it off, who knows. That wouldn't have been a problem – it happens. But he made it very, very obvious that he didn't give a monkey's. While the rest of them, and Adam in particular, were doing their utmost to make the performance look real, he just slung his bass about the place, making no effort to mime at all. And that, in my book, wasn't just letting the band down – it was letting the kids down. I mean, we all know that there are times when it's just not possible for the band to play it for real – but it's not fair to disillusion the fans by making it obvious. But that wasn't the worst of it. In a vulgar parody of a curtsey to the Queen, the bastard suddenly lifted up the front of his horrible little white skirt to flash the thinly disguised tackle under his grotesque white tights to an audience of royalty, all sorts of dignitaries and ordinary families and children. In other words, not your normal rock 'n' roll crowd, which wouldn't have turned a hair.

When they came off stage Adam was as white with anger as the stripe across the middle of his face.
'Sack him!' he grated under his breath as he strode past me.
'What...?' I mumbled.

62

'Sack him. Sack him,' he said, now quivering and livid with rage (Don't forget that this was Adam Ant, still in full costume – not the mild-mannered, Clark Kent-like, Stuart Goddard!).

I took Kevin aside at the first chance I got and asked him to come and see me at the office first thing in the morning. He must have known why. Anyway, he turned up just as I'd asked and I unceremoniously fired him from the UK's biggest pop group.

Despite Adam's vehemence in demanding that I sack Kevin, he was mortified by the incident. I think the betrayal, combined with the ruining of the performance, nearly killed him – because his perfectionism wasn't just a pose; it was in his blood and I'm sure it still is. If you went to his flat you'd see that all his suits and outfits were neatly pressed and not just hung but filed in his wardrobes. His shoes and boots were perfectly laced and polished – as were his leather trousers and jackets. Every detail was neat and tidy, carefully maintained and utterly organised, which I suppose is a bit ironic considering his origins in the punk rock scene. That meticulous approach ran through every aspect of his life – he'd write everything down, no matter how trivial it might seem to anyone else. In fact he kept a diary, in which he would write religiously every day, recording everything that happened to him and his mates every single day of his life, including marks out of ten for all the different women he'd been with. Nothing about Adam was casual – and that included the way he treated his fans.

One time, on tour in Manchester, the hotel security people made me aware of a fan in the lobby whose obsession with Adam was so extreme that it went far beyond anything I'd seen in more than twenty years looking after groups that inspired just as much adulation as the Ants. It wasn't that she was physically debilitated or that she came across as unbalanced. But her fixation on Adam was so intense that she literally - and I mean literally - could not utter a single sentence without mentioning his name. Apparently she'd been that way for a good three years – so she was a bit of a diehard Ants fan – and she'd been through all sorts of treatment, including electro-convulsive therapy, which is a very unpleasant ordeal, none of which had been effective. Maybe meeting the object of her obsession could achieve what the psychiatrists couldn't, I thought. After all, apart from this affliction, she seemed to be a very normal, pleasant young woman who wasn't a threat to my protégé - and, seeing her sitting forlornly in the hotel lobby, alone without a hope in hell of meeting her idol, I was touched. I went to Adam's room and asked him to come down and talk to her.

'You don't have to,' I said, 'but she seems to have been through some terrible trauma and maybe if you talk to her it'll help her. I know it might be harrowing – and if you can't face it, I'll understand but...It may just help...'

I didn't need to say anything more. Adam agreed to go and meet her straight away. With hindsight, perhaps it was because he understood the pain of psychiatric illness. But actually, it was probably just because Adam was, and is, a very kind and caring man.

So Adam came down and sat in a quiet corner with this girl for about half an hour. I wasn't privy to their conversation but I know he tried as hard as he could to help her, to give her some kind of direction in her life that wasn't aiming purely at Adam Ant. Whether or not it helped her I suppose we'll never know – but I do know that it wasn't easy for Adam.

'I don't think I could go through that again,' said a drained and upset Adam when he came back upstairs.

64

Adam's need for complete control made itself more and more apparent as his career went from strength to strength – and the rest of the Ants soon found themselves surplus to requirements. By this time Adam and Marco were handling all the song writing and even the recording without input from the rest of the band – they played all the instruments, including the drums, at one time. I suppose Adam began to wonder why he was sharing all the money with the band in a five-way split when he and Marco were the only ones doing any work.

Now Adam's creativity was completely unfettered and he took total control over the way he was promoted – most significantly by virtually reinventing the promotional video as a piece of action drama with high production values. The record company had been touting showreels by the usual batch of video directors, mostly pals of the A&R people I suspect, and Adam was expected to pick one of their boys and sit back while he put the promo together. But that wasn't Adam's style at all. He came to me and said that he wasn't impressed by any of them. I didn't see why he should be restricted to the people the record company put forward so I introduced Adam to a very good friend of mine – Mike Mansfield. They got on like a house on fire! Mike was happy to give Adam's irrepressible creativity free reign and let him loose on the concepts and storyboards. CBS weren't too happy about being obliged to relinquish control to their artist together with a director who was also a producer in his own right – but they had to admit that the results were stunning and totally fresh. The first in the can was 'Stand and Deliver', a swashbuckling, swaggering mini-epic in its own right that set the tone for all the rest to come. Unlike the average pop promo, Adam's videos didn't try to replicate the atmosphere of live performance – that nearly always fails. Instead they captured the spirit of Adam and the Ants and amplified it to create images that were ten times larger than life – just like their creator really!

DIANA ROSS AND ADAM ANT AT NBC TV'S MOTOWN 25TH ANNIVERSARY SHOW

In 1983, Tamla Motown, the seminal soul record label whose name defines a whole musical style, was celebrating its 25th anniversary with a big televised event featuring many of their own legendary stars and a select few major pop stars of the time. So, when I received an invitation for Adam Ant to appear, I accepted it like a shot. Adam's music was a million miles away from Motown but it was a fantastic chance to reach a massive new audience. When you look at the list of names that appeared when the show was broadcast on 16th May you can see that Adam really was right out of the left field!

Michael Jackson – with the Jackson 5 for the first time in years
Diana Ross and The Supremes
The Four Tops
Linda Ronstadt
José Feliciano
Smokey Robinson
Marvin Gaye
And....As they say, many many more!

We just had to go for it and off we went to LA to record Adam's track for the show. Arriving at LA airport, I drove Adam in a hired car to the studio in Pasadena, California and we were both pretty excited about the whole thing. So I was taken aback when we arrived in the studio car park and Adam suddenly froze in his seat.
'No!' was all he said.

I had a horribly familiar sinking feeling. The one I get when I've set up something for my artist and suddenly, inexplicably, they refuse to do it. And guess who looks a fool – yours truly!

'Adam...Why?' I asked quietly, summoning all my patience.

'I just can't go through with it...I just can't...I won't,' he stuttered under his breath. He looked pale; frightened even.

Of course I knew him well enough to understand what he was going through. Once he went through that studio door he would be Adam Ant – not Stuart Goddard – and the upstart white boy pop star from England would have to perform with all those Motown legends. He was just terrified.

But it was way too late to back out now. I cajoled, coerced, lectured and persuaded him until finally I got my quivering wreck of an artist through those doors, where we immediately met the legendary Berry Gordy before being ushered through into the studio area. Adam stopped, frozen again. Through the glass we could see a sea of mainly Black American faces, maybe thirty or so of them, all with greying and white hair and beards. He was absolutely bricking it. He'd rather have been anywhere but in that studio – and I wasn't exactly cool as a cucumber myself. If someone had dropped a bomb on that studio that day the world would have lost just about every one of the great geniuses of soul music!

Only the hefty soundproofed door separated Adam from these legends – and after a lot of hesitation, I got him to push it open...The reaction he got was incredible. All of them looked up, saw Adam Ant and spontaneously broke into applause! Talk about gobsmacked! And it wasn't just politeness – their applause was genuine and heartfelt. They loved him!

That was it – Adam was captivated and filled with a new confidence. So much so that he got his track down in a mere two takes – and the performance was among his best ever. In retrospect, I'm convinced that walking through that studio door was, literally, one of the most important steps of Adam's career. He was afraid to perform alongside his peers; worried that he'd be found wanting. But he wasn't! He proved himself – to himself more than anyone else and he was a resounding success!

Mind you the show itself, at the Civic Auditorium in Pasadena, California on the 25th March wasn't without its problems! Sitting at the side of the stage watching Adam's performance on a monitor I suddenly noticed that someone was on stage that shouldn't have been. And they were interfering with Adam's act! I couldn't allow that. Not at an event as important as this one – or any other come to that. As I leapt to my feet ready to manhandle this overenthusiastic fan off the stage someone caught my arm and whispered in my ear. I was right! An over enthusiastic fan had run onto the stage all right. But it was the fan's identity that stopped me in my tracks!

'That's Diana Ross!' the bloke said fervently.

Well! I did a Disney cartoon-style double take. And sure enough, the queen of soul music had got carried away with Adam's performance and run from her position in the wings to join him, dancing provocatively round him as he struggled manfully to carry on regardless! When Adam's number was over he ran up to me, overwhelmed with excitement.

'Don! Did you see that??? Did you see what happened???' he babbled, beside himself.

'Yes,' I replied, hardly less hysterical myself.

'Diana Ross, dancing with me! I couldn't remember my words or anything...She just floored me!'

By now Adam didn't need anyone. He was unstoppable. He didn't need me anymore – or my protection. Or so I thought...

Towards the end of 1983 it became clear to me that it was time for Adam and I to go our separate ways – not that there was any ill will between us. It was just that our association wasn't bearing fruit the way it used to. My other businesses were suffering by my continued and increasingly prolonged absences and anyway I wasn't comfortable with the musical direction he was taking. Never one to rest on his laurels, he was keen to develop a new sound and image – but the trouble was, in my view, that it was one that the kids weren't quite so interested in.

In general Adam was being just a little bit difficult and when the next US tour came up there were plenty of other good reasons why I should stay behind this time round. For starters, he was a lot more confident and the tours were organised like military operations - I'd made sure of that - so he didn't need me along to hold his hand the way he once had. Obviously, the saving on flights and accommodation wasn't to be sneezed at either.. Instead my son Bradley went along to work with Pete Clark from Supermick Lighting Co. on the lights.

A couple of days into the tour I got a call from Adam in a frantic, almost hysterical, state. The problem was the manager of The Romantics, who were the support act and an up and coming band in the States at the time (They were the second support act we'd had – on our first major tour it was a then little-known band called INXS!).

It's probably worth explaining the way tours work in America at this point. The uninitiated would probably imagine that performers are simply paid a fee to perform on the dates they're booked for – but it's not as simple as that. In the UK any band that wants to be the support on a major tour has to 'buy on'. In other words, their record company coughs up a not insignificant amount of money in 'tour support' – a contribution to the overall cost of the tour and to the support act's use of the PA and lighting. In the states there's also an element of 'tour support' involved but because the scale is so much bigger the main act's management is always on the lookout for a support band that's already making its presence felt but which hasn't yet become a serious live contender. That way, you hope, there's a good chance that they'll achieve a high chart placing while the tour's still going, thereby guaranteeing sell-out shows. Needless to say, The Romantics were just such an act. It's the nature of the beast that there's a conflict of interest. The support act wants to get the best sound and lighting it possibly can – in short, they'd ideally like to steal the show. On the other hand, there's no way the main act's going to allow these upstarts to upstage them – so their sound and lighting people will keep a strict eye on the levels, ensuring that the support doesn't sound too good. Friction, therefore, is almost inevitable.

And in this case the friction had gone way too far for Adam's liking. The Romantics' manager wasn't just pushy – just doing his best for his band would've been perfectly professional and completely understandable – he was so downright aggressive and obnoxious, that I wondered whether he was also a serious cokehead to boot (which would have explained why he was such a pain in the arse – they generally are!). It was bad enough when he commandeered the mixing desk in the soundcheck on one occasion, despite our sound guys' protests and just whacked the faders up to full blast, way over the maximum support band's levels we'd previously agreed. What was much worse was that he did it again in the middle of his band's gig. He stormed the desk, bodily throwing our sound man off the rostrum and pushing up the volume again. Well, up with this we would not put!

Anyway, I told Adam, as always to 'leave it with me' and got onto our US contact at CBS New York about it. He was about as much use as a chocolate teapot. He just said he'd have a quiet word and ask him to calm down a bit.

It didn't have a lot of effect because Adam was on the phone again the next night.

'Don, he's getting even worse. He's been threatening me and threatening the band...He's totally off his head! Something's got to be done about him Don!'

'Leave it with me,' I said again, just for a change. And after briefing the Road Manager on a few measures that would make the little sod think twice about getting uppity, I went off to make some more calls to Mike Piranian – CBS' New York Artist Liaison man and Al de Marino. CBS might have thought they had some corporate clout – but they couldn't control this wayward manager. But I had mates with a very different kind of clout and I knew they'd get results.

I made a call to a very good friend of mine, Billy Brindle, who was from a well-known London family but wasn't your usual 'face' in that he was an artistic sort who wrote and sang his own songs.

'I need some help in the States,' I said, 'Have you got anyone out there?'

'Yes mate,' he replied, 'What exactly is the problem?'

'Well,' I said, 'We're having some trouble with this manager of a pop group out of Detroit that's supporting Adam. I believe he's a right cokehead and he's becoming a right pain in the arse and if he keeps going the way he is, he's going to ruin the tour – if you can call it a tour...We're only two or three days into it and it's already more like World War Three!'

'Yeah I can sort that out no problem.' my mate replied, sounding just like me! 'Leave it with me,' he went on, before hanging up, promising to call me back ASAP.

The phone rang a very short while later and he said, 'Right, OK – it's sorted. I've called in a favour and some friends of friends from Chicago are going to sort it out. I just need all the tour details – halls, hotels and so on and a contact name.'
'Thank you very much!' I said. Done job!

The next day, though, I had several more frantic calls from Adam, who was now in a right old state of panic.
'Don,' he said, 'I've been thinking about it overnight and he's still acting like an arsehole but he hasn't been quite so bad...But I know what you're like Don...I don't really want any problems, if you know what I mean...'
'Look Adam,' I interrupted, 'there are no problems – just forget about it! It's all been arranged.'
'Well I want it all cancelled,' he said emphatically. 'I'm just going to have to live with it and sort it out myself.'
'Well, it doesn't sound like anyone there can control this guy – and it's going to get a lot worse before it gets better,' I said. But Adam Ant, characteristically, was adamant!
'No! Whatever it is you're going to do – don't do it!'
'All right, have it your way then,' I said – although he'd put me in something of a predicament.

I rang my friend back to ask him if he could call off his Chicago boys.
'Look Don,' he said impatiently, 'you should have thought of that before you called it on. It's too late now – it's all in hand...So you're just going to have to deal with it.'
I had thought as much. I knew full well that before you call something on you have to weight up all the pros and cons very carefully because once you start that heavy ball rolling it's bloody difficult – dangerous even – to get in its way!
'Fair enough,' I said to my mate.

I rang Barry Mead, our Road Manager, and talked him through the situation.

'Look,' I said, 'Adam's suddenly got cold feet about having this guy dealt with. How do you feel about it?'

'Well,' he replied in exasperation, 'the guy's a complete nightmare! If he's like this at the start – what's he going to be like by the end of five weeks? It's going to be absolute chaos!'

'OK,' I said. 'Look, something is going to happen, don't you worry! All that's going to happen is this: some people are going to come down and get him on his own and give him a good talking to. Now, when you see it happening, for God's sake don't interfere and let them have their head...They're not mugs...There's not going to be any bloodshed' At least I hoped there wasn't going to be any bloodshed! The Road Manager grunted his assent – but without much conviction.

'Just let it run,' I reiterated firmly. 'If they ask you anything, if they say they've been sent by me, just co-operate with them and just let it run...'

'OK,' he agreed, a little more confident now.

Well, two days later my son Bradley and Fay, one of the other lighting guys reported back to me. They'd just finished the soundcheck and most of the crew had headed back to the hotel for a rest before the concert started. These two guys in dark suits like something out of The Godfather suddenly turned up at the stage door and asked where The Romantics' manager could be found – and from the look of them it was bloody obvious that they weren't just popping in for a social visit. These guys meant business. Bradley and Fay directed them to The Romantics' dressing room and almost the moment they disappeared through the door, everyone else in there came flying out, clearly scared shitless!

It was a good quarter of an hour before the two stereotypical hoods emerged and quietly left the building. Anyway, from that moment on, the formerly stroppy git was bending over backwards to be nice and to oblige our crew and the Ants in any way he could! Funny that!

Of course, Adam wasn't aware of what had gone on. But he did phone me to say that the formerly obnoxious Romantics manager was now as nice as pie.

'He's being unbelievably nice!' Adam exclaimed.

'Ah, well, I can explain that mate! Look, if you check with the crew you'll find that he did have a visit from someone after all – I couldn't stop it once I'd called it on. It's just not done Adam. Anyway, it's nothing for you to worry about – there's no reflection on you. But I can guarantee you won't have any more trouble with him!'

A few days later I flew out to New York, where Adam and the Ants were appearing at the famous Radio City Music Hall. Of course by this time everyone had got wind of what had happened – and if they hadn't, they'd have guessed from that manager's miraculous transformation into mister nice guy – and were eager to see what would happen when he and I came face to face for the first time! I wasn't fazed by it at all because he was bound to be scared of me after whatever those hoods had said or done to him – he'd certainly know who'd sent them – whereas I had nothing to fear from him at all. So I wasn't all that surprised when I turned up to discover that he was nowhere to be found. In fact no-one saw hide nor hair of the bastard for the entire two-day stint at Carnegie Hall! He'd just completely gone on the missing list.

It just goes to show what you can achieve - often without violence, or at least without much - if you know the right people and make the right noises!

*   *   *

Some time after my management contract with Adam was finished and he was living in Los Angeles, I got another call from him – we were and still are very good friends – to say that he was being threatened, yet again. And he was very scared.

'What's the story then,' I asked.

'Well,' he said, 'there's this Scottish guy who's going out with Lelia (I believe she's one of Adam's ex-girlfriends)...'

I should explain at this point that Adam always managed to break up with his girlfriends on the best of terms and they'd almost always remain the best of friends. Not only did he keep in touch with them all, but he'd also send them postcards, letters and even some of his drawings from wherever in the world he travelled. A very nice, friendly gesture, you'd have thought, but sometimes their possessive new boyfriends didn't agree.

This was just such an occasion. This guy saw Adam's letter and got the raving hump – obviously threatened by the girl he wanted to marry (or at least use to get his green card to stay in the States!) receiving a friendly letter from a guy who was not only an ex-boyfriend, but also an exceptionally handsome one who also happened to be one of the biggest pop stars in the world! Now, I could understand the bloke feeling a bit insecure – but threatening Adam was going way too far. Apparently he'd got hold of Adam's number (presumably from the letter) and phoned up several times, each time leaving a threatening message. Before the most recent message, he'd evidently got drunk and wound himself up into a frenzy of paranoia and what he said on the phone was very, very heavy indeed. It really got to him. Adam was downright terrified – so terrified, in fact, that he was considering getting out of the house he'd bought in LA. He just no longer felt safe living there, since this nutter obviously knew the address.

75

I asked Adam for the guy's name and anything at all that he knew about him. He told me the name and went on to say that he was an ex-professional Scottish footballer who'd moved to LA and become some sort of choreographer and/or fitness trainer.

With that I made a call to a very close friend of mine in London.

'Do you have any help up in Scotland?' I asked, 'Because I need to speak to someone...'

'Yes – I know the man, in fact!' he replied and said he'd get this man to call me straight away.

No sooner said than done – the phone rang minutes later and a voice asked in a thick Scottish brogue what he could do for me. It was a Glaswegian called Billy.

'Hello, thanks for calling so quick,' I said. 'My problem is this. I manage Adam Ant and he's got a problem with a Scotsman out in Los Angeles who's getting very excitable and leaning on him...threatening him big time...'

I told him the guy's name, mentioning that he used to be a footballer, and he immediately cut in.

'Oh I know him!' Billy said and went on to give me chapter and verse on the bloke.

'He's a complete jerk,' he said. 'He's not even worth worrying about!'

'Well, look,' I said, 'Would you do me a favour? If I give you his number, can you give him a call?'

'No problem mate – a favour call? Love to!'

So I gave him the relevant number, thanked him and said goodbye.

A day or so later I got another call from a pleased but incredulous Adam.

'What did you do to him?' he marvelled. 'He's just phoned me up and he's absolutely terrified!'

I laughed.

'Well, Adam – you know I've got friends. I just called in a favour.'

'Some favour!' he went on. 'How can I say thank you?'

'I'll tell you how you say thank you,' I said. 'Take down Billy's phone number in Scotland and give him a call and have a chat with him. Maybe you can send him some signed photos or albums or something for his kids.'

Adam took my advice and called Billy – and this extremely hard Glaswegian gangster was absolutely over the moon when Adam chatted with him and his kids and send them all sorts of presents!

This was another example of what you can do with the right contacts. Poor old Adam was six thousand miles from home and his friends, and completely mortified by the threats that were spewing out of his answering machine almost on a daily basis....Yet all it took was one phone call to the right man and the whole thing goes away for good!

It's always the same with guys like that pathetic ex-footballer. He's all full of himself when he's got the hump, making death threats he hasn't got the bollocks to carry out – but as soon as someone with a bit of clout turns the tables on him, he's like a little puppy dog! Obviously, since I was no longer Adam's manager, I didn't have to sort out this problem. But he was still my friend and I was still concerned at the thought of him sitting there alone and scared in that great big house in LA, living in fear and totally unable to resolve the situation. After all, he had more pressure on him than most people could take – and he certainly didn't need this shit!

It might sound a bit gangster-like to you – but let's face it, all it took was a couple of calls, a favour called in and it was done. Finished. And what's more, everyone was happy! Adam could get on with his life and work without looking over his shoulder. I no longer needed to worry about Adam's safety and our Glaswegian friend's kids were ecstatic about going to school and bragging that they'd been talking to Adam Ant. And of course their big hard Dad was happy that his kids were happy – especially since it hadn't really been any skin off his nose to make that call because he hadn't really liked the jumped-up ex-footballer in the first place and had quite enjoyed putting him in his place!

Looking back at how he was then and at how he is now, I can't help wondering whether Adam's almost schizophrenic transformation into that stage persona has something to tell us about the state he's in now. Isn't it possible that now he's lost that outlet for the other side of his character he's having trouble just being Stuart? Who knows? I know I don't!

It would be ridiculous to write a chapter about Adam's career without acknowledging the fact of his recent tragic tribulations. As someone who came to know this very troubled, complex, incredibly talented and creative, yet kind and decent man very well, I hope that my perspective will counteract the misinformed, misleading and even downright cruel speculations we've seen in the press following Adam's unfortunate recent dramas.

In that spirit, here's what I've garnered from my brief phone conversations with Adam and Marco about that awful time when Adam got sectioned.

I rang Adam as soon as I heard.
'Hi Adam. How are you?' I asked.
'Oh, hi Don,' he replied, 'thanks for ringing. I've had some terrible problems...'
'Well I can see that – what happened?'
'Well,' he replied, 'this guy had been saying I owed him some money for something I'd asked him to do for me...I

don't know what...So I went round to see him and he started getting very nasty - violent in fact. Worse than that, he said some very bad things about my daughter...'

'What do you mean?' I interjected, my concern now redoubled.

'Well,' Adam replied gravely, 'he said "have you ever seen what a grown man can do to a four-year-old girl?"'

This sounded far more serious than I'd expected. I pressed him to tell me more. Among other things, he told me that he'd then stalked the guy for four to six weeks.

'You'd have been proud of me Don,' he said, going on to detail the intricate plans he'd laid in preparation for neutralising the threat of this man. He'd finally gone down to this pub that the bloke frequented. But what he didn't know was that it was a National Front pub – a private members' place. And in case you're not familiar with them, the NF extremists are not the nicest of people at the best of times – and certainly not the kind you want to take on all on your own!

Having heard all this I didn't know what to think – or how to reconcile it with what I'd read in the papers. Not that I was any stranger to the concept that the press tell lies – it was just that Adam's interpretation of events was so very different. I phoned Marco to see what he knew.

'It's a complete load of rubbish,' he said, quite emphatically. 'It's all in his mind. He's been trying to have it with the guy's wife – and the guy's had a pop at him, simple as that!'

'But Marco,' I said, confused. 'If you'd heard what Adam said the bloke said about Adam's daughter...It was horrible...'

That phrase has stuck in my mind ever since – it's not the kind of thing you forget: 'Have you ever seen what a grown man can do to a four-year-old girl?' I mean, just making that kind of threat...It was just sick! I'd never seen any corroboration of this threat until very recently Adam mentioned it in a press interview, which was the first time I'd seen it in print.

But before I continue with Adam's version of the story, perhaps I should outline what the press said. We'll probably never know the real truth – but the following is an agglomeration of the facts I've gleaned from the various and often self-contradictory reports in the press.

According to The Sun (August 14th 2002) Adam went to the pub – The Prince of Wales in Kentish Town, North London – dressed 'in a white Stetson and combat jacket to pistol-whip a besotted fan's jealous husband who had been harassing him.' This, at least, seems consistent with Adam's version of events. But on entering the pub (though later reports say he was never allowed in!) he was apparently faced with a crowd who clearly didn't recognise him and who mocked his appearance by humming the theme tune to 'The Good, the Bad and the Ugly'. Adam stormed out and allegedly came back and threw a car alternator through a window, which hit one of the drinkers in the head – at which point Adam is supposed to have pulled out a starting pistol and threatened the crowd with it. The report goes on to say that the pub's customers then chased him out of the pub and called the police. Far be it from me to suggest that The Sun plays fast and loose with the facts – but it is interesting to note that the 'starting pistol' mentioned in their piece on August 14th 2002 had become a 'wartime revolver' by the time their August 16th 2002 report went to press. On the 23rd, the Daily Mail also described the weapon as a 'revolver' before going on to say that it was an 'imitation firearm'!

That said, half of the rest fits roughly with what Adam told me. He did say he was wearing combat gear – but he also mentioned 'five or six guys in a car' after him that I haven't seen reported.

Adam went on to say, admittedly in a very feverish way that suggested he wasn't entirely balanced, that he'd escaped by hailing a taxi. One comment that sticks in my mind was when he said, 'I knew what you'd have done Don – I hid the gun under the seat!' Which made me laugh despite the sinking feeling I had in sympathy with Adam's plight. Of course, that would have been the last thing I'd do. If the police know a guy's got a gun they'll take the whole car apart till they find the thing. And, of course, they found it – and Adam was in deep trouble.

'They bashed me...Threw me to the ground...' he went on, in a tone of complete terror, 'And one of them nutted me...Just smashed my face up. I was saying I didn't want to cause any trouble...But they took me off out of there...'

The police had arrested him, kept him overnight, charged and released him on that occasion. He then went AWOL and, once Social Services realised that he was unstable because he hadn't been taking his medication, they sectioned him. In this respect, the press reports are roughly right, although theirs was a simplified version of events – reporting that the police caught up with Adam near Camden Lock and took him in a van straight to the Royal Free Hospital just up Haverstock Hill in Belsize Park where he was detained 'for his own protection and "for the safety of others" under Section Two of the 1983 Mental Health Act.'

And from that point on, the press account rings true – because The Sun, on 16th August 2002, reported that Adam had phoned them from the Royal Free, saying that 'I've been abducted by the police......They've sectioned me – I've been here all night. The whole thing's a conspiracy and they're just out to get me. I'm not mad.'

Sadly, this version sounds depressingly like the one Adam told me when I got a strange phone call from Chris de Niro from the band (thus nicknamed by Adam and credited on the albums because he looks like Robert de Niro), who was apparently at the Alice Ward at the Royal Free – the secure mental ward where people who have been sectioned are held for assessment! What the hell was he doing there? I wondered – until Adam's voice cut in and all became clear. He was frantic, pleading with me to send him two or three of my best very large security men that night 'because they're coming to get me, the police and the SAS!' I didn't know what to think – but although I've been out of that game for a good fourteen years now I said I'd get Sid Sofos down there. Adam told Chris to write Sid's name on the wall by the phone so that he could get a visitor's pass for him. Having made sure that Sid was available, I thought it wise to check with Marco before sending him down to fend off Adam's attackers! It was a good thing I did! Marco filled me in on Adam's worsening mental state since I'd last seen him: he'd been sectioned before in LA and had committed himself a couple of times in the UK and Marco was convinced that he needed to be sectioned for his own good. He was a danger to himself. There was some truth in what Adam was saying but he'd built it up into an epic drama in his head, exaggerating it and embellishing the facts with film-like fantasy that he believed completely. The fact that he seemed to have stopped taking his medication didn't help matters.

But I don't want to close this chapter about Adam on that rather tragic note. That would look like these unfortunate events are the end of his story – and I'm sure that won't be the case. Certainly Adam's been plagued by mental illness and certainly that's manifested itself of late in ways that have provoked mockery in some quarters and sympathy in others. I, and all of Adam's other real friends and fans, are in the latter category.

Who knows whether or not he'll ever reappear as a pop performer. It doesn't really matter because, in his time at the top, he achieved more than most could ever hope for. His talent was, and is, outstanding – but in the end it's what the man's like as a normal human being that's important from now on.

So I'll leave you with a tale of a little-known persona that Stuart Goddard adopted on an annual basis – the time when Prince Charming, the Dandy Highwayman, the King of the Wild Frontier was also Santa Claus.

In the run-up to the first Christmas of the time I was with Adam, he came to me and said that he wanted to spend Christmas Day with kids in hospital – specifically, kids who were seriously or chronically ill.
'OK,' I said, and got on with making the arrangements, about which Adam was very specific. No-one – and I mean no-one – other than the kids and their friends and families and, of course, the hospital staff was to know about his visit. On Adam's instructions, I told each of the hospitals on our itinerary that if there was any leak to the press or any other media the whole thing would be off.

Emotional blackmail's a powerful thing and we persuaded the record company to provide us with a vanload of records, posters, photos, Adam Ant dolls and any other sort of merchandise.

Anyone can blag a load of swag from their record company. But it's not everyone who spends the whole day hanging out at several London hospitals just talking to seriously ill children. Personally I was disturbed and upset by the visible evidence of each child's ordeal – the tubes and electrodes protruding from painful-looking points in their slight and delicate bodies. But Adam seemed undaunted – and his unannounced Christmas hospital visits became a kind of top secret tradition. And every time Adam would come back to my house afterwards for his Christmas dinner – because his own family didn't feel like a family any more, for obvious reasons. He'd eat his meal with us – but every time it was obvious that the experience at the hospitals had utterly drained him and as soon as he felt it was polite to leave the table he'd slump onto our sofa and fall deeply asleep.

When he went to visit those kids, knowing he had the power to brighten their lives and alleviate their suffering, if only for a short while, it seemed to me that he was just as committed as when he was playing the most important performances of his life. He gave himself, heart and soul to those kids, just like he did with those other kids – the fans – when he was on stage.

As I mentioned earlier, it seems that Adam's now drinking and smoking – and I've heard that his new friends play up to him all the time. They probably don't realise that their constant flattery and approval is just what his illness makes him crave and therefore is just what he doesn't need. But of course, that's out of my hands now and that's the end of this chapter on Adam. But I'm sure it's not the end of his story!

STARS GET STARSTRUCK TOO!

SCARLET & JIMMY PAGE

Once, when Adam Ant was appearing at the Dominion, Tottenham Court Road, I'd driven up there with my daughter Lyndsey and we met Jimmy Page (a very old friend of mine by this time) and his daughter Scarlet. Of course I had things to do and people to see, so I asked Lyndsey to stick with Jimmy and Scarlet for a while. I could hardly fail to notice that Scarlet was made up with the complete Adam Ant look – obviously a fan. And the irony was that Scarlet, the daughter of Jimmy the legendary Led Zeppelin guitarist, was madly jealous of my Lyndsey. Why? Because Lyndsey's dad, little old me, was the manager of her idol, Adam Ant!! The fact that her dad was, if anything, more famous meant nothing to her. It just goes to show that even the superstars and their families can be every bit as starstruck as the rest of us mere mortals!

CHAPTER THREE

1959

MY FIRST BITTER TASTE OF PORRIDGE

Her Majesty's finest arrested us – Kenny, Freddie, Twinkle and me – in 1958 after we'd been on a little mission down in Farnborough where we'd broken into a place, having carefully bypassed a complex system of alarmed doors and floors, or so we thought... When we blew the safe all hell broke loose; the safe's alarm was pressure-triggered. So we legged it pronto and sat back on the hill for a while watching the cop cars swarm in like bluebottles round rubbish and enjoying the sight of them buzzing about the place. Not what you might call normal procedure for a firm that's just set off the alarms on a pretty serious job! But when you've been getting away with it for years and running rings round the Old Bill you tend to get a bit complacent, blasé even. And that's what we were, I must admit, getting too cocky by half! We broke our own golden rule: that we would never travel back into the Smoke (London) during the early hours and would always wait up till there was plenty of other traffic on the roads as people headed into town for work.

So we shouldn't really have been surprised when, driving back into the Smoke on the A30 about an hour and a half later, we were stopped and nicked in short order! Back at Farnborough Police Station we were charged and while we were waiting to come up before the local magistrates court there was this big hoo-ha and headlines in the local press about a big firm of London safe blowers.

For a pleasant change, the Old Bill were actually quite nice about the whole thing. They gave us breakfast in our little rooms and even kept us supplied with cakes and sweets and cups of tea and so on! Mind you, they weren't that generous – we paid for it all out of whatever cash we had on us. We even had books to keep us occupied in one of the rooms while we reserved another two for sleeping in until finally we were up in front of the beak and packed straight off to the Scrubs, where I was to get my first bitter taste of 'porridge' – a taste with which I was to become depressingly familiar.

Prison at the back end of the fifties was a very different proposition to what it is today: it was harsh.

After the obligatory searching and hideously cold bath and delousing procedures – which I reckon had as much to do with the ritual humiliation of new inmates as it did with institutional hygiene measures – you had your formal date with the governor to look forward to. For this cosy little *tête à tête*, the prison officers would march you in and make you stand to attention on a mark on the floor in front of the Governor at his desk. Then the crimes with which you'd been charged or sentenced would be read out to him and he would lay down the law to you in no uncertain terms, all the time looking at you the way you'd look at a piece of shit on your shoe. And then you'd be shown to your accommodation for the duration of your stay with Her Maj, which you'd generally be sharing with at least two others. Now the Scrubs was, and is, a Victorian building, with a touch of the gothic horror about it and it certainly wasn't designed to make you feel good about being there! Not the kind of boudoir that makes you dive enthusiastically onto your bed to test the springs. If you did, you'd probably have broken your back. The beds (well, bunks) were of steel – and instead of springs they featured taut metal straps, topped by unyielding mattresses made of coir (fibre from the husk of coconuts) or horsehair, which were a right pain in the arse, back, legs and pretty much every other part of the inmate's anatomy! To make the discomfort complete, you had a rock hard 'pillow' and the blankets were made of a puke green tweedy material that made you itch like crazy. Obviously, if you were in there your life wasn't exactly going to plan – but at least no-one could say you didn't have a pot to piss in! On the contrary, the luxurious amenities included just that – one pot each, with lids provided in a vain attempt to stifle the stink. Other mod cons included a slit of a window set high up in the cell wall, thickly and considerately glazed with strengthened glass and bars to spare you the view outside and to ensure the level of light was always a dismal shade of grey, and the metal pipes that clanked out a 24-hour soundtrack of rumbling Victorian plumbing combined with the ceaseless tapping of other prisoners communicating in Morse code (eavesdropping on these conversations was apparently quite entertaining as well as being a handy source of information, but unfortunately I didn't know Morse code!). The décor of your cell (or 'Peter' in prison parlance), perfectly in keeping with the other accoutrements, was a masterpiece of penal minimalism in raw concrete, hard steel and painted bricks and, as a final caring touch, the miniscule air vent was ingeniously designed in such a way that it provided a chilling draught without actually freshening the cell's rank and stagnant air.

Just in case the three of you felt lonely at any time, a spyhole was thoughtfully provided so that you were reassured by the comforting thought that a friendly screw was always keeping an eye on you!

In short, 'bleak' didn't begin to cover it! Breakfast meant porridge, always – hence the term 'doing porridge'. In fact there's an old lag's saying to the effect that if you don't eat your porridge on the day you're getting out, you'll be back for it. Luckily for me I like porridge (quite a bonus if you're going to spend any time in stir!) so I always ate mine up; a lot of poor sods hated the stuff and failed to eat it most of the time. But they always, without exception, ate every scrap on their last day inside, such was the power of that superstition.

Mealtimes were as regimented as every other aspect of prison life in those days. We'd be called down, one landing at a time, and we'd file through into the mess, collecting our 'cob' on the way (these large-ish bread rolls were about the only half-decent items on the menu!) There, the muck they laughingly referred to as 'meals' was slopped into our steel trays, which had separate compartments for main course, pudding and for cutlery, which, amazingly, was still made of metal in those days. You can't imagine them giving convicts metal knives these days can you! As well as your steel tray you had a steel bowl – much like the ones you use for dog bowls nowadays, but smaller. These were for your soup, which was doled out of a big pot, next to which was a bowl of salt, from which you had to take a pinch if you wanted it – no salt and pepper pots for us! Anyway, once you'd collected whatever it was that day, you'd all troop back up to your cells where you'd eat anything you found vaguely edible and swapped odds and sods with others with different tastes – not that there was a lot of variation; you simply got what you were given and that was that. To round the meal off you got a mug of tea – although even that was often little more than boiled water.

For life's little comforts, we were given the princely sum each week of 1s.8d, which is about 20p in today's money. As you can imagine, that didn't go a long way and I counted myself lucky that I wasn't a smoker because tobacco was what most people's money went on. 'Snout' as tobacco's called, was a major currency – and it probably still is, although I hear telephone cards are now the really hot currency – and as far as I can remember no one ever smoked ready-made fags. Roll-ups were far better value for money and there was always an eager queue when we were called down to the canteen for the buy-up and the screws guillotined out eighths of ounces of snout from the standard quarter-ounce packets that were unaffordable to all but the most miserly of inmates. You'd roll your roll-up as thin as humanly possible in order to eke out your baccy for as long as possible – and you never threw your dog ends away. They were pulled apart and the last precious shreds of snout put back in the baccy tin! Snout aside, you could buy anything your heart desired – as long as all your heart desired was toothpaste, jam, sugar and the wherewithal to write and post the single solitary letter you were allowed each week. At least, as a non-smoker, I didn't go short of those little luxuries, such as they were!

More importantly, I and anyone else who could live without all the tobacco their pittance would buy, could save up snout and then barter with it for whatever else you could get – and of course the all-powerful 'barons' had the means to get all kinds of contraband including, in later years, all sorts of drugs. At the time I'm talking about now, though, drugs hadn't taken their hold and tobacco was the only 'currency' worth a light and the 'barons' made fortunes (in prison terms) out of their loan shark operations in which they imposed terrifying rates of interest and even more terrifying penalties for failure to maintain your payments.

Anyway, while we were on remand we at least had a slight variation on the usual routine to look forward to in the shape of our almost weekly trips back to the magistrates' court in the vehicles unaffectionately known as 'sweat boxes'. The name couldn't have been more accurate. The old style of prisoner transport was a van that had been divided into tiny compartments, each with a little steel seat and one-way glass so no one could see in, into which we were individually locked for the journey to court. The sweatbox was bearable in the winter but in summer it was bloody torture in there! Court trips were handy for stocking up on snout! You were allowed to take your baccy with you when you left the prison and, because they never noted how much you had, it wasn't too tricky to bring some back in – that is if your family or friends managed to get some to you via your brief! Of course, once you'd been committed for trial and sentenced in the Crown Court these little day-trips came to an end and sometimes, at the height of banged-up boredom, you could almost remember those sweat boxes with nostalgia – and you certainly missed the privileges you'd enjoyed as a remand prisoner!

For starters, back then you were allowed a visit every day – which meant you didn't have to eat the prison food if you had someone willing to bring food in for you. Better still, with that one outside meal each day, you were allowed to have one drink brought in. And that could be beer if you wanted (and we usually did)! Also, you were allowed to wear your own clothes – which your visitors were allowed to bring in.

Of course we were all convicted in the end. Kenny got three years because he had a lot of form – which was unlucky because he'd only just joined our firm. I think this had only been his second job with us and, of course, his last! Freddie and I got two years apiece and Twinkle got eighteen months – and then we had to wait to be reassigned to another nick to serve our time. The way it works is that they send you straight back to the nick where you've been held on remand. Then, if you've only got a few months or so to do they'd just keep you there. But if you had serious time, anything more than a year, you'd be moved to another prison. You had no idea where you'd end up – all you could do was hope it was better than the Scrubs, which wasn't that unlikely given the state of the place!

Anyway, regardless of the fact that you knew it was coming, it came as quite a nasty shock once you'd been convicted and the whole regime changed literally overnight and you were only allowed one visit per month – even that was often cut short because of pressure of time and numbers on the visiting day and instead of an hour or more you sometimes had to make do with a mere forty-five minutes. If you picked the wrong day – such as a weekend – you might only get half an hour or less, which was particularly upsetting if your nearest and dearest were not very near at all – because it made the journey very dear, not to mention exhausting! Of course, you still had your one letter a week, as if that made up for the lack of visiting time and if you wanted to send more, you had to pay the extra in the canteen out of your shilling and eightpence a week allowance.

In those days absolutely every item of mail, incoming and outgoing was opened, read and, if they deemed it necessary, censored – so you had to leave your letters unsealed when you gave them to the screw for posting. This was partly to ensure that you couldn't make any illicit plans – such as to escape! But to be fair it was also for your own protection. If their snooping on your letters showed that you were a target, for example, or that you had troubles at home, your wife was having an affair or had threatened to leave you, they'd keep an eye on you. They'd even get you up in front of the Governor to see exactly what the trouble was and sometimes they'd try to help you resolve things, perhaps by giving you extra visits so that you could talk things over. In fact I get the impression that they took a lot more care of the individual in those days than they do now!

Having said that, it wasn't a bed of roses. Even on remand you were banged up for twenty-three hours a day in those squalid cells with just half an hour's 'exercise' in the morning and again in the afternoon – I say exercise, but that just meant walking round the yard because there were no sports or recreation facilities at all. The closest thing we had to a work-out was the thrice daily trip down to the mess and back for our meals – which was quite a stretch in itself, actually, hauling yourself up and down four landings!

Another abiding memory of being inside is of cocoa – the last drink of the night before lights out, which was reputed to have been laced with bromide to keep our sexual urges under control. You might think the late night cup of cocoa sounds rather cosy – well it wasn't if you were a nonce or a copper! When the rest of us put our mugs out to be filled as the trolley came round we got a nice hot cup of sweet cocoa – but bent cops and nonces tended to have scalding hot liquid poured over their hands instead, among many more severe punishments.

Morning ablutions were another favourite time for meting out jailhouse justice. Each morning we were let out briefly to slop out our pots, wash and shave and my God did it stink in there. The all-pervading stench of piss and shit that had festered in those pots all night seemed to invade every pore of your body and made you want to chuck up – and you never, ever got used to it.

Anyway, one morning, just as we were all ready to go round to the ablutions, the word went round telling everyone to go the long way round. Only one con didn't seem aware of the word on the landing – a copper. Off he trotted in the usual fashion with his pot in hand, presumably a bit bemused that the rest of us were going in the opposite direction. When he got back to his peter he realised that he was deeply and literally in the shit – because, one by one, we'd emptied the foul-smelling contents of our pots all over his cell and its contents before casually strolling off to wash the pots out in the normal way

Believe it or not, they gave us razor blades in those days too – and not your safety razors, the old-fashioned cut-throat jobs, which gave rise to all sorts of mischief, as you can imagine! Of course they were strictly controlled: for each prisoner there was a sort of sheath on the washhouse wall with your number on it. The screw would dispense a blade to each prisoner and once you'd shaved you had to return the blade to the screw, who'd replace it in your numbered sheath. There were always arguments about who'd swapped a blunt one for a keen one of course, but since I could get by with only two or three shaves a week I never needed to get involved!

But it was the boredom that really got you down – and you'd do anything to brighten up the day. So, when my mate Kenny said he was having an identity parade one day and asked if I wanted to take part, immediately said yes – well it was something to do! As I mentioned earlier, Kenny had only just joined our firm when we got nicked – so this ID parade had nothing to do with me. It was about some other job he was charged with. The appeal of the parade wasn't just to relieve the ennui – it was a chance to get out of our prison clothes and get suited and booted, if only for a little while. And boy did we scrub up well! To a man we had tailor-made whistles (that's rhyming slang by the way: whistle and flute – suit!) from Woods of Kingsland Road in Shoreditch, up near the old Metropolitan Hospital, which was where every face in London got his threads, including the likes of the Krays. In those days it was safe to say that if you weren't in a Woods whistle you were a nobody – at least in criminal terms!

Prison identity parades were much better than their police station equivalents – in fact they were entirely different and much fairer things. In a police station it was easy to fix an identification – all the cops had to do was tip the punter the wink and let them know that the one they wanted fingered was, let's say, number three (that's why experienced faces would switch places and clothes at the last moment as often as they could!). In contrast, the screws, were much more inclined to be on the prisoner's side. So it was the accepted wisdom among the criminal fraternity that a prison identity parade was by far your best bet. For starters you had such a massive choice of blokes in there – and none of them were going anywhere. Secondly the police had fewer opportunities to get at the witnesses. But by far the greatest advantage was the fact that everyone in there was a face – and that a lot of them looked pretty scary. That made it easy to get a load of blokes who looked vaguely like you in a line-up and confuse the witness – not to mention intimidate them. Often, faced with a row of extremely hard-looking men, they'd start thinking about the possibility that they'd be got at on the outside and suddenly develop amnesia!

In the event that seemed to be what happened in Kenny's line-up. The witness didn't pick out any of us and we all trooped back to our cells very pleased with our day's work, which meant that the police had no positive identification and therefore couldn't nick Kenny! Unfortunately for him, though, it wasn't that cut and dried. The next day, Kenny told me that the police had had a word with him and said that they knew he'd done the job and, more to the point, they knew who he'd been working with. If Kenny didn't put his hands up to it, they'd nick his mate, Roger Barclay. Obviously they didn't have a concrete case against Kenny but were confident that they could nail Roger.

This was a terrible dilemma for Kenny.

'What am I going to do Don?' he said. 'Roger's only a young lad and his wife's just had a baby...I don't want to be responsible for him going down...Specially at a time like this!'

'Well, Ken,' I replied, 'it's your liberty we're talking about...I wouldn't presume to try and advise you on that. It's your freedom or otherwise, mate. Only you can make a decision like that.'

With that I wished him the best of luck and left him to mull it over. It didn't take him long to decide that he couldn't do it to Roger – so he pleaded guilty.

He'd already done more than six months of his original three-stretch by this time – and the court wiped that out completely, sentenced him to five years and moved him over to D Wing (we were all in C Wing at the time), which was where the lifers and long-termers were – that basically included everyone serving five years or more. That might sound like a bad thing – but in prison lore it's actually a kind of promotion because the regime for lifers was a lot more relaxed. Long-term prisoners got more free association time and various other little perks that were denied to us ordinary cons in C Wing. After that, of course, I didn't get much chance to see him – other than through a little scam he'd told me about when we'd first arrived at the Scrubs.

'Put yourself down as a Roman Catholic, Don,' he'd said.

'But I'm not...' I began.

'I know – but do it anyway. They get more church services – so if we get separated we'll be able to meet up at church!'

I took his advice and, sure enough, we managed to meet up several times in the prison chapel just as he'd said we could. If it hadn't been for that bit of advice I might never have seen my mate again – even though we were in the same nick!

Of course you meet a lot of interesting people on the inside – and most of them you'd rather not have met at all! The

96

guvnor on our wing in the Scrubs, unofficially speaking I mean, was a geezer called Jack Buggy who was later murdered in Mayfair and his body was finally found bobbing about offshore somewhere. He was in for a shooting outside the Pigalle Club in Piccadilly sometime earlier – whatever it was, he wasn't a bloke to be messed with. Not that I had any problems with him – I used to keep my head down! Another particularly charming character I met in there was a big long-haired, long-bearded lifer who had fed his partner to the pigs! Slightly worryingly, they'd put him in charge of tending the prison gardens.

The thing with lifers, in particular, was that often they just didn't give a toss about anyone or anything – their own life being over to all intents and purposes. One such bloke was Emmett Dunne, who'd murdered his wife's lover while in the army in Germany. A huge, terrifyingly powerful man who was all the more terrifying because he didn't possess a scrap of sympathy or empathy for anyone. He had his own boyfriend in there – but whether or not the poor sod was a willing lover I'll never know because the word was that if Emmett wanted you, he took you and you didn't get a say in the matter! As an indication of how fearsome he was, he walked around constantly with a radio to his ear. This was strictly prohibited – but who dared tell him that or try to take it away from him? Certainly not the screws! It's hard to get across just how intimidating he was – but I'll never forget a picture of him in the paper once holding a fully grown bloke off the floor, by the neck, at arm's length, which gives you an idea of just how powerful he was! Again, although the sight of him was enough to put the wind up me, I never had any problems with him – mainly because he was in the lifers' wing and the only times our paths crossed was when being marched from one part of the prison to the other – and then we were always supervised by a 'Red Band' or a 'Blue Band'.

A word of explanation: there were two types of 'trustee' prisoners who were entitled to walk around the place and supervise other prisoners to varying degrees. A 'Red Band' would take charge of a group of other prisoners but wasn't allowed to go anywhere on his own – for example, it was these guys that marched me to and from the tailor's workshop where I worked for a while. A 'Blue Band', however, had a bit more freedom, and could wander about more or less at will. Some of them were grasses – and that was how they'd got this coveted job. Others, though, were quite helpful chaps who'd run messages about the place and handle the all-important snout deliveries. Either way, though, you had to watch yourself with them – unless you knew for sure that they were kosher you had to assume that they were toadying up to the screws to keep their precious job and would stitch you up at any opportunity.

After a while, though, I was sent off to another prison called the Verne on the Isle of Portland in Dorset, which is connected to Weymouth by a causeway.

It was like an old castle, complete with a long-drained moat and what looked like battlements so even if you were to attempt an escape by scaling the inside walls, you were faced with a thirty-five or forty foot drop to the ground – and since the moat hadn't been filled in, the drop from the top was even longer. Worse still, it was separated from the mainland by a causeway that was flooded at high tide so if you actually breached the walls it was you against the elements – specifically time and tide in this case because if the tide was in you could find yourself sitting trapped outside the prison for hours until the screws strolled outside at their leisure to haul you in again. Even if you got your timing right you were by no means home free: there was only one way you could possibly go, so all they had to do was put a couple of screws at the other end of the causeway to wait for your arrival. I suppose if you had a boat you'd be laughing but as far as I know very few people ever got away from the Verne.

It was a formidable place – and the horrendously bitter winds that swept its starkly exposed location only added to the sense of total desolation as if their howling was a warning to stay inside and never attempt to break free. The gale force storms that thrashed us into submission made the Scrubs look like a breeze by comparison and just walking from the dormitories to the canteen was an epic struggle against the forces of nature. Lest you think I'm over egging the pudding – or should I say over thickening the porridge – I should point out that there were ropes provided for the bedraggled inmates to hang on to as they staggered about the place to prevent them being swept off their feet. I've never experienced anything like it! You literally had to cling on for dear life. Letting go was not an option – although a few of us did give it a try, for want of any other source of entertainment. It proved to be just about possible to stand unaided and take the wind head on – but God forbid you started running. If you did the wind would catch you as if you were a sail and drive you forward faster and faster until your legs could no longer keep up and you were flung like a sack of potatoes against the cold wet stone at the foot of the dormitory walls. From there, almost without exception, the next stop would be the prison hospital. To add insult to injury, taking your hands off the rope was considered a deliberate act (which it was) and the inevitable injuries assumed to be self-inflicted, which meant you got punished too!

We slept about twenty to each of the dormitories, which all led off a single corridor. Each had a toilet at one end and a washroom area in the middle where hot water was available –

if you were lucky, or very diligent. I was always the latter, making sure I was up at the crack of dawn to get my share of the hot water. Shaving in icy water in those conditions was no fun at all! It was a bit like an army barracks in the sense that we were all responsible for keeping the dormitory and toilets clean and tidy – and making the beds in exactly the regulation fashion and folding the blankets in a particular way.

I suppose it was because the place was so isolated and exposed to the worst the elements could throw at you that the regime was much more relaxed than that at the Scrubs. The reality was that you suffered a lot worse outside of those walls than you did inside. Nevertheless, escape attempts were a regular occurrence, especially as Christmas approached and even hardened cons were wracked with homesickness – or after someone had had an upsetting visit and lost the will to endure their confinement for a minute longer. And every year, around the week or so before Christmas, the whole place became a hive of illicit activity. You'd hear all sorts of whispers and then there'd be the sound of a lot of scampering about at night as people got their little escape plots ready. Then, after a while you'd hear the screws' shout go up.
'One away Governor!!'
And we'd laugh – a lot.

Personally I never tried it. It was futile – and anyway I built myself a separate mental place while I was inside. My prison state of mind, you could call it. I just thought of home, family and mates as an entirely different world; a world I'd return to one day but which, for the time being, didn't exist. It was only by living in my prison world and mentally fencing off the one outside that I kept my sanity really – that and just biting the bullet and getting on with my work in the blacksmiths' workshop. As prison jobs go, that was a pretty good one. They taught us how to temper steel and make all

100

sorts of wrought iron stuff – and they even let you go on outside courses.

Thinking that I might as well alleviate the boredom a bit and learn something while I was at it, I joined a painting and decorating course, which was run by a civilian decorator who came in daily to give us lessons on all aspects of painting, wallpapering, graining, staining, stippling and so on. It was impressive – I still remember a lot of what I learnt then and if you wanted to take it up as a trade when you got out, it was a bloody good start!

It was also a good way of seeing a bit of life outside those awful walls. Once you'd completed the course you could go out on working parties to practice your new skills – doing up the screws' houses generally – and I jumped at the chance to break the monotony. The only trouble was the little git who was responsible for supervising us. Not a screw – a civilian. But he might as well have been a screw considering his attitude. He was an obnoxious little bastard! What was worse was that he seemed to have it in for me. One time as we were going back into the prison, after the little Hitler had already had a couple of pops at me, he called out my name and number.
'449. Murfet!!!'
I looked back at him.
'I want to search you!' he said with a smug and decidedly nasty leer.
'You ain't searching me mate.' I said. 'There's a couple of screws there and they haven't searched me.'
'Well I want to search you!' he said, all pumped up and full of his own misguided sense of importance.
'Why?' I demanded indignantly. There was no way I was having this jumped-up little pipsqueak rubbing me down – and I didn't see any reason why he'd feel the need anyway. It

was completely unjustified. Maybe he was gay and wanted to get a little grope – who knows? There was a lot of it about!

He declined to give me a reason – so I declined to co-operate. 'I'm not objecting to a search,' I said firmly. 'But I am objecting to you searching me!'

A screw approached with an enquiring look on his face and I caught his eye.

'Look – *you've* got to search me,' I said to him with a certain amount of respect – or as much as I could muster.

'Sorry Murfet,' said the screw, 'he's entitled to search you...'

'Well I don't care if he's entitled or not – he ain't laying a finger on me!' I shouted. 'I don't want him touching me...If you want to search me yourself, well you go right ahead!'

'Well all right,' the screw replied. 'But you're gonna be up on Governor's for this!'

That meant 'Governor's Report'. After a perfunctory search, in which he found nothing (and I had nothing to be found!), I found myself up in front of the prison's governor.

'Explain yourself Murfet,' demanded the governor.

'Well I just don't like the man,' I said vehemently. 'He's a nasty little piece of work – and why he picks on me I don't know. I wasn't carrying anything I shouldn't and I wasn't doing anything wrong. But I just objected to the way he spoke to me. Maybe he thought I was an easy target – and if he did he was wrong...'

'Nevertheless, Murfet, you embarrassed him in front of the other cons,' the governor interjected.

'He embarrassed himself!' I parried. 'He didn't need any help from me!'

That got short shrift!

'Well I'm sorry Murfet, you're going to have to go and work in the block!'

I just managed to stop myself from swearing and incurring another punishment. I was utterly gutted. The appropriately named 'block house' was where they made concrete blocks – not the most fascinating or pleasant job of work really. In

102

fact, on a hot day (yes they did exist, even in that windswept part of the world), it was like hell on earth – knee-deep in wet cement and choking and half-blinded by the grey cement dust that hung in the air and solidified in your mouth, throat and, no doubt, lungs.

I managed to stick it out for three or four weeks and then went up in front of the governor again.

'Look,' I said, 'this is not fair! I went on the painting and decorating course and did the job properly and never gave you any grief at all and just because this one guy – not the nicest of people – decides to pick on me I've got to suffer...I honestly think I deserve another chance...'

'All right,' he said, to my surprise. And he put me back in the blacksmith's workshop, which, as I'd found before, was quite interesting – enjoyable even – and certainly a lot more bearable than the block house!

One night at about midnight, in the middle of the customary frenzy of stir-craziness that, as I've said, always set in during the approach to Christmas, we were all stirred rudely from our sleep by a God-awful clattering up and down the corridor that linked the twenty or so dormitories. Believe it or not, some cheeky git had managed to get a huge wagon wheel into the prison - and by wagon wheel I don't mean the popular chocolate and marshmallow snack biscuit, although that would have been extremely welcome at the time. I mean the four or five-foot diameter wooden-spoked thing off a farm wagon with an iron ring for a tyre! Anyway, they were rolling this bloody great thing up and down the corridor and it was clattering, clanging and banging against the walls like World War Three had broken out. How they got it in there I'll never know – or why, come to that. But it gave us a hearty laugh all the same!

The military history of the place also provided us with some excitement – and I don't mean that we were amateur historians! One evening the entire prison was at dinner. Unlike at the Scrubs, we all ate at the same time and in the one canteen, which was like a big school dining room with all us cons lined up on long rows of trestle tables and the screws eating up at one end at a long table of their own. Some of the guys had been working outside in the dungeons, where the French prisoners of war were once held in the times when the place had been a garrison, and one of them had found something very, very old and very, very interesting. And not just in archaeological terms!

Halfway through dinner this bloke pulled out his find, cupped it gleefully in his hand and then bent down and bowled it along the floor. It trundled with a hollow metallic sound towards the assembled screws at the top table. And suddenly the whole cavernous room was drowned in a terrified hush.

It was only a bleedin' hand grenade!

There was a sudden explosion – not the grenade; just panic! It was utter chaos. Everyone who'd clocked what it was leapt out of their seats, upturning tables as they did so. The rest, who couldn't actually see, caught the hysteria like wildfire and erupted out of their seats, sending crockery and cutlery, food and drink flying all over the shop. It was absolute Bedlam! Luckily the grenade never went off – but you'd never have guessed it looking at the state of the canteen by the time screws and cons alike had stampeded out of the place!

Needless to say, we all got punished for that little drama – not only did we all have to slope sheepishly off to our dormitories without food but what little we had by way of entertainment and leisure facilities were severely curtailed for some time afterwards. But it was well worth it just to see the sheer terror on the faces of the screws!

Talking of mealtimes, among the questionable delights that appeared on the menu with depressing regularity, two dishes pissed us all off most sorely. One was unaffectionately known as 'afterbirth' and it consisted of something they described as minced 'meat' (what animal it came from we'll never know) floating in a revolting puddle of grease and oil. It looked revolting. It smelt revolting. It *was* revolting. But it was edible – just, the irony being that at least real afterbirth is apparently very nutritious. I doubt very much that our version was – and outside of a prison you'd be even less likely to want to eat it. But eat it we did – because it was infinitely preferable to the other culinary torture they inflicted on us. That was the cheese. Which was rank. No – 'rank' doesn't begin to describe its vileness. It was the cheese from hell. It was so foul that few of us could stomach the stuff. But since you'd go hungry if you didn't get the stuff down your neck you sometimes had to force it down, no matter how much gagging and retching you had to endure in the process.

But one day, we rebelled against the evil/vile cheese (evil being an anagram of vile, either of which describes the stuff perfectly!). I wish I could say someone rolled it along the floor like they did with the hand grenade – it would have caused similar levels of terror – but, no, this was a less dramatic form of protest. The word went out: DON'T EAT THE CHEESE.
We hardly needed telling twice. They might as well have asked us to go along with: DON'T STOP BREATHING. If you wanted to stay alive you just didn't eat that hideous cheese! So we all backed the idea and the very next day, what do we get offered up for our dinner – you've guessed it, it's that bloody cheese! And sure enough, not only did not a soul touch the stuff but everyone solemnly picked up their

uneaten wedge of the stuff and carried it outside, where the whole prison's cheese supply was left as a monument to its own unpopularity!

Of course we were punished...The sports day was cancelled and there was no film that week but soon things settled back into the old routine and the incident seemed to have been forgotten. Obviously it hadn't been completely forgotten though because they never served up cheese that rank again – at least not during my time there!

We had quite a few laughs in the dormitories too – and the camaraderie of sharing with twenty blokes more than made up for the lack of privacy – especially when you'd been used to being banged up with two others in a cramped Victorian cell for twenty-three hours a day. One night, as I came back in having been to the toilet, a mate of mine passed me on his way out and hissed at me.

'Oi Don, they've just put a snake in your bed!'

Bloody hell! I thought. But I got back into bed anyway because I couldn't let on that I'd been warned or my mate would have come in for all sorts of stick. So I sat there wondering what sort of snake they could possibly have got hold of and put in there. I could hear them all suppressing their sniggering and I lay there for a good five minutes, rigid with apprehension, with my feet pulled up almost up to my chin – not that they could tell. Finally I couldn't take the tension any longer – and although I hadn't felt anything (yet), I suddenly leapt out of bed shouting 'What the fuck was that??' of course they all fell about laughing, unaware that I hadn't even seen the thing – and when I pulled off the covers out came the snake, which was just a grass snake. Not a terribly dangerous beast – mind you they can give you a nasty nip!

Another enjoyable way of passing the time was having a bit of fun with the old night watchman who'd often come in after lights out to snoop about and generally check up on us. We used to get a long reel of cotton and tie one end to a broom, which we propped up against the wall at one end of the dormitory. Then we'd wait till we saw the beam of his torch sweeping past the doorway as he entered the room. Once he'd made his doddering way about half the length of the dorm, someone would give the cotton a little tug, then another, then yet another. At the far end, the broom would tap, tap, tap against the wall, and the poor old sod would swivel, sweeping the darkness with his torchlight like a lighthouse for the source of the noise. Of course it wasn't always a broom – each time we'd come up with a new noise to torment him with. And this went on for ages. I don't think he ever did work out what was going on. Of course it seems a bit unfair now, looking back, this poor old geezer in his sixties having to deal with a gang of twenty assorted, and mostly young, thieves and villains! But he was the only entertainment we had – weird though, isn't it? How little things like that can give so much enjoyment!

Newcomers – especially if they had made themselves unpopular somehow – had a special treat awaiting them. The usual trick was to balance a brown paper bag full of water over the top of the light above their bed with a long string of cotton attached. The bloke in the adjacent bed would have hold of this string and he'd wait till the victim had settled down in bed with his head on the pillow before giving it a hefty tug and dousing the bloke and his bedding. Another perennial favourite was the 'apple pie bed', where you fold the bottom sheet up and over the blanket so that the victim only has half a bed to get into.

Of course it wasn't all fun and games – and often we had our private version of jailhouse law. Our lockers by our beds were just hospital style cabinets really – no locks! Obviously snout and cash was too precious to leave in there and you'd carry that on you all the time. But because there were no locks, there had to be an element of trust with any other possessions you were allowed to have – and thieving from a fellow prisoner wasn't just a crime it was a deadly sin – almost literally deadly in fact! One time I remember, we noticed that things were going missing from everyone's lockers – so we got together and did a sort of Neighbourhood Watch job until we caught the culprit. And when we caught him, his fate was a lot nastier than the cops would have had in store for him. He got a proper kicking and was quite seriously striped up (slashed with a knife). He then made the mistake of grassing up the people who'd done him in and soon he was 'taxied' – which means he was shipped out *pronto* to another jail, as were the two blokes he'd grassed on.

Of course, even with our strict code and even stricter enforcement methods, a bit of thieving was inevitable given the kind of people you're locked up with. Because at some time or another all the lowlifes end up in stir alongside the misunderstood gentlemen of impeccable moral character such as yours truly!!

Around this time – '58/'59 – a new law came in to the effect that any remand time you'd served would be deducted from any time to which you might be sentenced if you were convicted – a concept most people would think went without saying! I'd got my home leave all planned out at the time – this was a concession you became entitled to about two months before you'd served your time and you got to spend a week at home with your family as a way of helping you acclimatise and readjust to the outside and start rebuilding your life. And it just so happened that when I came back from my home leave, they'd lopped the two months I'd spent on remand off my sentence. Result! I found that suddenly I only had about a week until my release!

I remember my brother and Freddie Welsh, a well-known face out of Tottenham, came down to pick me up for my home leave – and even doing that meant getting some crap from the cops. Apparently they'd already been pulled over by the Old Bill on the way down through Farnborough and, with tedious predictability, they pulled us again on the way back for no reason whatsoever, other than to let me know that they were still watching me. Thanks very much chaps, I thought bitterly.

The journey back to jail by train didn't go smoothly either. If you weren't back on the dot of the designated time you were in deep trouble and, typically, my train was late, which meant I missed the bus to The Verne. It wasn't like London down there – buses were few and far between and I had to wait ages for the next one. Anyway, being a responsible citizen – or at least starting to look like one – I phoned the nick to say that I was already on the island and only five or so miles away and that although I would be late getting back, I would be there as soon as my train arrived. The stakes were high. In those days you got a third of your sentence in remission – and failing to report back punctually from a home leave could mean losing the lot. Imagine it – less than a week from release from a two-year stretch, having served eighteen months, and I faced the gut-wrenching possibility that I'd be inside for another six months or more just because of a missed train! Luckily they weren't too unreasonable. I was still put on Governor's Report to explain myself – but, thank God, my new release date was intact!

ANOTHER TASTE OF PORRIDGE

In 1991 I had two or three years of brushes with the law and spent a fair bit of time in police cells and prison.

I spent some time on remand in Winchester prison – another Victorian monstrosity on the South coast. I'd been charged with fraud and, although the two mates with whom I'd been charged ultimately went down, I fought the case and was eventually acquitted. The layout and facilities were very similar to those of the Scrubs, with the steel staircases connecting steel gridded landings and the obligatory high tensile wire netting slung between floors to stop the inmates pelting the screws and each other from above – and of course to prevent suicides. All the peters ran down either side of the building with the ablutions area in the middle. As always, there were no cells up against the outside walls, presumably so that there was no way of scratching your way through the bricks. The screws would stand on the crosswalks or by the ablutions and now, a good thirty years on from my first taste of porridge at the Scrubs, the powers that be had separated the 'nonce' and Rule 43 cases from the rest of us. Rule 43, incidentally, refers to prisoners who need special protection from the other inmates. As well as the paedophiles, they included bent coppers, bent screws and grasses – anyone the ordinary prisoners might want to exact retribution against. And then, of course, there were the real nutters – and it was the rest of us who had to be protected from them!

While I was in Winchester, the next wing to us was the nonces' wing and when we went down for meals in the central ground floor canteen area there'd be a frantic scramble because no one wanted to be the last of our wing to go down. It wasn't that we were scared of the nonces – quite the opposite usually. But since there was no segregation once you were down on the ground floor, they used to start the nonces walking down as soon as the last of our lot had hit the stairs. So if you weren't careful; if you let yourself trail just a little bit behind your mates, there was the terrifying possibility that the kitchen staff might mistake you for the advance guard of the nonce parade! And when you know the

terrible, unspeakable things they used to do to the nonces'
food, you'll understand why the very thought put the fear of
God into us. Gobbing on their plates was the very mildest
thing they did – so on the odd occasion when I found myself
last in the rush for the canteen, I just went without my food.
It just wasn't worth the risk! Of course, after you got to know
the ropes, you'd always make sure you were first in line –
and it was generally the newcomers who hadn't yet twigged
that got the worst of it.

Another danger, which was quite a new development, mainly
in the more modern prisons, was the police plant. If you'd
gone down for a short stretch or were on remand and
pleading 'not guilty', and the cops knew you had your fingers
in some dodgy pies, they'd put someone in there to see if
they could coax some information out of you. Often you
could spot them a mile off – some bloke who suddenly gets
all matey with you for no apparent reason and then works the
conversation round to what you're in for, whether you did it
and so on. They could be quite cunning though. Say you
were in for armed robbery – they'd put someone in with you
who said they were in for the same thing. Then they'd talk
about their 'crimes' in the hope of getting you to open up.
You might forget all about it until you come up in court
pleading 'not guilty' and then all of a sudden a familiar face
pops up in the witness box giving evidence about your
jailhouse 'confession' and all the other people you'd named
and incriminated. The golden rule, therefore, was to stay on
your toes and keep your mouth shut about what you'd done
and hadn't done – especially if you're pleading 'not guilty'.
This never would have happened thirty years ago!

Some things have got better for the con though. In general,
for example, the screws are no longer allowed to open your
mail – so you can actually seal up your letters before posting,
unlike in my first years inside. Of course, I'm damn sure they

look at some of the mail – it's just that they'd have a job using it as evidence in court. Nevertheless, it's wise to watch what you put in a letter from inside because they can still gather intelligence to use against you somehow! Similarly there have been many cases of the police putting two defendants in the same case together and then bugging the cell. Again it's intelligence gathering, rather than evidence building but my advice to anyone who finds themselves banged up is never to assume that because they're not allowed to something they won't. They can and they do!

Later, in Pentonville, I couldn't believe my eyes when I saw how things had improved! I had a cell to myself – and in it were a flush toilet and a basin with hot and cold running water! Of course that's only on the remand wing – because it's another of these Human Rights laws, I suppose from the EU, of which I heartily approve, and which says that because you haven't been found guilty you have to be treated as innocent. Of course that was always supposed to be the case but you'd never have thought so in the old days! No more three to a peter – you might have to share with one other but that's the worst it gets – and there are proper beds with proper mattresses, a lot more space and really quite pleasant, clean and bright decor! It was Heaven compared to my first taste of porridge back in the late fifties! Still no pillows though, for some reason or other – maybe it's because they could be used to smother someone! Better still, remand prisoners these days get a lot more association time and get to play pool and watch telly – come to that a lot of convicted prisoners get those sort of privileges too these days and many more besides.

Conditions may change – but the routines and rituals of prison life remain pretty much the same. On the inside you don't just live by the letter of the law – you read between the lines and bend the rules to make life a bit more bearable.

That's why you've got to suss out the moves the moment you get in there; because the more you know the score the better off you'll be. For example, when you first come in you're issued with your basic kit: your clothes, toothbrush, towel, mug, water jug and comb and so on, none of which will ever be replaced unless you hand in the old one. And that's your lot until you get out as far as the screws are concerned. But soon you'll be wanting more. When you get your first visit after being convicted, for instance, you'll want to look as good as you can so you'll want to know how to get your shirt properly ironed. Your prison issue strides will probably be too long or too short or too baggy or too tight – you'll want to know who to talk to about swapping them or getting them altered. Things like that make a big difference to the way you feel when you're inside – and so does every little triumph over the system, just like on the outside in fact. In one joint I remember the best scam of all was knowing who to see about getting a steak sandwich delivered with your cocoa at lights out! Now that really was a treat! My point is that no matter what the prison – or when you're in there come to that – you've got to put yourself about and find out what's what – if not, you're missing out and making life unnecessarily unpleasant for yourself.

Digressing a little, I'll tell you how you can spot an old lag – or at least one from my day. There were never any pockets in the prison-issue trousers and, for want of something to do with our hands, all of us, to a man, used to walk around with our hands tucked into the waistband of our trousers. It's a habit that sticks. I still can't help doing it today and many's the time I've spotted someone doing the same thing and, on meeting them, they've confirmed my suspicion that they were inside at one time or another!

Basically the screws know what goes on and it's their job to stop you beating the system. And it's your job not to let them catch you – because the punishments can be quite severe. It's a game really – but a very seriously and subtly organised one in which no one tells you the rules. You just have to suss them out as you go along.

Of course you've got a big head start in that game if you're already a bit of a player. By which, I mean if you're in with the right people – and in that respect I've been very lucky because in almost all the nicks I've been in it was the London boys that ran the place. And because I was something of a London 'face' I had no trouble getting the right advice from the most powerful people. Of course just being from London wasn't good enough. If you were a complete mug or a nonce, of course you got no help. You had to be either a face or you had to be in there for something the boys admired; something they'd put you on a bit of a pedestal for, like a big armed robbery or a major fraud for example. Don't get me wrong though – none of these blokes back you up out of the goodness of their hearts. Most of the time they're heartless. No – if you're a face it means you've got connections, money or power that could be of use to them on the outside. In short – if they think you've got something they want you can get what you want out of them!

Now, I've talked about some of the things that had changed for the better when I found myself back inside. Well, some things changed for the worse too! I wasn't overly chuffed to find, for example, that they no longer let remand prisoners have food sent in and nor do they allow visitors to bring anything in for you. But what I found a lot more depressing was the difference in the people I was in there with – and it was absolutely *not* for the better. There were so many young flash gits; knife artists who were in for stabbings and other forms of violent crime...But this wasn't the kind of thing we'd have thought of as violent crime in my day. It was pointless, petty, nasty viciousness for its own sake and for no

114

purpose. At least with an armed robbery, any violence that occurs is incidental – a necessary evil. Frankly I found it shocking. I mean a mugging for money's one thing, but a lot of these kids were doing time for stabbing someone, killing them even, for 'respect'. In other words for no good reason at all. It just seemed to me that there were an awful lot of mindless people doing an awful lot of porridge for completely mindless crimes.

Of course, I can't say there wasn't mindless violence in my day, in the late fifties, but there was certainly a lot less. The word 'respect' is abused these days; it's become meaningless; an excuse to kill. In the old days we were crooks, just like these kids – but when we talked about respect it was about honouring your peers; people who were proven grafters. These days it seems to be a much more petty concept – they'll stab someone for slagging a mate off for Christ's sake!

That brings to mind the time when I and another twenty-four associates were arrested for a fraud worth £5 million to £25 million, depending which paper you read or which TV channel you watched. Of the twenty-five of us, only ten or twelve actually ended up being remanded and found ourselves in the good old, bad old Wormwood Scrubs. And as we all trooped into the reception area – depressingly familiar to me of course – I had to laugh because standing there was a very familiar figure: Handsome John from Hackney. Which was a right result because a few of us had a bit of illicit gear we needed to get past the screws somehow – snout and a few other things that would be like gold dust inside. Catching Handsome John's eye, I whispered to him, 'Listen mate, we've got a bit of gear we need to get through.'
'No problem Don,' he replied.
I went over to the others.

'Quick, give us your gear,' I said urgently. They complied without question and I handed the whole stash to Handsome John who slipped away double quick.

The rest of the boys, many of whom had never been inside before, simply could not believe it! Once they'd been thoroughly searched, rubbed down and had handed in all their other, legitimate, property and signed for it, they found themselves inside the Scrubs proper. And there, their snout and all the other bits and bobs that make life inside bearable were duly handed back to them. Of course, in their eyes I was God! And I didn't look half bad in the eyes of the other cons – after all our latest caper may have gone pear shaped but it had also made us into celebrities. We'd been all over the television and in all the papers and everyone in the Scrubs wanted to be our friend and do us favours – which I must say made life in there a lot more bearable.

Mind you, I wasn't there long. This was the third of my three big charges – and yet again I walked away. After a nine-week committal at City of London Magistrates Court there was a three-month case at Snaresbrook, halfway through which the prosecution case collapsed and we were all acquitted.

In the meantime though, every time you left the nick as a remand prisoner to make a court appearance there was the possibility that you wouldn't be coming back – you might be acquitted or at least get bail. That was all very well, but if they thought you were gone for good you'd have to go through the whole tedious admission process, seeing the doctor, the interview with the governor and so on. That was bad enough – but what was worse was being put in a new peter on a new landing with a new cleaner (the cleaner's the bloke you've really got to know on every landing) and possibly a new cellmate. That was a nightmare. Just when you'd got things sussed and made things cosy for yourself you'd have to go back to square one and start all over gain.

Nightmare! The thing to do was to let the governor know that 'this time' you definitely would not be applying for bail in the hope that he'd keep your cell for you. Usually it worked and you'd be sort of 'fast-tracked' through processing and find yourself back in your familiar remand landing and peter where you knew the score.

CASSIUS CLAY

Looking after Cassius Clay (later known of course as Muhammad Ali) for a couple of days at The Dorchester in London was a popular job with my boys because so many of them came from the boxing world, notably Danny and Billy Francis, the sons of Georgie Francis, neither of whom could wait to get down there and meet the great man. Of course, it seemed a bit unnecessary – protection for the world's greatest boxer...But actually our guys were perfectly qualified for the job, which meant spotting people who looked likely to pester him and spiriting them away before they got the chance.

You'd think Clay would have had plenty of his own people – and you'd be right. Trouble was, they were worse than useless. All they seemed to do was pose, mill around and look officious and businesslike with one eye on the crowd and the other making sure they weren't missing out on anything more glamorous! In fact they were so preoccupied with their own self-importance that they didn't notice our guys doing their job for them right under their noses – basically because they were manoeuvring the situation like the professionals they were and not trying to score points.

*   *   *

Frank Warren employed Artistes Services for most of the fights he promoted, usually at the Albert Hall – and my guys

117

absolutely loved it. Not only because they were all keen boxing fans – but also because the whole atmosphere made a pleasant change from handling hordes of screaming kids!

CHAPTER FOUR

Late 80's to Early 90's

WHITE COLLAR CRIME

Although you'll read a lot about some of my more physical criminal adventures, it wasn't always that heavy – or that dangerous. I've also been involved in a lot of what you might call 'white collar' crime in my time – and in this chapter, I hope to give you a bit of an insight on the way some of the moves worked!

Crime comes up quite a bit in this book. It has to because it's a book about a life in which crime was a recurring feature – whether in its blue-collar or white-collar varieties. That's not to say that I ever got involved in criminal activities out of any love for the idea of being outside the law. On the contrary – almost every time it was out of sheer necessity. Every legitimate business I've ever been involved in has faced some sort of threat, ranging from blackmail and scams, outright lies and rip-offs to literal daylight robbery. And the fact of the matter is that you have to protect your interests – it's either that or go under. As my good friend Adam said, it's Dog Eat Dog Eat Dog Eat Dog!!!

Combine that little phrase with the old cliché that life's a bitch and you've got the Don Murfet philosophy in a nutshell! All I ever did was make sure I was the dog with the sharpest teeth whose bite was a lot worse than its bark – and the one that screwed life before it screwed me! That's not as heavy as it might sound though. In truth, all I was doing was protecting my business. When things started coming on top, I put a stop to it before anyone really heavy got involved. In short, someone gets a few stitches in time and you probably save someone getting hurt much, much more seriously!

All through my life I've worked closely with people on both sides of that legal fence. I've worked with some good criminals and their connections and I've worked with a lot of police – you have to sometimes in my line of work, when you need them for crowd control and so on. It's odd really, but straight people – the police, in particular – are easily convinced that you're a 'straight' and 'proper' person like themselves. But the moment they find out that you're involved with some dodgy characters their attitude to you changes completely and you're *persona non grata*.

This goes back to a time when a very good friend of mine, Ginger, was arrested for what was called 'shopping' back then. In case you're not familiar with this particular scam, here's how it works. Firms go into a shop two or three-handed and wander round browsing and looking as unsuspicious as possible. Then one of them distracts the assistant and drags him or her off to enquire about some display item while the other nips round, clears out the cash register and leaves.

That's what Ginger and his two mates were up to – but on this occasion it all went pear-shaped. The shop assistant sussed what was going on almost as soon as they tried to leave the shop. She chased them outside to where their motor was waiting and snatched the key out of the ignition. They weren't going anywhere – so they had to sheepishly give the cash back. Now, in my book, no real crime had been committed – the shop had got its dosh back and no real harm done. But that wasn't enough for this 'have a go hero'! She put the keys in her pocket and made it quite clear she wasn't about to give them back. Just then, her boyfriend turns up

120

and, typically, he's only an off-duty copper! Ginger's two mates leg it down the road and somehow, one of them manages to melt away into the crowd of shoppers that's formed outside the shop. The other, affectionately known as Hedgy, keeps going, running like there's no tomorrow - then stops abruptly. He wrenches open the door of a nearby stationary car, drags its panicked and protesting driver out, flings him down onto the tarmac and leaps in before screeching off down the road, denting a few parked cars as he wrestles the car under control and hurtles away.

In the meantime Ginger's stuck outside the shop with the off-duty cop – who's now threatening him with all sorts of punishments, legal and otherwise. So Ginger decks the bloke, gaining himself just enough time to have it on his toes and duck down a side road, then another, then another...Just as he's beginning to breathe easy, thinking he's lost the copper, a car roars up behind him – guess who! The cop jumps out of his car wielding a wheel brace – and he's clearly not averse to a bit of ABH with it. Ginger ducks as the hefty spanner whistles over his head and clocks the bloke with a deft uppercut that leaves him on his arse yet again. Ginger runs off leaving a dazed copper sitting in the road. But now more cops have arrived on the scene and it isn't long before Ginger's run as far and as fast as his legs would take him. Inevitably, the police cut him off and, utterly drained and breathless, he's arrested without much of a struggle.

First I heard of this drama was when I got a call saying that Ginger's in Barnet General Hospital and could I pop in and see if there's anything he needs. So, helpful as always, and concerned about Ginger, off I went to the hospital where I found him in a private room. But he wasn't the only one in the room – guarding him was a copper called Bill Jardine. Now I knew Bill very well indeed – he lived in a street adjoining ours and all our kids went to the same school together.

'Hello Don!' he said, more than a little surprised to see me. 'What are you doing here then?'

'Hello Bill,' I replied. 'I've just popped in to see my mate here.'

At this, I could see the questions running through his mind as his brow furrowed. 'What,' he was clearly thinking, 'the hell are you doing associating with known criminals?'

After all, Bill knew me as a showbiz guy – I was quite well-known as such by this stage – and I used to be invited to all the police dances and other social functions and used to hang around with quite a few other friends and acquaintances who happened to be policemen.

Anyway, Ginger applied for bail and, of course, I stood bail for him at the courthouse in Barnet. With all my police connections, not to mention my showbiz reputation and all the favours it allowed me to provide for the cops, I thought they'd accept my surety for Ginger without question. But no, they CRO'd (contacted the Criminal Records Office) me like anyone else. They'd obviously done a bit of digging into my activities and hadn't been all that impressed with what they'd unearthed. Funnily enough, that was the last time I ever got invited to any police dinners or dos! Old Bill Jardine kept his distance after that too – but Andy and Leslie, bless them, remained the greatest of friends until, sadly, Leslie, who was a lovely, lovely person, died recently. Andy and Leslie weren't the usual police couple, though. He was a highway patrol cop – and that meant he had a much more relaxed attitude to the likes of yours truly than the CID boys, who, by nature, were always out to trip you up and score career points.

Anyway, the upshot was that my credibility was blown as far as anyone connected with the police was concerned –

something that happened quite a few times over the years! Like the time when Ginger's brother Patsy and a mate of his got involved in a very big altercation and got arrested. While they were being interviewed down the nick, one of the cops interrogating them made it quite clear that the cops were well and truly on my case.

'So, you're Murfet's men are you?' He wasn't asking – he was simply stating a fact, and enjoying their discomfort.

I know there was always a big police file on me – but it seemed it was growing particularly quickly at the time. And this was the beginning of what proved to be a long series of brushes with the law – on the showbiz side as well as in what you might call my 'extracurricular activities'.

On the crowd control side of my music business operations for example, a lot of the guys I used had form and knew people – but they were good blokes, straightforward cockneys with no 'side' to them at all. And they were streetwise. They could suss people out almost at a glance – that was why I had them in the company to start with! So, ironically, there were times when the police were very appreciative of our 'powers of persuasion' as you might put it politely.

There was the incident when Rod Stewart was threatened up in Newcastle, for example, which was reported in all the papers at the time. All his road crew had got themselves embroiled in a situation and there had been some very nasty gang fights. As usual, when the shit hit the fan, yours truly got a call!

'Rod's very definitely got some major problems up here,' they said. 'Can you help us out Don? Can you send a couple of boys up here to mind Rod for us?'

Is the Pope a Catholic? Of course I could!

The two guys I sent were no ordinary minders – they were faces. And almost as soon as they arrived in Geordie land and checked into their hotel there was an authoritative knock on their door. It was, of course, the local CID.

'Look, we know who you are,' they said. 'We know exactly why you're here...'

What can you say when the cops tell you that? Not a lot. And my two guys were initially speechless. What the cops went on to say, though, was nothing like whatever they'd expected!

'And we're going to help you,' said one of the cops.

'How d'you mean,' asked one of my blokes, more than a touch gobsmacked.

'Well, we'll take you to where these bastards are, you do your business and we'll mind you...'

'You're gonna work with us?' my blokes spluttered in amazement.

'Yep,' said one of the CID blokes. 'Because these people are an absolute pain in the neck for us. They've given us so much aggravation round here you wouldn't believe it and, frankly, we've just about had enough of it. You sort 'em out and you'll be doing us a big favour! Of course, none of this ever goes outside this room you understand!'

And that's exactly what happened. The cops guided my men to where these people hung out and gave them all the intelligence they had so that they knew exactly when they'd catch them with the fewest of their men around them for backup. My boys did their business with their usual efficiency and taught these north-eastern lads a very severe lesson and warned them off making any more of their silly threats. That wasn't unusual. What *was* very unusual was the fact that they then had a police escort back to their hotel, where they packed their things before being escorted to the station and onto a train bound back to London! End of story!

This is a typical example of the way police co-operation with villains' works! And don't let the coppers tell you otherwise! What you'd got was a potentially dangerous situation where known villains or tearaways are threatening a rock star, for publicity or whatever other reasons. Defusing such a situation was almost impossible for the police. It would take a lot of manpower they could ill afford, not to mention the paperwork. Worse still, for them, was the fact that the police have to be seen to behave themselves. Unlike us, they can't just go steaming in and take these arseholes by the scruff of the neck and give them a good talking to (or seeing to!). They have to be very careful. By realising that we had a goal in common and making use of my boys it was all done very discreetly. We slid in quietly, did the business and were back in London before anyone was any the wiser.

In short, everyone had a result. I had no problems. The firm in Newcastle knew that we could come back after them any time we liked, so they were good boys from then on. And the police were very happy indeed because they'd resolved an aggravating situation without getting their hands dirty or having to do anything unpleasant – and, best of all, the local firm didn't even know they'd had a hand in the whole affair!

There have been countless other examples of this kind of collaboration between what you might call the law and the lawless, where we were pointed in the right direction and then blind eyes were conveniently turned because the cops knew that although we might cross that fence from time to time, we were nowhere near as lawless as some of the types they had to keep under control! Sometimes it was just some thug who was making a nuisance of himself. Other times it would be someone whom the police just couldn't touch for legal or political reasons – about which we, of course, couldn't give a monkeys! Whatever it was, they knew they could rely on us to be subtle, yet extremely effective.

When the newly built Harpers shopping centre in Bedford was overrun by nasty little thugs, 'Murfet's Men' again came to the rescue of the police, the appointed security firm, the terrorised shopkeepers and the ordinary people of the town. The problem stemmed from the fact that the land on which it was being built hadn't been formally 'adopted'. What that means is that it was still effectively private land and the Highways Act and various other legalities didn't apply, which made it difficult for the police to provide anything like effective policing. Sterling Security approached me because their own staff were being laughed at, ignored and even attacked, the police had had one of their officers assaulted and little old ladies and shopkeepers were being terrorised by hooligans who were spitting down on people off the walkways, mugging people and vandalising everything in sight. One guy was even going around the nearby estate with a rat on his shoulder to scare the living daylights out of the old dears. Of course, the shopkeepers, with justification, were up in arms about the lack of protection but in reality there was only so much that anyone could do. The poor little sods working for Sterling Security were just part-timers, probably students supplementing their grants – and you could hardly expect them to go steaming in against these hardened and apparently downright vindictive yobbos. And even if they did have a go at the little slags they'd only go crying to the police saying that they'd been assaulted. Anyway, the security guys' job was just to provide a reassuring presence, sign deliveries in and out and patrol the place at regular intervals, presumably between catching up on their studies. Understandably, they were right out of their depth and scared out of their wits! I felt sorry for them. And anyway it's one thing dealing with serious professional villains who don't hurt anyone without a very good reason; it's quite another dealing with vicious little gits who just get their kicks out of bullying people. I can't abide that sort of behaviour – and I

126

was happy to take the considerable money on offer and sort the little bastards out once and for all!

I sent a very proficient team of ten or twelve of my best guys up there. They staked the whole area out for a week or so and came back to me with copious notes – from which we put together our battle strategy.

The following week when the little thugs turned up in the car park to start their usual troublemaking we intercepted them and gave them a serious talking to. Most realised they were punching way above their weight – but a few fancied their chances. They got hurt. Others tried to leg it but when they ran for the stairwells we pounced, had them cornered like rats in a trap and flung them unceremoniously out of the stairwell fire exits – and once outside they got a thorough seeing to. Over a period of a couple of days we read them the riot act and completely terrorised the little sods – an eye for an eye and all that! But we were determined to make sure they didn't dare to start up their shenanigans once we'd headed back to the smoke – so we 'interviewed' each of them separately in a style that was a bit different from the methods employed by the local constabulary. Like the local bobbies, we asked each of them for his address. Unlike the bobbies, we had ways of making sure they told us the truth!

Isolating them, one by one, from their mates, we'd demand their address, pointing out that we would be asking their mates for the same information. If the two versions didn't agree they would get a slap. Funny enough, we didn't have a lot of trouble getting all of the gang's correct names and addresses. And now that we had them, we issued them with a promise – not a threat:
'Right, if we hear of one more incident on this estate you'll be seeing us again. It won't be anything like what we've done to you here. In fact nothing will happen to you in this

area. We know where you live – every last one of you...So one night, maybe a week, maybe two, maybe three weeks after you do something to annoy us, you'll be walking along the street and a van will pull up alongside you. You'll be slung in the back of that van and you'll be hospitalised. That means, boys, that your legs and arms are going to be damaged – so damaged that you won't be able to terrorise anyone ever again. Understood?'

They understood all right. No-one ever had a moment's grief from those little thugs from that day on! There are other instances – such as the time when a major uniformed security company used our services for jobs that required some manhandling. But more of that later...

That's not to say that my work with rock 'n' roll bands was entirely separate from the criminal element – in fact my time with Led Zeppelin was the perfect example of the way that Rock, Pop and Crime often go hand in hand. It all starts, of course, with fame. When you're an internationally renowned rock band with virtually unlimited cash, and especially one that's notorious for its insatiable appetite for illicit drugs and women, you become a magnet for all sorts of lowlifes.

I'm sure it won't come as much of a surprise to you when I bring up one time when Jimmy Page had been arrested for possession of a little bit of Class A. By a little bit, I mean an amount modest enough that it was clearly for personal use (as if a major multimillionaire international rock star would need to get involved in dealing drugs to supplement his income!!).

The Kensington and Chelsea police had spotted this scruffy looking guy buying something from a dealer and swooped down, arrested him, run him in and charged him. As always, the first I heard of it was when I got a call from Peter Grant, Zep's manager. He asked me to meet him at the Old Mill House, Jimmy's Windsor home. When I got there I got another call. It was Peter asking me to meet him in a lay-by up the road. I left my wife June with Charlotte (Jimmy's wife) and headed off.

'Look Don, we've got this problem,' came Peter's familiar words. 'We're just about to go off on tour to the states and we can't have Jimmy busted...It just can't happen...'

I should point out the seriousness of the situation. Once you've got a criminal record for illegal drug possession in the UK there's no way you're going to be admitted to the USA unless you get a waiver (special permission from the US Embassy) – and you're certainly not going to get a green card allowing you to work there. In short, the entire tour, and by extension, Zep's US career, was hanging in the balance of the scales of UK 'justice'.

'Leave it to me,' I said, for a change, after asking for the details of the police station he was held at, the name and number of the arresting officer, dates and times and so on.

After making a couple of calls, a good friend of mine arranged a meeting for me with Matty, a very well-known face (and a grass, now dead) about town who was particularly renowned around Hatton Garden at the time. I explained the situation and asked if there was anything he could do. A man after my own heart, he said, 'Leave it with me!' and we parted company. Then, at our next meeting he said:

'OK Don, here's what's going to happen.'

I was all ears.

'He will go to court,' he said, with a certainty that was very impressive. 'And at the last minute they're gonna move him to a small side court, right...'

'Yeah, go on...' I said, intrigued.

'Where he'll plead guilty,' he went on, 'and there'll be police in there but no press – no press at all. No-one will know...And then he'll come out of there...And as he comes out we'll pass you something well worth having...'

'What...' I started to question what use all this was if Jimmy was found guilty.

He waved my question aside and went on.

'What we'll pass you will be Jimmy's file. The whole thing – and none of it will ever go on his record – end of story.'

Impressive! But what was this going to cost?

'OK – but what's that gonna come to,' I asked, with more than a little trepidation.

'Seven grand,' he replied.

Could have been a helluva lot more expensive – even though seven grand was a lot of money back then it would have been cheap at twice the price if the alternative was cancelling a major Led Zeppelin tour of the states at the last minute.

I went back to Peter Grant and told him what was required if Jimmy was to get off scot free and Led Zep were to go ahead with their tour unhampered by the powers that be.

'That's how it's gonna work,' I told him.

'OK,' Peter said. 'But look, I've got this guy over here working for me. He's CIA. He's serious – and I want him to run this thing for me.'

'Well, I'd rather not have to involve any more people than necessary in this – but if you're saying that's the way it's got to be, then so be it...'

And that's how we left it. I was waiting to meet these people and get from them the seven grand as agreed when I got a call.

'Hello – is that Don?'

'Yeah,' I said, cautiously.

'Well I've got some papers here with me. Is it all right to pop in and see you? Anyone about?'

'No, no – no problem, come on over,' I said.

I was living in Normandy Avenue in Barnet at the time. I sat there waiting for these people to show up. I don't know what I was expecting – maybe a Jag full of heavies, or a Merc or a Roller...

130

Soon enough, there it was. It was a Merc all right – but not the blacked-out windowed luxury gangstermobile I'd pictured in my mind's eye. Right outside my front door, a Mercedes private ambulance saloon rolled up, complete with blue light on the top – obviously it wasn't switched on. Inside, I could see a guy who was no paramedic or ambulance man – it was the earpiece he wore that gave it away. That and the fact that he looked as hard as nails – and the fact that another heavy looking guy with his own earpiece then appeared out of nowhere, approached the ambulance and said out of the corner of his mouth, 'OK. It's all clear – there's nobody else about – you can go in.'

I watched all this going down open mouthed and stood back as these high-tech heavies invaded my house like it was a small country they were conquering. I couldn't believe it – this was like G-Men protecting a presidential motorcade. And it turned out that I wasn't far wrong! They produced an envelope. I opened it and inside were crisp notes to the value of seven thousand quid.

'What's all this about then,' I asked. It all seemed a bit over the top to me.

The guy with the money was absolutely huge, intimidatingly so. He was Danish I think – but whatever else he was, he had hands like shovels. He turned to me and said:

'That's just the way we work, y'know...'

'Well fair enough,' I said, 'but I never thought there'd be any need for all this business – bloody ambulances turning up and God knows how many blokes with their bleedin' earpieces watching the whole street! Call me old fashioned, but it's only seven grand being delivered! I'd have just picked up the money, dropped it off and been done with it!'

Well anyway, that was the end of that part of the process – overcomplicated in my book, but never mind. So I went down to see the bloke we had to pay with the seven grand.

He lived in Whetstone, only a couple of miles from my gaff. He seemed all right, and we got talking.

'Anyway, I've got the seven grand,' I said.

He went strangely quiet. Disturbingly so.

'Look Don, I'm sorry, but I'm gonna have to bale out of this deal,' he said, apologetically.

'What do you mean bale out?' I protested. 'You can't bale out now – there's more riding on this than you realise mate...'

'Oh I realise all right – what you obviously don't know is that there's been a lot of other people making enquiries – the kind of enquiries we ain't happy about...'

'Rubbish – you're just being paranoid,' I snapped.

'No, mate. I'm telling you now; someone's sniffing around and making themselves busy. And all that's gonna come out of it is that someone's gonna get nicked! So we don't want no part of it.'

'OK then,' I said. 'Let's have the seven grand back.'

He complied – a bit too willingly for my liking. He obviously wasn't joking – he was genuinely worried.

So I left and as soon as I got home I phoned Peter.

'I've got your money here Peter – I mean I've still got it. There's been a snag...'

'What sort of problem,' Peter boomed in the huge voice that matched his physical presence.

'Well I'll explain it all tomorrow – but there was all sorts of crap going down...Bloody ambulances turning up at my place and people sniffing around and making people get all uppity and nervous...'

The next day I went to see Peter in person.

'Look G,' I said (as Peter was called by his close family, Led Zep and the crew). 'I don't know exactly what's been going on but we had it all sorted out nice and sweet, no problems at all. By this time next week it would've all been done and dusted. But someone's making themselves busy and sticking their nose in making what they call "enquiries..."'

'Oh yeah,' said Peter, suddenly seeming to understand what I was on about. 'That'll be Herb – this guy I've got working for me.'

'But why?' I said, exasperated.

At this point Peter suddenly looked a bit sheepish – if you can ever use that adjective to describe a mountain of a man like Peter Grant. In stature, he was a lot more like a grizzly bear. So let's just say he looked like a sheepish grizzly bear. Not much less frightening than usual in other words.

'Well, Don, it's just that he thought...Well, we thought...You might have had an angle on this whole thing...that you might have been trying to have us over...'

That gutted me. I was appalled.

'Peter,' I said in hushed tones full of reproach, 'you know me better than that!' I wouldn't do that to you...I wouldn't do that to Jimmy. In fact I wouldn't do that to anyone! I can't believe you're accusing me of that! I was just handling a perfectly straightforward, easy little operation like I've done for bloody years with no problem at all until you get some arsehole to interfere...'

'Well,' Peter mumbled, well and truly (and bloody rightly) shamefaced now,

'maybe my man thought some of the money might be going into your pockets...'

Before he had a chance to finish that sentence I cut in angrily. 'For Christ's sake Peter, it's bad enough that you went along with that – that YOU started thinking of me like that...'

'But..' Peter stammered.

'No "buts" Peter. You thought I was out of order – that's not good. But I'd have thought the least I deserved was that you asked me straight – instead of having some geezer going around checking up on me and all these other people behind my back and undermining my credibility in the process!'

'But my people need to be....' he started, trying to justify himself.

'No,' I cut him dead. 'Forget about it.'

So, thanks to Peter's CIA buddy's interference all deals were off. No skin off my nose, I thought.

Anyway, subsequently Jimmy got nicked and of course had a criminal record for drug offences that was going to cause him all sorts of grief. What's more, I found out later that his fine was an outrageous amount, all of which went down the drain (or into the coffers of the court) for no result at all. The deal I'd sorted out would have been so much better all round – especially because Jimmy wouldn't have had a record and he'd have avoided all the bad publicity – but no, Peter's new associates knew best.

I wasn't at all happy about the kind of people Peter was getting involved with because although they claimed they could make all sorts of problems go away they just didn't deliver. He was obviously enamoured with the glamour of these big time agency people – and I must admit that they did seem to be very well-connected. One time I was going to see Peter at the Montcalm Hotel and I clocked a car sitting outside with three guys sitting in it. They were obviously watching the hotel. I could tell at a glance – and I should know – that these were no just three ordinary blokes sitting around having a chat. This was a professional little firm. I took a slight diversion and entered the hotel from a different direction that was just out of their view and went straight up to Peter's room.

'Peter, did you know there's three guys parked up out there watching the place...You got any problems I should know about? Or are you expecting any trouble? Are they working for you or what?' I interrogated him, determined to get to the bottom of this.

'No,' he said, evidently as much in the dark as I was.

I'd taken the precaution of writing the car's registration number down. I handed it to Peter, who left the room to talk to his new CIA buddy. In less than ten minutes he was back, with a satisfied look on his face.

'No sweat Don. They're police – an undercover team.'

The fact that he could get that information so fast – not to mention find out that they were police on an undercover operation – meant that this guy was even better connected than I'd imagined. To get that kind of info you have to have security clearance at the highest of high levels – so clearly he was serious! There was no question that this CIA fellow was capable. My worry was whether he was streetwise – and I mean streetwise London style. After all, he was an American dealing with English people, most of whom were pretty shady characters. Fact of the matter was that I could get things done more quietly, more effectively and for a fraction of the price these yanks were obviously charging – but that didn't stop Peter referring almost every little snag to the guy.

CRIME AGAINST CRIME – BEATING THE BOOTLEGGERS

There were many areas of my work with Zeppelin that meant sailing more than a little close to the legal wind. A case in point is the way we approached destroying bootleg stock in record shops. In case you're not familiar with the term, a 'bootleg' is any record, tape, CD or piece of merchandise that's manufactured and sold illegally without coughing up the royalties due to the band/record company/publishers/management and so on. In the seventies they were rife, presumably because the technology didn't exist to keep track of what's been sold where like there is today with bar codes and what have you. It was my job to turn up team-handed at any record shop that had been reported to us as flogging dodgy product and destroy it. Now I'm not saying that charging into someone's shop and destroying stock is strictly legal – course it isn't! But, unlike my CIA-connected friends, I like to think I took a relatively discreet stance on the whole operation – and we always had one of the record company people with us so that the retailer knew we were coming straight from the top. I even went as far as to seek the permission of the store's owner before trashing their bootleg stuff - not, of course, that they had a lot of option faced with me and a team of my most intimidating men! In any event, since they were selling fraudulent products and depriving the copyright owners of a lot of money, they couldn't exactly go running to the Old Bill could they! I would politely point out that if they declined to co-operate and allow us to destroy the relevant stock we'd be happy to leave it in their racks – but that we'd score the records across both sides to make them completely unplayable and therefore unsaleable.

If the shop owner didn't let us trash the dodgy stock, the implied threat was they'd pass the word around that this shop was stocking bootlegs and they would almost instantly find that they couldn't get stock from any of the major distributors. Sure, there were ways round it and they'd manage to get some stock one way or another – but not without a lot of unnecessary hassle and extra expense. All in all it was hardly surprising that almost every shop became instantly co-operative in the war on bootleggers the moment we showed our faces!

It's another example of something I've been involved in that's technically illegal – but which is working on the side of the law and preventing serious fraud. I suppose you describe the area I work in a 'grey area' but that makes it sound boring and I can assure you there was never a dull moment in the life and crimes of Don Murfet!

We always took a similar stance with ticket touts and people flogging counterfeit merchandise (T shirts, posters and so on

136

with the band's name, images and logo printed on them). Even legitimate merchandise is known in the business as 'swag' – but it was just the really bad rip-offs that we clamped down on and confiscated. Again, that ain't exactly legal – but then neither is producing and selling counterfeit swag and flogging it right under our noses! It wasn't just Zeppelin and the record company who were getting ripped off – it was the fans themselves, who often thought they were buying the genuine article and would be gutted to find that the quality was crap and the designs not a patch on the ones the band had commissioned for the official merchandise. Again, though, I reckon we were more than reasonable and if they toed the line and didn't take the piss too much we would tolerate them. It was the ones who persistently and blatantly touted really crappy stuff right under our noses that we came down hard on. We simply wouldn't let them work! Like the record shop owners, they could hardly call the Old Bill when we confiscated their stock – but if they played the game, we'd often actually give them it back after the concert. You can't say fairer than that can you!

The men at the top of the big record companies weren't averse to a bit of dodgy dealing themselves – I mention this lest you get the impression that it was only me and my associates that were doing all the ducking and diving! A prime example was one time I was in a meeting with Maurice Oberstein, the head of CBS, discussing Adam Ant's career and trying to negotiate his record deal up a bit – like you do. Maurice wasn't having it and he trotted out his usual response to such requests, which was along the lines of:
'Tell Adam to make a list of all the things we've done for him and are doing for him and then to make a list of exactly where he'd be if we hadn't done any of those things and see if he still thinks the deal isn't a fair one.'
The upshot of which was that he had no intention of budging. But he did mention something I could help him with – and

which could be worth a lot of money to me! Part of the reason for my appearance at CBS that day, and the main reason why Oberstein was not in the best of moods for negotiating was that the workers at their main distribution depot were threatening to go on strike. This could be disastrous for a record company; if the records aren't in the shops they can't be sold. In that respect the music business is just like any other. The big difference, though, is that chart placings mean everything – and a glitch in record deliveries could mean a drop in the charts, or even a failure to appear in the chart. That would be bad enough but a poor chart showing could also mean the loss of a Top of The Pops appearance – and TOTP was, and still is, crucial to the promotion of a single in the UK.

Maurice was singularly unhappy about being held to ransom by a few workers and he asked me whether I could send my boys down there and do a bit of strike breaking. I was up for it and so were my boys – but as it turned out the strike didn't go ahead and our services weren't required, more's the pity for my bank balance. I only bring this one up to emphasise the fact that these corporate fat cats don't mind stumping up money and breaking the law if it suits their corporate purposes – and I don't mind saying that I agree with them!

RIDING ON A WAVE OF DOSH

In the sixties and seventies, and even into the early eighties, the big record companies were awash with money. The Artist Liaison guys at your EMIs, your CBSs, Warners and so on seemed to have endless cash to flash about and lavish on their artists – not to mention themselves. They were just given credit cards with which they ordered up seemingly endless streams of booze, motorcades of luxurious Limos and almost any other luxury item or service the artist demanded that you could name – as well as quite a few you probably couldn't!

For a guy like me, these loaded Liaison blokes were rich pickings. They wanted Limos and drivers and I had as many as they wanted. And to make sure I got more than my fair share of the money pot, I'd simply give them a kickback in the form of a personal percentage of anything they put my way. Not strictly legitimate practice, I know, but hardly the crime of the century! Needless to say, my car service to the stars, Artistes Car Services was rolling the money in, and the Limos out, almost round the clock and quickly became the biggest operator in the showbiz world. In fact the company was growing so fast and branching out into new areas of business and we found that we had more coming in than we could handle and we had to start subbing it out.

One of the beneficiaries of this development was one Stan Addersman, an impressively smart, well turned out chauffeuring professional with manners as immaculate as his uniforms and his motors. You'd never have thought so to look at him, but he was also a complete bloody lunatic of a driver! And, never one to miss a trick when it came to squeezing a bit more dosh out of a deal, I made sure there was something extra in it for yours truly. And here's how it worked. First of all the Artist Liaison guys were putting their invoices through the accounts system in the normal way – and of course some were directly from my own Artistes Car Services and others were from the people I was subbing work out to. Because most of those guys were more expensive than my outfit anyway, they had a problem with paying me a commission on all the work I put their way – which I simply split down the middle with the Artist Liaison guy concerned. All of which was very nice for me – and even nicer for the Artist Liaison guys because they were also getting a drink off the top of the work I did directly for them!

And those commissions didn't half build up! At one point I had a look at how Stan's account stood – and he was into me for a whopping nine grand! I couldn't have that!

'Stan, mate,' I said to him, 'we've got to talk about your account. It's run right up to something like nine grand! You're going to have to cough up soon or I'm going to have to stop giving you work mate!'

I was bemused by his response.

'All right Don...Look, I'd like you to come and meet my partners...'

'What partners?' I butted in impatiently. 'You haven't got any partners...I thought you were your own boss!'

'No. I'm owned by a bank,' he said.

'Oh,' I replied, not really any the wiser.

Anyway, I decided to go along with him and, a short while later, the two of us rolled up at this bank in The City that was funding Stan's operation. We were escorted through the hallowed portals and ushered into this great big swanky boardroom where a couple of toffee-nosed bankers (I'll leave it up to you to decide whether or not that's rhyming slang!) sat looking down the aforementioned toffee noses at me.

'Now look,' one of them piped up. 'We understand that you're threatening to remove your business from Stan unless your commission is paid.'

'Quite right,' I replied. 'I've made a deal with Stan – and it hasn't been honoured and I'd like to know the reason why.'

'Well that's not quite the way we see it,' the little banker replied. 'After all we – Stan and his men – are doing all the work. We are doing all the invoicing...So it seems to us, if you really want your commission, that a more conventional approach would be for us to invoice for the amount in question and for you then to invoice the record company or companies.'

I wasn't having that.

'But that wasn't the deal,' I spluttered indignantly.

'Well that's the only way it can be. We've done the work, we've invoiced them and been paid and we're not prepared to give you any commission.'

'Well that's bloody marvellous isn't it,' I protested. 'So what would you do if I cut you off without any work – nothing, *nada, zilch*? Eh?'

'Frankly, Mr Murfet,' the supercilious git went on in his increasingly oily and officious manner, 'we don't really see that as a problem. On the contrary, we feel that our operation is in a position of great strength with all of the current and potential clients. In short, we're confident that we can keep these accounts in our own right – hence our reluctance to pay you commission for work which we are capable of retaining without recourse to your company...'

'I see,' I said quietly. 'You got it all worked out haven't you. But there's one thing you haven't factored into your cosy little equation.'

The two little bankers smirked. One waved his hand to say, 'Do go on...'

So I did. And now in a tone that was a lot less acquiescent.

'What you people need to realise is that you haven't got any idea of how strong I am – or how I operate.'

With that, the smirks on their smug faces shrivelled a little. I went on, anger now evident in my voice.

'You banking people always want guarantees don't you. Don't like that element of risk, do you! Well here's a couple of cast iron guarantees for you. First I'll guarantee you that within a week your tinpot outfit will have absolutely no work whatsoever. Secondly, when that happens, I'll guarantee you that if you come crying back to me because you're on the brink of bankruptcy you'll get nothing – repeat, nothing – until you cough up every last penny of what you owe me.'

They were considerably less smug-looking now. But still they pressed their point.

'Well Mr Murfet, you must do whatever you have to do. Nevertheless, we feel that our position is such that we can dispense with your services entirely and secure more than enough work under our own steam.'

I'm quite chuffed to say that, true to my word, within a single week they had not one poxy driving job. No-one in showbiz and none of the record companies would touch them with a bargepole.

And then things really started to kick off. I had a call from the Artist Liaison guy at Polydor.
'Listen Don, what's going on? We've got this Stan Addersman geezer down here in Reception parading up and down with a bloody great sandwich board thing that says we're nicking his business!'
Apparently he was really laying it on thick, claiming that we were taking the bread out of his family's mouths, bleeding him dry...You name it, he claimed it!
'Yeah?' I said, not entirely surprised. 'Don't you worry about that. Leave it with me!'

Like a shot I rounded up a couple of my guys and we went steaming over to Polydor in a van. I had a plan – and like all the best ones it was very simple.
'Go in and get the bastard, sling him in the van and throw him in the Thames,' I ordered, now determined to teach to cocky git a lesson he wouldn't forget.
They were nice blokes really, the guys who worked for me.
'No...We can't do that!' they said.
'All right, if you're not comfortable with that, do whatever you think fit – but I want him frightened...really frightened. Just you make sure he knows that he'd better not show his ugly mug in that street again – ever. Or around any of the other record companies. OK?'
'OK,' my two boys agreed almost in unison.

142

I never did get round to asking exactly what they did to him. But whatever it was it worked. The boys went and did their work in their customary efficient and thorough style and Stan learnt his lesson.

And guess what. The phone rang a few days later and it was one of our little bankers again – but he didn't sound anywhere near as smarmy this time.

'I wonder if we might arrange a meeting Mr Murfet,' he simpered.

'Why?' I demanded, as if I didn't know.

'Well, you've clearly made your point and we are forced to admit that we had sorely underestimated your powers. We were hoping that you would be willing to discuss the situation in a civilised manner,' he said with a humility I'd never have guessed he possessed.

'Yeah?' I sneered, loving every last grovelling mouthful of his humble pie. 'Well, we can talk all right. We'll talk when I get the money you owe me.'

'Yes but, can't we talk about th....'

'No!' I cut in, shooting him down in flames.

They were reluctant to say the least to cough up the £9K and wanted to negotiate. But I wasn't having that and I told them so, adding that nothing would change till I was paid. After hearing nothing for a few days, I paid their garage in King's Cross a visit one evening. All their Daimler Limousines were sitting pretty in the yard outside their offices and, under cover of darkness, I proceeded to bomb them with loosely-bound bags containing a high quality cellulose stripper, which began eating into the pristine paintwork the moment it hit those gleaming roofs and bonnets.

The following morning, when the drivers arrived to prepare their vehicles for work, it was immediately apparent that the

143

Limos were unusable in that state and they had no choice but to let down their corporate clients. It was bad enough for them to lose a full day's revenue – but what was worse was that this would be very bad for future business. To cap it all, the people they hired to respray their fleet found it wasn't as easy as they'd thought. Assuming that they were dealing with the effects of a normal commercial stripper, they used the standard neutralising agent – not a good plan. Every time they tried to respray the vehicles the paint just blistered – and that meant that their precious Limos were out of commission for a lot longer than they'd expected, with disastrous financial consequences!

Needless to say, I never got my commission – in fact the company, Beaufort Cars, went out of business, largely due to my efforts. I was left with a useful weapon to use against those Artist Liaison people. They'd missed out on their kickback for all the work they'd put through Stan's outfit – so it wasn't long before they brought all their business back to yours truly, knowing I'd make sure their got their kickbacks!

You may wonder how I stopped Beaufort Cars getting any work. The answer is that I simply made the Artist Liaison people show my tariff, and Beauforts, to their Accounts Department. Mine was considerably cheaper – so they instructed all departments to use my company. Repeat that process through all the other record companies, agents, publishers and so on and you've got the market cornered completely legitimately. And that's exactly what I did!

Adam talking to his fans in 1981, flanked by myself and Dave Moulder.

Me trying to persuade The Pig she'd look better with a pork pie hat and sunglasses for the *Ant Rap* video

145

For those who went

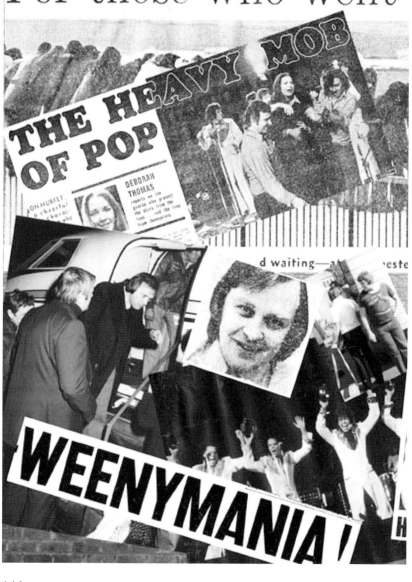

THE HEAVY MOB OF POP

DEBORAH THOMAS

reports we the search who protect the stars from the fans — and the fans from themselves

ON MURFET a cheerful charac who

d waiting—a ...este

WEENYMANIA !

to the wrong airport

... here IS David Cassidy

Girls rush stage at David Cassidy's first British show

By MAURICE RICHAR

FIVE HUNDRED girl of pop singer David Ca crowded on to Manch airport's international

Airport arr

Introducing ...the heavy mob of po

SECURITY

Glitter

NYDS

lf a ton of gentle persuasion

147

The typical fans' reaction when they catch sight of Adam Ant or the group.

Yours truly being used as a stand-in while Adam practised for the *Friend or Foe* video

148

Me revisiting the Scrubs 44 years after my first visit. I like this view better!

CHAPTER FIVE

1965 – 1972

DONOVAN AND THE LEECH

I was very close to Donovan Leitch. He was a lovely bloke, very gentle in manner and outlook and extremely well educated and clever with it. And, surprisingly for a pop star, along with Donovan came his mum and dad! His dad, Donald, was a very amiable chap who just seemed to like travelling around the world with his son, of whom he was very proud. In fact, as soon as Donovan became successful enough, his father quit his job at British Aerospace in Hatfield and hardly left his son's side, becoming what you might call Donovan's general factotum. But his mum, Winifred, was a very different kettle of fish – she was an absolute horror, a bit of a bully and a hard taskmaster to boot! Makes me shudder to think of the run-ins I had with her. She always had to get her twopenn'orth in – whatever the issue, and whether or not it was any of her business. She drove me nuts – and Donovan wasn't her greatest fan either! I had the impression that she didn't approve of Donovan dropping out of college – as almost everyone did in the sixties – and the pressure she constantly put on him was responsible for his leaving home. Not that she was happy about what he did once he'd gone! Far from it – he went on the road with an itinerant kazoo player known as Gypsy Dave Mills, travelling around the country scraping a living by busking and generally living the hippy life.

Early on, Donovan had been struck by polio, which had left him with a slightly gammy right leg and a bit of a limp –

something we had in common, although my polio didn't leave any significant damage. Now I come to think of it, maybe his illness accounts for his mum being such a control freak; she probably just couldn't get out of the habit of trying to protect him all the time.

Anyway, we'd been working for Donovan for a while on the security side, driving him, Ashley Kozak (Donovan's double bass playing manager) and Gypsy Dave about the place to TV shows like Ready Steady Go – the Top of the Pops of its day. This was around 1965 and soon Donovan was really cracking it and being hailed as the British answer to Bob Dylan! Before long he was a genuine, 24-carat superstar and his lifestyle followed suit. And he made the front page news in 1966 when he got busted for marijuana possession and got weighed off at Marylebone Magistrates Court in Marylebone Road – I took great delight in outfoxing the journalists and getting him away by a side door! He'd been living in Wimbledon, but as his new wealth piled up he invested in an Aston Martin DB7 with custom made interior (including head lining in blue Paisley silk) and a house in Little Berkhamsted, Hertfordshire, which made life easier for me because I was living in Barnet at the time. Less convenient was the hippy commune he set up on the Isle of Skye, which was a bit of a schlep to say the least! I remember one time bringing the Aston Martin back from there with Donovan's father as a passenger. When Donald fell asleep I got up to 145mph on the motorway and, when he woke, he was amazed that we'd got back to Hatfield so quickly!

Once the rock stardom rollercoaster really got rolling, Gypsy Dave was just along for the ride really – but it was clear that he loved Donovan dearly and took great care of his friend. Even back in their busking days, Donovan would sit there strumming away and it would be Gypsy Dave who did the hustling, going round with a hat and cajoling cash out of the punters and generally making sure Donovan was OK.

Donovan had promised Gypsy that, in return for all the care he'd lavished on him, if he ever made it big, Gypsy would get half of everything. And, to Donovan's great credit, he was true to his word. As soon as the big time beckoned Donovan, Gypsy moved into his posh new gaff with him and for a quite few years did absolutely bugger all. And I mean that literally. He was always around but he would not lift a finger – not even to carry his own guitar. He had the same size room as Donovan and lived the same lifestyle – which was pretty lavish! I suppose he had the right, if Donovan didn't mind but still, maybe it's the grafter in me that finds it hard to bear someone doing nothing at all, the whole bloody time, but anyway, one day I took him aside and had a word.

'Look Gypsy, you've got to start doing something mate. Why don't you find yourself a niche – something you enjoy but that'll make yourself useful to Donovan. What about learning to handle the live sound mixing or something like that? Surely you don't want to be a ligger all your life?'

In his hippy naivety Gypsy was convinced that their friendly agreement would go on forever and ever amen – but obviously it wouldn't. I knew damn well that the moment mellow mannered Donovan got married, or got himself a new, more ruthless management firm, Gypsy would be out on his heavily earringed ear!

Before too long I was proved right and Donovan's increasing intimacy with his girlfriend Linda Lawrence, whom he'd started seeing just as he became well-known, meant that there was no room left for Gypsy in his life – at least not as the full time leech he'd become. He didn't take it very well – well that's an understatement. Donovan rang me from his cottage in Buck's Alley, Little Berkhamsted after he'd broken the bad news to Gypsy, urgently seeking my help. Gypsy had gone completely apeshit and backed his Land Rover into the Aston Martin!

'He's still here...And he's going berserk Don. He just won't accept that it's all over...You've got to come up here and sort him out!' spluttered a rather less than mellow Donovan.

'All right. Leave it to me,' I sighed. Here we go again, I thought as I got in the motor and headed for Little Berkhamsted.

No sooner had I pulled into the drive, I was faced by an irate Gypsy – no longer the gentle hippy I'd been used to.

'I won't stand for this,' he ranted. 'He's changed! He's not the same person since he's been with her.'

'Look Gypsy,' I said firmly. 'The fact is that he's with her – and he's gonna be with her for good. He's marrying her for Christ's sake – and nothing you've got to say's gonna change that. I told you before that you needed to find a niche in the band; be something more than just a ligger but you wouldn't listen.'

He wasn't having any of it and started making wild threats and going on about what he was going to do about it. I cut him short.

'Look Gypsy, you can't do anything about it mate. I'm looking after Donovan and I'm telling you now it's over. It's finished. You can't come round here smashing things up – and if you do I'm gonna have to get involved. And you won't want that I can assure you.'

'But...' he began.

'No buts,' I cut in. 'You're just gonna have to bite the bullet and go mate. There's nothing I can do about it. You're not allowed on this property unless Donovan says so – and certainly not if you're gonna start smashing things up again. Because if you do, I'm gonna have to get my men down here – and you can't win against them. Do you understand? You can't win against them.'

154

So off he went to who knows where to do God knows what. I did hear from him a couple of years later – and was pleased when he told me he'd got married and was trying to settle down with his new wife in Norfolk somewhere. It was a shame though. He'd had an opportunity to make something of his life that a lot of people would give their right arm for – but he just didn't try.

Before Linda, Donovan also used to go out with a very attractive American girl – a former model called Enid Stulberger, with whom he had a couple of kids: Donovan Leitch junior (or Donno to his American friends) and daughter Iona Skye. He first started seeing her amid the usual cloud of marijuana smoke of an American tour and, one morning after they'd all been off for the night camping and getting high in the hills outside LA, I had to drive up there to pick up Donovan. When I arrived, Enid (with whom I did get on with very well, incidentally) emerged from a tent – but to my surprise it wasn't Donovan that appeared behind her. It was John Sebastian of Lovin' Spoonful. Well, you know what hippies are like – it didn't occur to me that there was anything untoward going on till a long time later.

Anyway, Enid fell pregnant shortly after that and throughout her pregnancy I got on very well with her and young Donno and spent quite a bit of time with them at Donovan's Hampstead apartment. Donovan was having to spend more and more time out of the country on tours – so he wasn't around the day the baby was born. Just after the birth I received a very strange phone call from him and I congratulated him on being a dad again. But he was weirdly cold about the whole thing.

'You coming to see the kid then?' I enquired, more as a statement than a question. But to my amazement, his reply was a chilling, 'No.'

Odd! I thought. Whatever's up with him?

155

'Don, I need you to do something for me,' Donovan's strangely shaky voice said.

'OK,' I said, mystified.

'I want you to go up to the flat, tell Enid it's all over...'

'But,' I began to protest, only to be overridden by an unusually insistent and authoritative Donovan.

'I want you to pick up Enid, Donno and the baby, take them to the airport and put them on a plane back to America,' he said flatly.

'But Don,' I pleaded, 'she's only just had a kid...'

'I'm telling you, that's what I want. OK. Give her the tickets, give her some money but tell her she's got to go.'

I was shocked. He'd been with her for a few years by now – and I'd assumed Enid and the kids would be a permanent fixture...But there was no changing his mind and he flatly refused to see the baby.

'Well, if that's what you want...' I said.

'It is.'

'OK, leave it to me,' I said and off I went to perform one of the most unpleasant duties of my life in the rock and pop world – well beyond the call of duty, I'd say, in fact! Arriving at the Hampstead flat I sat Enid down and broke the news. She couldn't believe it. She just could not take in what I was saying to her.

'I want to see him,' she said.

'He won't see you love,' I said gently.

She sat there stunned, in total shock, struggling to grasp the appalling fact that her whole life had just been pulled out from under her. Leaving her grappling with her abandonment, I slipped out to call Tim Poulton, our regular travel agent (and the one most of the industry used).

'I've got a bit of a situation here mate,' I briefed him. 'And it needs to be handled delicately.'

I didn't give him all the details. I just mentioned that there was a lot of heartache going on, that Enid and the kids were leaving and that I'd need some help at the airport, what with

156

all the crying that was bound to happen – and I didn't just mean by the newborn baby! With the help of Tim and his people and Eddie Faulkner, TWA's Special Services guy, I made things as bearable as I possibly could and finally got the stricken remnants of Donovan's broken family onto a TWA flight to the States. And that was the end of Enid as far as Donovan was concerned.

Many years later, while I was in LA with Adam and The Ants, I met up with Enid and her daughter. I was relieved to find that she bore no animosity towards me – because none of it had been my doing. She understood that once Donovan had made up his mind, all I could do was make the terrible news as bearable as possible. Nevertheless, some people might have found it hard to resist the temptation to 'shoot the messenger'. It was one of the hardest things I've ever had to on the behalf of any of the artists I've been associated with – because it seemed so unjustified, downright cruel really. And I never really got to the bottom of it. I can only assume that he'd convinced himself that he wasn't the baby's father. I suppose that when you've got a load of people all free and easy, camping in a sort of commune in the hills and getting completely stoned, all sorts of things can happen. Frankly I wouldn't know. So I guess I'll never know whether Enid was with John that night – or if not why Donovan ditched her so abruptly. I will say, though, that when I met Iona in LA that time, she looked a lot like Donovan and Donno, for what it's worth – and incidentally both children have since become successful actors in LA.

For a full time hippy and Ban the Bomb protester, Donovan didn't half drop a lot of bombshells. One time he was in New York with Linda and he went out for a walk and came back with the latest piece of earth-shattering news.
'I've just signed with Allen Klein. He's my new manager,' he announced brightly.

Anyway Donovan took me along to meet the famous Mr Klein at the cinema he owned in Times Square where he was, as usual, showing a seriously weird film. I only remember odd flashes of it – a guy with no arms running round with a guy with no legs on his shoulders, so that together they made up a complete body...Well, kind of. And there was a shocking rape scene. According to the hype it was for real! The director had duped some young starlet onto the set, giving her the impression that she'd be acting – and then set the camera rolling and actually raped her! Mary Poppins it wasn't – and it certainly wasn't my cup of tea! Nevertheless, there were queues right round the block and it played to packed audiences night after night. I didn't have a lot to do with Allen Klein after that night and, with hindsight, it's now clear to me that this was the beginning of the end of my association with Donovan.

Allen Klein was the guy whom the Rolling Stones brought in to co-manage them alongside their original *svengali*, Andrew Loog Oldham, whom they eventually ditched, leaving the field clear for Klein to take control. Suffice to say Klein was, and is, a big shot in the biz. As if to prove it, Klein immediately set about getting Donovan out of his deal with CBS Records and signing him to Warner, who stumped up a ludicrous amount of dosh for the privilege. Unfortunately for Donovan, even the likes of Klein can't mess with CBS and get away with it and the subsequent litigation meant that he couldn't record or release anything for over two years. Pop fans have short memories – and those of Donovan fans were probably even shorter, having literally gone to pot (you know what they say about cannabis and the short term memory)! With no new tunes being aired, no new records on the streets and precious few gigs on the books, poor old Donovan was forgotten; he was yesterday's man. CBS had literally, unilaterally, finished him. His superstar days were over. Very

158

much the same happened to Gary Puckett and the Union Gap. He had a dispute with his record company and he was locked into litigation for two years – and again, from having been a massive star with 'Young Girl', with no exposure of any kind he quickly became history.

*   *   *

In 1969, just after the murder of Sharon Tate, the young wife of film director Roman Polanski (one of the horrific spate of killings perpetrated by Charles Manson and his followers), Donovan was still on his year out of the UK (for tax reasons) and we were staying at a house on Sunset Boulevard in LA where I remember a particularly bizarre party. It was a typical LA party of the time – loads of exotic people from all parts of the entertainment industry, along with glammed up wannabes of all descriptions. Among them was Richard Beymer who starred in the film of 'West Side Story'..

Anyway, as the evening progressed, I couldn't help noticing that Donovan was getting very friendly with Richard Beymer's other half, who was also in the film. Strange, I thought as I watched them slope off to a room together – unnoticed, it seemed, because later she went home with Richard as if nothing untoward had happened. It obviously had though, because before long the girl was showing up all over the world, wherever Donovan went – in Japan, then on his luxury 100ft motor yacht in Piraeus. (Incidentally, he'd bought the yacht from 'Magic' Alex Mardis, an electronics wizard who worked with The Beatles. I don't think Donovan quite grasped what he was getting into. The thing was so vast that it needed two crews – one for the engine and another for the sails!) Anyway, this went on for quite some time while Donovan was on his year out, though I wasn't with them at this time, having other fish to fry. Then, about nine months into his year's tax exile, I got a call from Donovan in Japan.

'Hi Don. Look I'm coming back. I'll be flying in tomorrow morning – can you pick me up at the airport?'

'Don, you can't. What about the tax?' I protested (if he so much as set foot on British soil during the year out he'd become liable for an absolute fortune in tax).

'I know what I'm doing,' he said. 'Just meet me at the airport.'

'All right,' I replied. 'Give me the flight number and your hotel phone number – I'll check out the times and get back to you.'

Putting the phone down I thought for a moment – this could be disastrous. So before calling Donovan back I called Vic Lewis, who was still involved with Donovan and whom I still considered my mentor.

Vic was horrified and got straight on the phone in an attempt to dissuade him, but to no avail. Vic called back later to say that Donovan must be completely mad but that he was insisting on flying in so I'd better go and get him.

'Leave it to me,' I said and before long I was parked up outside Heathrow in the early hours of the morning – just for a bloody change! As we drove towards Donovan's place, he told me why he was so desperate to come home. To say he'd had a bad time would be an understatement – he'd been through the emotional wringer and had come out crushed flat. He was so disturbed that he'd even contemplated suicide and had been on the verge of throwing himself off a tall building – and in that state of mind I suppose all you want to do is get back home and surround yourself with your friends and family. The monetary loss meant little by comparison – I have no idea what it amounted to but it must have been huge.

I never knew exactly what had happened to tear him apart so savagely – but you can't help thinking sometimes that life has a way of getting its own back on you. And if you were a bit of a hippy, as Donovan was, you just might think of it as

160

Karma and life was paying him back for the harsh way he'd treated Enid Stulberger!

Anyway, thank God, the damage wasn't permanent and in October 1970, Donovan went on to marry Linda Lawrence, the former girlfriend of Rolling Stone Brian Jones, in a lovely church ceremony in Windsor, followed by a sumptuous reception at Linda's parents' very large house nearby – which they used as a Bed and Breakfast. So soon after his dramatic break-up and virtual breakdown it would be easy to jump to the conclusion that he was on the rebound. Not so – he's still married to Linda to this day! I think Linda and her warm, friendly and accommodating family, for whom I had a lot of time, provided Donovan with the love and stability he was dying for and more than made up for his tense relationship with his mother.

*　　　*　　　*

Donovan's dad, Don Leitch, had never been a driver – but was suddenly inspired to learn and get his licence, so Donovan bought him a brand spanking new Jag! And it was in this that he showed up outside that church in Windsor, where happy crowds of family, friends and fans were spilling out into the road. I noticed the Jag approaching and went outside to meet him and direct him where to park. As I got close, he got out of the car and started towards me and the wedding party. Trouble was, so did the bloody Jag! He'd only left it in drive with the handbrake off! Luckily it wasn't going that fast – but then again, you try stopping a motor of that size and weight once it starts rolling. I lunged for the door, wrenched it open and leapt into the driver's seat, just in time to slam it into neutral and pull on the brake before it bowled everyone down like so many skittles. Another disaster narrowly averted!

Tragically, Don senior was to be involved in another disaster soon afterwards that could not be averted. Driving homeward from the pub in the Jag somewhere near Welwyn Garden City, his three-lane carriageway on the A1 narrowed to two lanes, then to one lane, the oncoming traffic taking over the oncoming two lanes. Somehow he failed to notice the signs or the bollards and continued to drive along the middle lane. A man had the misfortune to be driving his pregnant wife in the opposite direction. And in the head-on collision the woman was fatally injured. Don was charged with dangerous driving – and perhaps drunk driving, but I'm not sure about that. I know he'd had a couple – but anyway, as I so often do when friends are in trouble, I suggested that he used my people for his defence but he went with someone else. Which was a big mistake. I'm not saying he wasn't at fault. Obviously he was in the wrong lane – but I was convinced he had at least some defence based on the fact that the road signs hadn't been at all clear. But this stupid moron of a lawyer defending him advised him to plead guilty. Then he capped that insane decision by going on about the fact that his son was the immensely rich and famous pop star Donovan, who'd bought him a big flashy car that he clearly wasn't capable of handling. This rambling speech about the suffering of the parents of pop stars was supposed to be in mitigation, believe it or not. I couldn't believe what I was hearing. And apparently nor could the judge because he basically said, 'Thank you very much, I sentence the accused to nine months!' Obviously he got a driving ban too. It was the most pathetic defence I've ever witnessed – and as you know by now, I've seen a few!

Not a very lucky fella, old Don. Some time later he was happily mowing the lawn at their house in Old Welwyn, Hertfordshire when he swung his rotary mower about with a little too much enthusiasm – he was a stocky, very heftily built bloke, so maybe he didn't know his own strength. And

162

he chopped his toe off! I don't know if it's a good or a bad thing, having one of your more silly accidents immortalised in song, but anyway Donovan immortalised the incident in the lyric which went: '...my father cut his toe off with a rotary lawn mower'. I'm sure the whole thing displeased Donovan's mother immensely. On the other hand, maybe not. She only seemed happy being miserable!

*   *   *

Having been on tour with Donovan in America for about six months, I flew into England one Friday looking forward to a well-deserved bit of R&R. But it wasn't to be. On the following morning Donovan's mother phoned me to tell me that Donovan's brother Gerald had been arrested in Morocco. Apparently he'd bought some kif (part of the marijuana family of narcotics). And he wasn't messing about – he and his mate had bought a kilo of the stuff and put it in their brand new Land Rover (either Donovan's or Donovan had bought it for Gerald – I can't remember which) and off they went, headed for God knows where. Not a tricky transaction, you'd have thought – but it was if you didn't know whom you were dealing with. And they didn't! Having asked around for the name of a dealer they'd gone and found this complete stranger, who was happy to take their money. Unfortunately for them, he was also happy to grass them up to the local cops and make some more! That's the way it often worked: the guy would be allowed to deal to the local market as long as he gave up the big deals to the cops – preferably foreigners with luxury vehicles.

So they didn't get far before the police ambushed them, found the gear, confiscated the motor and slammed them in jail. What made Gerald and his mate think they could just turn up in a strange country and do a deal like that without being stitched up I don't know. They were only young guys, aged about eighteen or nineteen and just out of college, so you can't blame them for being naive I suppose. In fact, you could say they were lucky it was only a Land Rover they had confiscated – in my experience, the police in places like that will take anything they can lay their hands on. If you got caught on a bus, they'd nick the bus. If you got caught in your house, it became their house. These blokes made your average British bobby look like Dixon of Dock Green!

And here's the rub! The problem wasn't that the Kif was illegal – it was that it was mixed with tobacco, on which they hadn't paid the tax. Which, again, was bloody stupid, because if they'd taken the trouble to research the local laws they have known that, and could easily have stumped up enough to make the whole deal legal. Anyway, Gerald and his friend were banged up in prison in Rabat and someone had to get him out. Guess who that was!

I phoned Donovan in America.
'Do whatever's got to be done to get him out of there Don,' he instructed, like I was some kind of miracle worker (well, I've had my moments I suppose!).
So my first call was to the British Embassy.
'What's the story,' I asked them. 'And what do we need to find?'
The voice on the line went silent for a moment and then said, 'Well you're going to need a few thousand pounds – there'll be a sizeable fine to pay, not to mention some serious backhanders in various quarters...'
'OK,' I said.
Paying out large sums of money wasn't a major problem for the likes of Donovan. Getting hold of it in cash on a weekend was though – for me at least.

Tim Poulton my good friend and travel agent to the stars who helped me with that heartless exile of Enid and the kids some time before, came through for me once more. Despite his agency being closed for the weekend he sorted me out with all the cash I needed as well as the flights and hotel and I was on a plane bound for Morocco that Sunday morning. That might sound quite exciting – jetting off to Africa on the spur of the moment. But it bloody well wasn't. It was the last thing I needed after six months away! I was not chuffed at all.

If I'd been a bit pissed off about having to go in the first place, I had the right hump when the next Donovan-related bombshell dropped. Mrs bloody Leitch, the mother from hell, decided unilaterally that she was coming with me. This I did not need! I'd been prepared for all sorts of horrors. I could end up in jail, or in the hands of ruthless knife-wielding drug-crazed Moroccan dealers or ripped off by corrupt Moroccan cops.... But none of these terrible fates compared with the horror of an enforced trip to Africa with the dreaded Mrs Leitch. I'm a hard man – but not that hard. I did my damnedest to talk her out of it.

'Look Mrs Leitch,' I pleaded on the phone, trying to hide the utter desperation in my voice, 'it's a North African country and it'll be too dangerous for you. They simply don't have any respect for women out there. You'll be in terrible danger the whole time and I really don't think I'll be able to guarantee your safety...'

It wasn't working.

'I've had years of experience protecting people in high-risk scenarios and it's my assessment of this situation that it's simply too dangerous. We may not escape alive,' I warbled on, laying it on as thick as my imagination would allow. But no, she wasn't having any of it. Either she was very brave or she knew, as I did, that she'd probably scare any drug dealer or bent cop shitless!'

'Well that's as maybe Mr Murfet but I shall be coming regardless. Gerald is my son and I intend to give those people a piece of my mind...' she barked.

And on and on and on and on she went – and I had to admit defeat. She was a better man than I.

So off we flew, Rabat-bound, with this nightmare nag bending my ear every mile of the hellish journey. And it was one jet lagged and nagged old lag that finally rolled up at the best hotel in Rabat. The only consolation was that those hard-nosed cops, cynical embassy officials and dodgy drug dealers would be like fluffy little bunny rabbits compared to the unbearably indomitable Mrs L! Anyway, I rose above it enough to call the British Embassy the moment we'd booked in and arrange an appointment for the following morning. And they were very helpful; they told me the name of the prison just outside Rabat in which Gerald and his friend were being held and said they'd put me in touch with an English-speaking lawyer. Having hooked up with said lawyer, Winifred (Mrs Leitch to you!) and I went with him to the prison, where Gerald and his friend told how they'd been set up and stitched up. Worse than that, their captors had shown them what they called 'The Torture Room' – and as they described this little chamber of horrors I realised that I'd seen it on my way through the jail to meet them. In a room separated from us by iron bars they had two tripod-type arrangements supporting an iron bar between them about four or five feet off the ground. This sophisticated apparatus (I don't think!) was used to extract information from prisoners. Gerald went on to tell me that they used to hang the hapless prisoner upside down from this bar with his knees over it and his hands tied behind his back. Then they would pour water up the prisoner's nostrils, filling up his sinuses. If he was lucky he'd be able to blow it out. If he couldn't they'd beat him on the soles of the bare feet until the pain caused a sharp intake of breath that rammed the water deeper into the sinuses. The resulting pain was excruciating – but of course, there'd be no bruises on the prisoner and these evil bastards could keep doing this until they got whatever it was they were after. Terrifyingly, Gerald had been promised that he and his friend could look forward to this treatment very soon.

In another room, next to the reception area I'd passed on arriving, the staff showed me a sizeable storeroom that was stacked floor to ceiling with bundles of confiscated kif. It was quite incredible the amount they had in there.

Anyway, from the prison we were taken on to the courthouse by the English-speaking lawyer who, weirdly, had his father in tow – a dignified-looking old guy who clearly didn't understand a word of English but who was evidently an important and respected figure in the court going by the way they all kowtowed to him and kissed his hand. I looked on, not at all sure what to make of it all. Then the lawyer turned to me purposefully.

'Now, Mr Murfet. We will need the money,' he said.

Here we go, I thought. I'd been waiting to see exactly who's palms needed greasing first – and it looked like this guy wasn't too proud to be first in the queue for backhanders.

'Whoah - hold on a second,' I said. 'Who needs the money?'

'Well,' he said, 'we have to have money to pay the fine and to pay bribes.'

Well! What can you do? I didn't see that I had much alternative than to cough up and trust the bloke – at least the British Consul was there, and since he didn't raise an eyebrow it looked like this was kosher. Well, as kosher as anything got with the Moroccan authorities in those days! Our lawyer man was standing there looking expectant – so I handed over a wad of dosh. I think it was about four grand – which was a fair amount of money then (Well it's a fair amount of money now, come to think of it!). The father stood there silently and handed his son a briefcase, into which his

167

son placed the money. Just a couple of minutes later, I happened to glance out of the window and out of the corner of my eye I spotted the father, briefcase in hand, stumbling towards a parked car!

'Where's your father going?' I demanded of the lawyer, the Murfet rip-off radar kicking in and sounding alarms in my head.

'Nowhere. He's here,' he replied innocently.

'No he bleedin' well ain't,' I shouted. 'He's out there in that car...And he's got our money!'

With that I legged it out of the courthouse, only to see the old guy speed off in the car. I leapt into my rented job, put my foot down and sped after him. It wasn't easy to stay on his tail – he was flying along like a lunatic through Rabat's maze of streets. I didn't have a clue where I was going – or any way of second-guessing which way he'd swerve next. All I could think of was the fact that the snide git had our money and I hung on that bastard's tail for all my life was worth – or more accurately for all Gerald's life was worth! He had the knowledge of the streets. He knew he could outrun me in the end – and so did I. Unless, of course, he made a mistake. And he did. Busy looking over his shoulder to see how close I'd got, he lost concentration and BANG – he hit another car! This was my chance. Skidding to a halt, I flung the car door open and leapt out, leaving my car skewed across the road, and ran full pelt towards the old guy's crumple-fronted motor. It was only as I left behind the protection of the car that it dawned on me what kind of area I was in. Dark and dank-looking tenement blocks loomed over me from all sides. And, it seemed, most of their inhabitants were rushing out onto the streets to see what the commotion was. I was surrounded by hundreds of Africans and Arabs, all babbling to each other and at me...I had no idea what they were saying. And I had only one thought in my head – to get our money back. Reaching the crashed car, I leaned in past the stunned driver and, before he could react, snatched the ignition keys.

168

The babbling turned to a roaring in my ears as I opened the car's boot, took out the briefcase and flung the keys as far as I possibly could. Now it wasn't hard to get the gist of what these street people were shouting at me. They weren't on my side, that was for sure. They probably assumed I was the robber. But I didn't have time to worry about that – at least they were only making a noise. Not one of them made any attempt to come near me as I jumped back into my motor, did a screeching U-turn and hurtled back down the streets whence I'd come. Of course, this time I wasn't following anyone – so I didn't have a clue where I was going...

It took me a very long, very frustrating time to find my way back to that courthouse. But, finally, I found it. And before leaving the car and venturing back inside, I checked the contents of the case. Thank Gawd for that! I thought when I found the money. But that wasn't all the case contained! The sneaky old sod had all his cheque books and other important looking papers in there – so I hurriedly gathered them all up and stuffed them into a carrier bag and hid it in the car.

Back in the court, I approached our lawyer 'friend', who was still in the company of the British Consul.
'Your father's a thief!' I shouted at him.
He started waving his hands about in frantic, but unconvincing, denial.
'No, no, no!' he was saying.
'What d'you mean no?' I demanded, less than impressed.
'Look I've got the money back...But your father ran off with it! Where was he going with it?'
And with that, surprise, surprise, suddenly our lawyer's previously excellent command of English failed him and he lapsed into what I can only assume was Arabic. So I can't tell you what explanation or excuses he was giving in his hundred-mile-an-hour babble. I can, however, tell you that it was 100% rubbish!

I turned to the bemused-looking British Consul.

'Thanks very bleeding much mate for recommending these thieving gits. Fat lot of help you'd have been if he'd got away with the money! What was I supposed to do then, eh? Leave my poor mates in jail while I went home and tried to raise some more?'

He reddened and began to huff and puff the way these official types do.

'Well I can assure you Mr Murfet that I shall be taking the matter up with higher authorities and...' he blustered, until I impatiently cut him short.

'And I can assure you, that this money doesn't leave my hands until I meet the people who I'm meant to be paying. And I will give money to those people. Not some bloody lawyer or his dodgy dad or anyone else. If any payments are going to be made, it's gonna be me paying them, in person. You got that?'

He nodded. And I shut up, satisfied that I'd made my point.

Now you might be wondering what had happened to the normally vociferous Winifred Leitch. Well, she was there the whole time – except for my Italian Job style car chase – and for once, she'd found herself in an environment where what she had to say meant absolutely bugger all. Oh she tried to stick her oar in at several stages in the proceedings I've just described, but these Moroccan guys just dismissed her as if they couldn't even hear her voice, let alone pay it any attention.

Women don't get much respect out there at the best of times – and her shrill shouting got short shrift from the Moroccans. I wasn't particularly tolerant either, come to think of it. She kept bombarding me with questions, demanding to know what was going on – but her words went in one ear and out

170

the other. I was much too busy dealing with the situation to keep breaking off to explain myself.

Anyway, after some long and extremely annoying negotiations and a short trial in the courthouse I finally stumped up a fine of about £2000 and doled out various amounts to all these petty officials and jailhouse screws with their greedily outstretched hands and Gerald and his mate were released.

Gerald's huge relief on walking out of that awful place must have been tempered by the ear-bending he received from his mother in the back of my rented car as we headed back to our hotel – she'd been saving this up for days! Meanwhile, our lawyer sat next to them looking shell-shocked and his father was still nowhere to be seen. If I was being uncharitable I could suspect that the lawyer was in on the sting from the start – but it's more likely that when his father saw what amounted to a fortune to a Moroccan he reverted to type and had it away on his toes before thinking it through.

Back at the hotel, I'd booked rooms for the boys, in which, no doubt, they were looking forward to luxuriating after their ordeal. But that wasn't Mrs Leitch's plan.
'Right – I'm taking Gerald up to my room to give him a bath!' she barked.
Well I couldn't believe my ears. Nor could Gerald – and his face was a mask of humiliation and horror. I felt sorry for him; a grown man being treated like a school kid!
'Well, he has got his own room, Win,' I suggested.
But no – she wasn't having any of it. He wasn't to be trusted to take care of himself and she was going to take him in hand and give him a proper scrubbing to clean away the last traces of that disgusting place. And that's what she did! Poor young Gerald didn't stand a chance – he was Mummy's boy and she was never going to let him go. On the plus side, he was now

taking the brunt of 'Madam's' constant nagging so I could finally relax and enjoy myself wandering around the bazaars and engaged in a bit of haggling for a nice Moroccan wallet and a few other knickknacks. Having booked flights home for the following morning I went back to the hotel and, while Gerald was absorbing all of his clucking mother's attention, took the chance to have a chat with his mate and find out what had really happened. By the sound of it they had been set up from the start – as I'd thought. The police who stopped them already had the registration number of the Land Rover and knew what they had bought. So, before we left the country, I made a formal complaint about the Land Rover, which was still on the missing list – or more accurately, was probably being driven around Rabat by some bent copper! I also lodged a complaint with the British Embassy about the lawyer's father attempting to steal the money.

They assured me that the complaint would be taken very seriously – but I wasn't convinced. Anyway, I didn't care that much. It wasn't as if he'd got away with it and Donovan wouldn't miss the price of a new Land Rover. So we went home and did our best to forget the whole sorry story – although I doubt very much that Mrs Leitch let Gerald forget it for a moment of the rest of his life!

Would you believe it, about a year later, the British Embassy in Morocco got in touch. They'd only got us the Land Rover back!

All in all, a job well done!

*   *   *

On Donovan's first US tour we had a lovely guy with us called Sid Maurer who used to run Roadrunner Records out of New York and who also did all the graphic design for

172

Donovan's record sleeves. Now, as part of the promotion for the shows, Donovan had hired a huge billboard on LA's Sunset Strip – but not to plaster with a 48-sheet poster like everyone else. Donovan was going several steps better by personally doing a drawing right onto the billboard, with Sid's help. Anyway, the day before they were going to do this mammoth drawing, we'd run into a very pretty hippy girl called Rona – and as a finishing touch to their masterpiece they wrote in the corner of the billboard, 'For Rona'.

That friendly little touch started a brief affair at the Beverley Hills Hotel whose aftermath was to go on and on – long after Donovan wanted it to be off! It was only for a relatively short while that Donovan and Rona were genuinely close but she became part of our lives for the next year or two. The trouble was that when, inevitably, Donovan had had enough of her she wasn't getting the message and she'd turn up everywhere we went. And guess who had to deal with the problem!

Long after that tour was over we were back in England when, completely out of the blue, I got a call from Heathrow Airport asking for verification that Donovan's American wife Rona should be granted entry to the country! I told them in no uncertain terms that there must be some mistake because Donovan wasn't even married – but somehow she managed to enter the country. And that's when the problems really started. Donovan didn't want to see her at all, but being such a gentle soul he didn't want to hurt her feelings. Come to that nor did I   she was a lovely, very pretty girl and sweet with it but, frankly, she was off with the fairies! Worse than that, she was with the Murfets! She used to do a lot of child-minding and would often ask her customers to drop her off at our place in Barnet and then end up staying when we didn't have the heart to ask her to leave. Not a major problem, I agree. But then one day our neighbours approached us asking if we'd seen this strange apparition wandering up and down

Fitzjohn Avenue. We went and had a look and found Rona dancing barefoot in the street, dressed in a flimsy dress that looked like a nightie, garlands of flowers in her hair, waving at everyone that passed and telling them all what a beautiful day it was.

Another time, backstage at Donovan's concert at the LA Forum, I was called to sort out a terrific commotion that had kicked off. Someone was kicking up a shocking fuss about being refused entry backstage. You've guessed it. It was Rona – now heavily pregnant and claiming again to be Donovan's wife. She really had lost the plot by this time – and it was a terrible shame because she was a very gentle and kind girl really. It broke my heart to have to turn her away – but she'd become a stalker and there was nothing else for it.

Donovan had a lot of qualities that I'd describe as 'magical'. I can think of no better word. Although I can imagine he's not everybody's cup of tea, he was a sort of throwback to the old-fashioned minstrel who'd entertain the court by putting every event and everyone into rhyme and song – it just came so naturally to him.

For example, one time in Houston, he started singing to himself in the lift down to the hotel reception, and then again in the Limo on the way to the gig.
'I love my shirt, I love my shirt,' went this little refrain.
I thought little of it. Just Donovan humming away to himself as usual. By the time we arrived at the venue it had evolved considerably and he'd added a couple of verses. Nevertheless I was amazed when suddenly he included this little ditty in the gig that night! Not only did he pull it off with aplomb, he'd added several more verses and he had the entire audience singing along to a tune that had never been rehearsed, let alone recorded. Coming up with half an idea in the lift before the gig, finishing it off in the Limo and

performing it to a massive crowd straight afterwards and getting them to sing along – now that is a star! In 1968, Donovan recorded 'I Love My Shirt' in Los Angeles and put it on his album 'Barabajagal', which was produced by Micky Most.

Do you have a shirt that you really love,
One that you feel so groovy in ?
You don't even mind if it starts to fade,
That only makes it nicer still.
I love my shirt, I love my shirt,
My shirt is so comfortably lovely.
I love my shirt, I love my shirt,
My shirt is so comfortably lovely.
Do you have some jeans that you really love,
Ones that you feel so groovy in ?
You don't even mind if they start to fray
That only makes them nicer still.
I love my jeans, I love my jeans,
My jeans are so comfortably lovely.
I love my jeans, I love my jeans,
My jeans are so comfortably lovely.
When they are taken to the cleaners,
I can't wait to get them home again.
Yes, I take 'em to the cleaners
And there they wash them in a stream,
Scrub a rub dub dub
And there they wash them in a stream -
Know what I mean.
Do you have some shoes that you really love,
Ones that you feel so flashy in ?
You don't even mind if they start to get some holes in
That only makes them nicer still.
I love my shoes, I love my shoes,
My shoes are so comfortably lovely.
I love my jeans, I love my jeans,

My jeans are so comfortably lovely.
I love my shirt, I love my shirt,
In fact I love my wardrobe.
I love my shirt, I love my shirt,
My shirt is so comfortably lovely.
I love my shirt, I love my shirt.

*   *   *

PAUL Mc CARTNEY

I was in Paris once, staying at the George Cinq Hotel with The Osmonds. Now, when you're staying in a place that posh you're entitled to expect a bit of privacy. Having got back there, I thought I could relax, but almost blew my top when yet another bloody fan came round the corner in the corridor asking the Osmonds for an autograph. But this time it wasn't a problem – the autograph hunter was none other than Paul McCartney!
'I've never done this before,' said Paul humbly as he waited for the boys to finish signing their names for him.

CHAPTER SIX

1990

HELICOPTER

'Don, I don't want to worry you but I think we're being followed,' June said in a voice filled with trepidation. For some time I seemed to have become the object of the Old Bill's attention but I had no particular reason to be looking over my shoulder – at least not on that particular day! Just to be on the safe side, though, I glanced in the rear view mirror. Nothing. At least no sign of a motor that had been behind us for any length of time.

'Nah – you're getting paranoid love,' I said breezily, backing up my air of confidence and stopping June getting the wind up by pressing my foot down a touch and accelerating along the A10 towards home. She didn't answer. Her eyes were fixed on the sky. Craning my neck out of the window to follow her gaze, I clocked the reason for her alarm. Just 'cause you're paranoid, it doesn't mean they're not all out to get you, as they say! And, hovering up above us like a giant wasp, a little behind and maintaining a parallel course, was a chopper. As my sun-dazzled eyes resolved into focus I made out the POLICE insignia emblazoned on the helicopter's side.

Oh shit, I thought. I had a distinctly uneasy feeling about this. But, then again, I thought, I wasn't exactly public enemy number one! A chopper on the case is a bit over the top for the likes of little old Don Murfet, I thought, and chuckled to myself to dismiss my own growing – but surely laughable – sense of paranoia. Then the turning for Stansted, onto the A120 and home, was looming up ahead. Now we'd find out whether they were really tailing us. And sure enough, they veered off in parallel, matching our every move. They had to be spotting for their ground forces, which I assumed would be lurking in some leafy lay-by nearby, eagerly awaiting their chance to pounce.

But why? I was on a perfectly innocent expedition. There was nothing out of order or incriminating in the van, on our persons or involved in the day's activities. I'd only been dropping off a piece of perfectly legit antique furniture at a dealer's gaff in London and June had come along for the ride. (We'd dabbled in antiques dealing for thirty-odd years).

Hang on a minute, I thought. We were carrying something, namely five assorted suitcases and holdalls belonging to Simon, a mate of mine who'd been staying with us for a few days. Not that there had been any suggestion that there was anything dodgy about them. His Fiat had been playing up – it only seemed to run on full choke – so he'd asked to borrow my car for his own trip into town, and had left his ailing motor parked in our drive. Having dropped off our bit of furniture, I'd called in to my office and yard in Tottenham Hale, North London, to give things the once over, since I was in the area and, as luck would have it, Simon happened along at the same time. All that luggage was crammed into my car, because he had several more calls to make, and he was worried that it would all get nicked if he left it in the motor all over the shop while he did his rounds of wheeling and dealing and ducking and diving. I should point out at this juncture that Simon was a 'runner'. That is, someone who borrows an antique item that he knows another dealer will be interested in buying. It's a way of dealing in antiques without having to lay out money up front for stock – all they do is broker the deal and get a nice day's work out of it with their commission, mark-up, whatever you want to call it.

178

'Lucky I ran into you Don!' he said. 'Can't leave 'em all in the motor. Do us a favour and take 'em back to yours and dump 'em in my car there would you?'

'No problem,' I replied.

'Thanks mate – you've saved me running all the way back out to your place and then back into the smoke again! Would've taken bloody hours!'

Anyway, my new load was the last thing on my mind as I drove carefully along the A120 in the chopper's looming shadow. I was frantically trying to second guess the police's motivations. What on earth could justify the vast expense of putting helicopter surveillance on the likes of me? Even more disturbing was the fact that this was the second time in a few weeks that I'd found the cops on my tail. About a month previously I'd been followed all the way from my Hertfordshire home to Kilburn in north-west London. I had June along for the ride that time too – and I was going to pay a visit to a legendary entertainment business character known as Terry The Pill (real name Terry Slater). Terry had been the manager of Amen Corner but he's probably better known to this day as the man responsible for the overwhelming majority of the fly posting activity done on the behalf of the major promoters and record companies. Anyway, it was when I pulled up at the traffic lights just three or so miles from my house that I noticed that a dark green car had appeared from nowhere behind me, occupied by two men, one of whom, I distinctly remember, wore a Barbour-type waxed jacket. They hadn't been behind me along all those convoluted country lanes – I'd have noticed them straight away. So where the hell had they sprung from? I wondered. For the time being I kept my mouth shut about it – no point worrying June unnecessarily.

Drawing away sedately as the lights went green, I kept driving through the leafy lanes with one eye subtly monitoring the rear view mirror, biding my time until I saw my chance to lose the bastards. So I saw it – and seized it. Up ahead was a skip blocking my side of the road. Between my Audi and the skip were a bus and a couple of cars making steady progress towards the bottleneck the skip created. I gunned the Audi past the two frustrated motorists, zoomed past the dawdling bus, nipped past the skip in the nick of time before the bus got to it. Leaving my pursuers stuck behind the snarl-up at the skip, I toed it again through the winding lanes I knew so well that I could take them at high speed without any real problem. As I turned left at the Sawbridgworth turn-off a few miles further on, I could see no sign of the dark green car – just a red car, followed closely by a motorbike. Either I'd lost them or they hadn't been the 'other people' in the first place. Maybe I was just getting jumpy, I thought as I drove on, still pushing the car to its limits on tortuous lanes, tricked out with blind bends until I reached flatter, open countryside where you can see for miles in every direction. Still no sign of the green car. I inhaled deeply, savouring the sense of relief that washed over me like a cool shower on a hot day – but my sigh caught in the back of my throat when something in the mirror caught my eye. That red car again. A tiny red spot in the distance – but getting bigger. . Hard on its heels was the motorbike – but why? It was a big powerful machine – easily capable of overtaking it. It was obvious to me that these two had taken up the baton from the green car the moment I'd lost him. I needed to find out once and for all whether or not these guys were after me.

Spotting a lay-by on the wide open road I stopped abruptly and checked my mirror again – just in time to catch the motorcyclist veer wildly off the road and take cover behind a couple of trees and an abandoned World War Two pill box at the roadside. That clinched it. No paranoia here – my suspicions were justified. The other red car drove past and its occupants weren't very worrying – just an elderly couple.

June twigged that something was up.
'What's happening?' she whispered urgently.
'We've got company,' I said with a wry grin.
I wasn't doing anything illegal. I wasn't carrying anything illegal. Now it was time to have some fun with the bastards! How? You might ask. Well, I should explain that once you've established that you're under police surveillance for intelligence gathering purposes – which I had – you know there's no way they're going to nick you for minor traffic offences, or anything much else come to that. It would blow their cover in an instant! So little details like running red lights and speeding, for example, aren't going to get you pulled.

From that moment on I used every trick in the book – and a lot that weren't – to lose them. Those boys were good though – I'll give them that. On that trip of thirty odd miles I had the dubious pleasure of the company of no less than two motorcycles and another two cars – not that I let on to them that I was aware of their presence. Rather than give the game away with excessive use of my rear-view mirror, my trusty co-pilot Murfet J. Mrs. had discreetly positioned the nearside door mirror to give me a clear view of the road behind and backed this up with a running commentary informed by her view in the make-up mirror on her sun visor. We got as far as the waterworks roundabout on the North Circular (London's inner orbital road) in Woodford before our shadows caught up with us again – at least as far as we could tell. It was that green car I'd first spotted three miles from home. Full marks for perseverance, I thought, as I headed towards the busy Montague Road and Dysons Road junction with an escape plan coalescing in my mind. They'd recently put up a NO ENTRY sign at the entrance to York Road on the left, putting a stop to its use as a 'rat run' to avoid the snarl-up at the Fore Street and Silver Street lights (incidentally, Fore Street was where the Regal Cinema was – where I first met Peter Grant). I was counting on my temporary 'immunity' from traffic offences to save me By the way, at the time it was a two-way, three lane road – now replaced by a massive underpass and a dual carriageway.

I ran a red that had just changed from amber and hooked a sharp left straight past that NO LEFT TURN sign and shot up the one-way street like a bullet backfiring before deftly (though I say it myself) negotiating at speed a series of chicane-like right and left turns that took me across Fore Street and through another couple of side roads before disgorging me into the Silver Street traffic four hundred yards up from the lights where, I was sure, my pursuers were revving their engines and grinding their teeth.

As I cruised nonchalantly towards Pinkham Way, my mug wreathed in a satisfied smile, I suddenly realised that there was a bike on my arse like it was stuck there with Superglue. My grin became a grimace as I wrenched a hard left hand down and sped up the off-ramp bound for Muswell Hill and Friern Barnet with the cemetery in my sights. I'll pay old Patsy Collins a visit, I thought wryly, he'll enjoy the company at his graveside and the Old Bill will have to hang around for as long as we please! Then again, it occurred to me, he'd be spinning in that grave like a lathe if he knew I was bringing the cops along too!

Another option was to nip straight back down onto the North Circular as if I'd just made the diversion to see if I was being followed. That was obviously what he thought I was up to because he didn't follow. He pulled up just past the off-ramp and waited for me to come down the other side and rejoin the North Circular.

182

Gotcha! I thought as I floored it up a narrow lane Muswell Hill-bound, leaving him with no way to get back to the off-ramp in pursuit.

Yet again, though, my triumph was short-lived. The bastard reappeared almost the moment I cruised into Muswell Hill Broadway. How he'd found me again I'll never know – it certainly meant that he'd had to ride against the traffic, the wrong way up the ramp. A bloody disgrace I call it! No respect for the law some people!

Anyway, it was only when I finally made it to Kilburn that I could be sure that my company had taken their leave for the day – and even then it was only because I couldn't find Terry's new premises and had to drive round the block a few times before I came across it. I had to admit to myself, however grudgingly, that these police guys were hot stuff – I'm no slouch and it had taken all my considerable nous to throw the bastards off my scent. The truth was, as I was reliably informed by a friendly copper some time later, that their superhuman ability to stay glued to my tail had less to do with their consummate expertise in the art of surveillance than the fact that they had a helicopter shadowing me and constantly radioing my position to their troops on the ground – just as they did that on day when I had all Simon's gear in the van. Bloody cheats!

Anyway, going back to that time when I'd actually seen the chopper following me down the A120, it became obvious to me that I was going to get a spin (That's have my house searched to those unfamiliar with the terminology!). As we neared home I gave June precise instructions as to what she should do on our arrival – if we got there before the predators pounced. When we pulled into our driveway June shot indoors while I transferred the cases and holdalls from my van into Simon's Fiat. Just as I'd stowed the last case and discreetly wiped the steering wheel, door handles and mirror clean of my prints, all hell broke loose. You'd have thought it was an Al Qaeda terrorist they were after – not Don Murfet. Four cars hurtled up the drive and screeched to a halt, disgorging hordes of plain clothes coppers, none of whom looked remotely like friendly old Dixon of Dock Green. It was like Raid on bleedin' Entebbe or the storming of the Iranian Embassy!

'Mr Donald Murfet?' said the burly main man in a brusque voice that tempted me to jump to attention and do a *sieg heil* style salute.

'That's me,' I confirmed levelly, as if they didn't know exactly who I was.

'We have a warrant to search these premises,' he continued without doing me the courtesy of looking me in the eye.

'What for?' I enquired – not unreasonably, I thought.

He swatted that polite question with distaste, like it was a gnat in his face and about to bite.

Whereas I, of course, had a bluebottle in my face – and there was obviously no getting rid of him.

'We're going in, Murfet,' huffed DCI Atkins (as I later came to know him).

Still I resisted.

'Not until I see that warrant you don't,' I said defiantly.

Now, considering I was one bloke, and not a very big one at that, surrounded by something like twelve to sixteen burly coppers, you might think I was either very brave or stark raving mad to stand my ground like that. But the fact was - and is - that I knew my rights. I was determined to know exactly what they were looking for and precisely when and where the warrant had been issued. Of course they knew I was stalling; they were having none of it and were trying to push me aside and barge into my home – which as everyone knows is an Englishman's castle! It took them some time – and a lot of resentment – to go and get the warrant from one

184

of their cars. And that was enough time for June to do what I'd instructed her to do before the cops came on top.

Anyway, when I finally clamped eyes onto the document, it was with some relief. The object of the search, it said, was bearer bonds and treasury bills or certificates of deposit – none of which were on the premises or ever had been. Nevertheless, I knew exactly what this was all about! It was about something in the City...

In those days, the City's financial institutions relied on a body of fairly elderly gents who acted as messengers, running – or perhaps more accurately doddering – between banks to deliver all kinds of documents – including, believe it or not, those of immense value such as the bearer bonds, treasury bills and so on that the cops were so keen to find. By and large these guys were professionals at their job with great integrity worthy of the trust placed in them. What they weren't, though, was hard! So they weren't much of a match for your average robber. Why the police seemed so surprised when, on 2nd May that year, someone mugged one of these guys and made off with documents with a face value of some three hundred million I don't know. Must've been like taking candy from a baby!

Anyway, that's what had happened – and suddenly all these stolen documents were flooding the streets as the robbers and their fences and their fences' fences in turn all tried to flog them – obviously for a fraction of their face value.

As a little aside, I was amused to find that the unfortunate messenger's name was John Goddard! Funny to think that it was one Stuart Goddard who'd come into my life ten years earlier and ensured my financial security. Mind you, it would have been nice to have had the best part of £300 million!

None of this had anything to do with me though. Of course I'd seen some of them – or photocopies at least – and people had approached me to see if was interested but I'd certainly never had them at the house so I had nothing to worry about.

Of course, it didn't matter what I said or did – the cops were coming in. And in they came. The Detective Inspector in charge was from the Regional Crime Squad based at Whetstone. With him was one DS Leader and the appropriately named DC Mooney (another of those weird coincidences – the same name as the Ants' bass player!). These three gentlemen (and I use the word ironically, in case you were in any doubt!) were to be my interrogators - the ones who'd later be messing with my mind and, ultimately, trying to fit me up! They weren't exactly Holmes and Watson, mind you. I didn't see a lot of intellect and deductive reasoning going into their little operation – it was more a case of charging about my place tipping out drawers willy nilly and stuffing their contents into big plastic bin liners. Very professional, I thought!

Throughout this whole home-wrecking process I kept schtum and let them do their worst – a matter of policy with me any time I have a run-in with the police. While this lot were poking around in my drawers (not my underwear, you understand – although that probably wouldn't have felt any more rude and intrusive or any more of a pain in the arse!) a couple of their mates had been scouring the grounds, garage and outbuildings – all of which are quite extensive. To my chagrin they returned looking pleased with themselves.
'Guvnor, there's something dodgy going on in them barns over there,' one of them reported in a gruff yet self-satisfied tone.
That was a relief.

'They're rented out,' I said. 'Whatever's going on over there's nothing to do with me – in fact they're all sealed off from my land and have their own separate entrances.'

The officer appeared to disregard this and he went on.

'Well it looks like somebody's making wine up there,' he stated, looking directly at me. All eyes turned enquiringly to yours truly.

'Look it's nothing to do with me,' I protested, temporarily abandoning my policy of keeping it zipped. 'I advertised the barns for rent in the paper, these people took me up on it and I've got a lease contract to prove it.'

''Oh yeah? Well where is this contract then,' the boss sneered without bothering to disguise his scepticism.

I couldn't help smiling as I indicated my desk, or rather its carcass, with the drawers torn out and hanging empty from their runners.

'Well it was in there!' I said.

They were not amused – especially the two junior PCs who were obliged to tip out the bin liner they'd just stuffed to breaking point with the contents of my desk and go through every document one by one. Of course they still didn't believe me as they carried out this new search with deep resentment, punctuating each rummaging with a sigh of irritation and a glare raid in my direction. So you can imagine how pissed off they were when they found the document that proved I'd been telling the truth! They were absolutely gutted. I, on the other hand, was visibly tickled pink!

'Well, where's the money they paid you then?' they insisted contemptuously, now clutching at straws.

'Like it says in that contract, I've been getting five hundred quid a month for the exclusive rent of that barn and if you care to check my bank account – which I'm sure you will – you'll find I've been paying in that amount every single month for the five or six months they've been renting it!' I replied with quiet confidence.

Predictably, they weren't very happy about this. I suppose it was selfish of me to make completely legal contractual arrangements, thus denying them the pleasure of nicking me. Anyway, since they'd failed to find anything untoward in the arrangement, they decided to get in touch with HM Customs and Excise to see if they could stitch me up somehow instead.

In the meantime, of course, the rest of their little posse had been continuing the ransacking of my home and had turned up some crockery and a series of photographs relating to it. The information documented with the photos made it clear that the crockery had been salvaged recently from the wreck of a ship that had sunk in the early 1800s and the position and provenance of this 'treasure trove' was clearly detailed. Well you can imagine the glee on their faces as they started to accuse me of 'interfering with shipwrecks' and thereby contravening the treasure trove laws under which the Crown owns the lion's share of any such find! Again, they were less than chuffed to be told what had actually happened, which wasn't any use to them. Because I'd been dealing in antiques for some time, I'd become known as something of an authority on values and the people who'd salvaged this crockery and other artefacts from the deep had come to me for an opinion on their value. Well, the china had been made in England and then shipped out to Holland, where young kids were employed to paint on it the well-known tulip patterns. It wasn't an unusual design, so their find was unlikely to be worth a fortune, I'd opined at the time. Then again, since the wreck had happened sometime between the late 1700s and early 1800s, the sheer antiquity of the stuff suggested it would be worth a bit – depending on how much there was, whether there was a complete set and so on. The upshot was that all I'd given was an opinion and all I'd received was some documents, thereby selfishly neglecting to break any laws!

Yet again the cops had been thwarted in their desperate attempt to nick me. They weren't happy bunnies – so they kept on going through the house with a fine-toothed comb until they came across some papers relating to Greenpeace. They turned to June and said, 'What's all this then?'

Presumably they now had me down as some sort of eco-terrorist! The truth, as always, was a lot more ordinary!

'It's my daughter's – she's a member of Greenpeace.'

'Oh really,' said DS Leader, suddenly with genuine interest. 'My wife and I are members too!'

I think it worth reiterating at this point that whenever I get a spin – and I've had a few – I make a point of committing to memory every last detail of everything that goes on, from the coppers' names, and that of the man in charge to the precise wording of the search warrant. Then at the first opportunity, which is usually in a police cell, I write copious notes on everything. I don't let any little scrap of information fade from my brain before I've downloaded it all onto paper.

Anyway, just as I was talking to June about getting hold of Martin Lee, our solicitor, they took a completely new tack, clearly trying to catch me off my guard.

'What's in those bags in the car?' one of them spat suddenly at me.

'How should I know?' I replied.

'You must know,' they said, 'because you put them in the car!'

'Look,' I said, 'someone asked me to run them back here and drop them off into their car, which is sitting out there by my garage. Now you might be the type of person who pulls into a lay-by on the way home to go through people's cases when they ask you the simple favour of dropping something off. I don't. Those cases are nothing to do with me. I just brought them home and put them in the guy's car as he'd asked. He'll be here soon to pick 'em up – so you can ask him about 'em!' But of course they weren't willing to wait for Simon to show up – it was me they were after.

'I think we'd better take a look for ourselves!' they said smugly as they strolled outside and over to the Fiat where one of them picked out a holdall, which made a telltale clanking sound as they did so. This gave rise to telltale triumphant smiles all round as the holdall was ceremoniously unzipped and one PC pulled out a beautiful antique porcelain vase, which he held aloft like it was the FA Cup. This was quickly followed by the other one of the pair, then by a selection of exquisite paintings and all sorts of other valuable-looking trinkets, gewgaws and bits and bobs.

'We've gotcha now!' the smug grins all round said, while I, on the other hand, said bugger all.

It wasn't what they'd come here to get me for – but the clear consensus was that they'd got me on something, and that would do for now. Anyway, they made it clear, they were hoping that the Customs and Excise people would find something amiss as well, so they were happy to call off the search for the time being.

While all this was going on, the police failed to spot a peculiar figure in the distance, waddling awkwardly in his dressing gown and carpet slippers down the lane and off to the phone box in the village. It was the bloke I'd rented the barn to. He was living in a caravan next to the barn and, having noticed all the commotion and instantly sussed that I was getting a spin, was phoning a mate for some transport out of the place. The cops who were still searching the barn and the surrounding area entered the caravan and found it apparently abandoned. So, not realising that its occupant was just a few yards down the road frantically dialling in the phone box, they didn't go after him. Thinking he was long

190

gone, they left the sniffer dogs tied up and simply called Customs and Excise to say that the maker of illicit wine had done a bunk. Which he had – but only minutes earlier!

Back at the incriminating Fiat and its obviously moody contents the cops, unsurprisingly wanted to know whose car it was.

'Just a bloke's who's been staying with me,' I said, trying to fudge the issue because I really didn't want to get Simon any deeper in trouble than he already was.

'Look, it's not my car. The Fiat's not working so he's borrowed my car and he'll be back later to pick it up.'

'Why's he borrowed your car?' they insisted.

'Cos it won't start,' I said with some irritation. 'I told you that.'

Bet you can guess what happened next. Yep, they got the keys off me and turned the ignition and the bastard started first time, eliciting another round of smug look-at-that-what-did-tell-you-the-bastard's-obviously-lying-through-his-teeth looks. I sighed to myself. There was no point at all in my attempting to explain that the Fiat only seemed to run on full choke and that therefore it made sense that it would start from cold when the choke was required but would cut out as soon as it warmed up.

'It seems you've been lying to us Mr Murfet,' one of them smirked, 'Again!'

And then they gleefully informed me that I'd be going along with them to the station. There was absolutely no point arguing. As far as they were concerned I was lying and that was that. I asked where they were taking me.

'Barnet.' They said.

I asked June to get onto Martin and tell him that I was being taken to Barnet cop shop, that I wouldn't be saying anything but to get someone down there as soon as possible. But just as they were about to cart me off a dust-laden, red-faced and sweaty young PC appeared – he was one of the party sent to search the loft, which was quite a task in my place I can tell you!

'Guv,' he gasped, 'Think you'd better come and have a look at what we've found up there!'

The PC's air of urgency said it all: there was nothing innocuous about whatever they'd uncovered now and DI Leader did what his name suggested and led his minions upstairs. It was as I followed them up to the loft hatch that it dawned on me what it could be that they'd found. And sure enough, when I got in there, blinking as my eyes adjusted to the dust and dim light, I followed the grim yet triumphant gaze of the assembled cops. In front of me, to my deep dismay, was a cache of about ten or fifteen assorted guns - enough to tool up a small army! It was an impressive collection by any standards, including Kalashnikovs, automatics, a rocket launcher, a deactivated World War Two Webley pistol and my son's shotgun, for which he, at least, had a licence. Apart from the shotgun, they were all replicas, I hasten to add – or had been deactivated like the Webley – but of course the police weren't having that. And if they'd believed it, they'd still have assumed that they were for nefarious purposes (quite rightly, to be honest!).

Now they really had got me! God knows what they thought they'd found – knowing my luck they had me down as some sort of international terrorist. Which would've been a stupid conclusion – no money in it is there! Anyway, what little I had to say about that discovery got short shrift and they lost no time in loading the haul, along with all Simon's bags, into their motors and whisking them and me off to Barnet cop shop. As is their wont, the cops left me to stew in my cell for quite some time – and it seemed like far longer – before the duty solicitor arrived and requested that she be allowed to sit in on the impending interview. We were introduced and I told her the way I operate.

'OK, this is the way I want this handled,' I said with the practised confidence of a man who's been through the mill with the police on more times than this lawyer had had hot dinners. 'I will not say a thing. Nothing. Understand?'
She nodded. I went on.
'I will just say what I've already told them: I've committed no offence and I decline to answer any questions. And that'll be the end of it.'
Again my nervous brief just nodded. Again, I went on briefing my brief.
'I don't want you to interrupt them at all. Don't object to anything they say, however out of order it might be in your book. Just let them talk and keep them talking for as long as we can so we can find out what they're talking about and what they think they've got. Because the more they talk the more they give away and the more we know about what this is really all about.'

With all that agreed, we entered the interview room where DS Leader and DC Mooney sat expectantly. What followed was pretty standard stuff – you've seen it all on The Bill and programmes like that I expect: good cop, bad cop, even worse cop and completely rubbish cop. On request I gave my name and confirmed my address but as soon as they put the next question to me I replied as planned:
'I've committed no offence and I decline to answer any questions.'
With that the four of us sat staring at each other from opposite sides of the table for what seemed like hours before Leader led with his first jab.
'Right. We've got a considerable collection of antiques, confiscated from a vehicle on your premises – and we know they're stolen. What have you got to say about them?'
No reply from yours truly.
Next he hit me with a question about the treasury bills. I didn't reply. Then followed a volley of curt questions, each

193

of which went unanswered. This lasted a good eight minutes until my brief finally cut in.

'Look, we've already told you he's not going to answer you – so why do you keep asking him questions?' she said, the irritation showing in her voice despite her polite and professional tone.

Leader's response was a dismissive shrug and a wave of the hand. He stopped the interview right there.

'Right,' I said to my brief, 'You stay with me and take me back to my cell – all the time. All the way.'

I should explain here that it's very important to be accompanied by your solicitor because sometimes they'll use remarks you make off the tape, even throwaway ones, against you. Whether or not these are in their notes, you're asked to sign them – which you should never do!

Once alone in the cell I confronted her.

'Why did you stop him?' I demanded.

'Well, he was just...' she stuttered, but I cut her short.

'I told you to let it run!' I said, not unkindly. 'Anyway, never mind. It's done now.'

She nodded, unsure how to respond. I was well and truly in the driving seat now.

'Now, you have got to inform them,' I went on authoritatively, 'and the Custody Sergeant, that they are not allowed to question me at all unless my solicitor is present – be it you or whoever it is. But they must not interview me any more without a solicitor. So off she went to do my bidding and, a little later, Leader and Mooney came into my cell and said they were taking me up to take my fingerprints and I found myself in this small room with just the two of them. I knew something was up. And I was right. They started giving it the big one.

'You think you're Mister Big don't you Murfet, coming in here shouting the odds and telling us what we can and can't do with you. Well let's get something straight shall we! I call the shots round here – not Don bloody Murfet. We'll do what

194

we bloody well like with you. And if we don't find exactly what we're looking for to make sure you go down we'll make sure you go down anyway don't you worry. And there's fuck all you, your bloody mob mates or your flash lawyers can do about it. You got that?' Leader spat at me.

Well I can't say I was overly keen on his attitude but it's safe to say that the message was coming across loud and clear and dripping with spit. Worse still, this wasn't going to be the end of it. They were obviously psyching themselves up to really put me through the mangle. By now there were three of them crammed into that tiny room – all glaring at me. I steeled myself for the onslaught, which, in my experience can take one of a few different forms. Maybe they were going to give me a good slapping about, being careful of course, not to leave too many obvious marks, in the hope that physical pain and fear would soften me up and make me more compliant. Equally likely, was that they intended to torture me verbally, goad me into attacking them, thereby adding another serious charge to their growing mental list. Whatever they had planned, though, I knew it wasn't going to be a walk in the park! I had to think quickly. I was at their mercy. And there was nothing I, or anyone else could do about it. Or was there? Out of the corner of my eye I noticed that the door was ajar by a good foot. Maybe, I thought, I can make a lunge for the door, barge through into the corridor and shout at the top of my voice that I was being assaulted. Someone had to hear me. My duty solicitor maybe. Or a decent cop perhaps (I'm sure there must have been the odd one or two!). I began subtly to angle myself, placing myself in the right escape trajectory to launch myself at the door. But Mooney anticipated me and kicked the door shut before going into the old tough cop routine and grabbing me savagely round the throat with a range of sneers and snarls along the lines of 'You think you're so clever' and 'You think you're Mister Big' and 'We're gonna fit you up' and so

195

on – and on and on and on and bleedin' on ad bloody nauseum. All incredibly witty stuff – almost Oscar Wilde-like really! But at least I didn't get a slap. On second thoughts though, I think it would've been less painful, or at least a lot less mind-numbingly boring! I hope it's true, as they claim, that they've been recruiting a lot of brighter, better-educated coppers – at least that'll mean today's villains won't have to put up with that kind of tedious plodding talk from the plod!

Anyway, I emerged unscathed from that little episode, if yawning quite dramatically and, as they bundled me back down to my cell I managed to catch the eye of the Custody Sergeant.

'Can I have a word with you?' I enquired politely.

'What about?' was his gruff, but not unfriendly response.

'Look,' I said. 'Are you in charge of me down here or are they?'

'Well I am!' he said quickly, clearly not happy that anyone would even question the fact.

'Right then,' I went on. 'They were told that on no account was I to be interviewed or questioned without my solicitor. They've done nothing but exactly that upstairs just now – and they've threatened me, slagged me off and said they're going to fit me up. And I want all that put down on the record.'

'But...' he began.

'Please,' I insisted, 'will you write it in because they are deliberately going against what they've been told to do and I won't stand for it. I'm under your care and if you let them do something to me that they're not supposed to I want it noted!' You might think I was being unusually trusting with a policeman there – but there was a reason: the police are not all on the same side! I knew full well that there's rivalry between the uniforms and specialists like the RCS (Regional Crime Squad) – and resentment too, because the RCS are so up themselves that really believe they're superior to the

196

ordinary coppers and the local CID. So it wasn't unrealistic to hope that the bloke would take my side – or at least tell the bloody truth.

To his credit he did comply and wrote something down on his records. Not that it was going to do me any good – as I was to discover later.

At this point I should explain the way the custody process works. The moment you enter those cells and the custody area as a prisoner they keep a custody record on you. This details when you were taken off for interviews, when you were fed, allowed exercise, allowed to wash and shave and use the toilet and what state you were in when they looked in on you – asleep, angry, tearful, composed and so on – and exactly when they looked in on you. Basically it's supposed to cover every single little thing that happens to you from the moment you enter till the moment you leave.

Anyway, the next thing I heard was a gruff, 'C'mon you!' as I was manhandled into my cell. I knew I was going to get at least a boot as a parting shot, so I kicked the door shut behind me as I tumbled in. Having confiscated all those antiques, guns and reams of paperwork from my place, the police stuck for somewhere to stash it all – so they had to fill up one of their custody cells with it. I was quite amused that they found themselves a cell short of a block – until I realised it meant I might have to share! I passed an uneventful few hours until sometime in the late afternoon the door opened and an Iranian bloke was shoved violently in. I wasn't impressed, not, you understand because I've got anything against Iranians, but because it's one thing being obliged to stay at the Old Bill hotel in considerable discomfort but at least in peace, and it's quite another when you've got a cell mate to contend with. I mean he could be drunk, smelly, violent or just boring – and even if I was sharing with a perfectly nice geezer I couldn't be bothered with being polite. Company, just at that moment, was something I could well do without!

Anyway, this guy wasn't so big that I had too much to worry about on the violence front – about five foot ten, I suppose.

'Alright mate, what you in for?' I asked by way of making conversation.

'Shoplifting,' he replied.

'Oh – so what happened then?'

'Well I was in this shop,' he said, 'and I bought something on a credit card...And it was a fake one and they sussed it and they nicked me for stealing from the shop.'

Then he went very quiet. I couldn't think of anything to say. Then suddenly he tensed up and blurted out, 'I can't stand it in here!'

'Well, sorry mate, but there ain't a lot I can do about it,' I said, shrugging, at which point he started acting very strangely – disturbingly, even – and working himself up into a terrible state. I didn't know who to be frightened for, me or him, so I banged on the door and almost instantly a copper looked through my hatch.

'What do you want?' he said long-sufferingly.

'Look,' I said, 'this guy's going berserk in here.

'Yeah, yeah, yeah, yeah,' he yawned, somehow giving me the tiniest of tiny hints that he didn't believe a word of it and even if he did he wouldn't have given a shit. And with that he shut the hatch.

Charming! I thought.

Meanwhile, my Iranian friend was stalking to and fro like a caged tiger, muttering something unintelligible (to me at least) under his breath and generally working himself up into a right old lather. All I could do was sit there and watch, helpless to help and helpless should he turn his madness on me instead of himself.

Then suddenly his hands flew to his throat. It was a couple of seconds before I realised why. He was throttling himself. This was getting scary. Very scary indeed. He wasn't

198

messing about, this guy. He wanted to die – and it looked like he was going to get what he wanted any second! Wedging himself into the tiny cubicle that sectioned off the toilet, he clamped his hands even tighter round his throat. I could see that every last drop of his strength was pouring into the job of squeezing every last drop of life out of him. I was horrified. But what could I do if the cops couldn't be bothered to do anything? I'm not gonna have a fight with him, I thought. If he wants to top himself I'm just going to have to let him get on with it! But then CRASH, his wiry frame collapsed on the hard concrete floor with a sickening crunch. His eyes began popping out of their sockets and his face turned bright blue and soon there was no sign of movement at all.

Just at that moment, the flap in the door opened and a voice called out, 'Tea up!'

'Only tea for one mate!' I replied as breezily as I could in the circumstances.

'Why?' came the bloke's reply.

'Well he's topped himself, hasn't he!' I called back.

That shut him up! You've never seen a face lose its colour so rapidly or completely. He went white as a sheet and hit the panic button. In a matter of seconds four burly coppers came charging into the tiny cell.

'What happened?' one of them roared.

'He just strangled himself!' I said. I could see the way they were looking at me and I knew all too well what they were thinking. 'I didn't bloody do it! He was in a right state and you lot wouldn't listen to him and...'

They shoved me out of way and grabbed the Iranian's prostrate form, dragging him into the corridor and trying every method they could think of to resuscitate him. Finally, after what seemed like an impossible time to go without breathing, the poor guy drew a spluttering, gagging, sickening breath. I'd thought he was a goner for sure. But then again, can you actually strangle yourself? I don't know, but this guy had certainly looked like he was succeeding! He obviously hadn't damaged himself too badly because then he became extremely violent – so violent that it took more than the four of them to restrain him. He was flailing his arms and legs about, kicking out at God knows what – it was complete chaos in that corridor until another two big plods arrived on the scene.

Meanwhile I sat in the cell and sipped my tea. It was nothing to do with me!

Finally the guy's ravings and assorted 'oofs' and 'ows!' and 'bloody hell that hurts!' from the coppers died down and they seemed to have restored the peace they were supposed to have upheld in the first place. A face appeared at the flap in my cell door.

'Sorry about that!' said the copper.

'That's all right,' I said, 'but do me a favour will you? Leave me alone tonight and let me have a bit of peace and quiet!'

'All right,' he said, 'we won't put anyone else in with you.'

'Cheers,' I said. At least they seemed to be a bit more reasonable with me after that little drama!

For once, they were true to their word and the rest of that night passed without further interruption. Anyway, having been charged with receiving stolen property, I was off to Barnet court in the morning to face the magistrates. More importantly, I finally got to see my own solicitor (as opposed to the duty solicitor I'd been lumbered with the previous day, who was a nice enough girl, but not streetwise enough for my purposes!).

'Look Don,' he said, in his bad news voice. 'I'm not going to go for bail, because you won't get it.'

'Fine,' I said. 'I won't ask for bail.'

This wasn't just me being helpful. I was being realistic. Knowing the rules of the game – and it is a game – I was aware that if you don't think you've got much chance of getting it you just don't waste your time asking for bail.

Why? you might ask. Because you'd be using up one of your chances – and there are only so many chances they give you! About two, in fact.

So the upshot was that I was soon off to Pentonville on remand – and it wasn't bad actually! They'd just refurbished the remand wing and I had a nice little cell all to myself complete with a toilet and hot and cold water. This was luxury compared to the pretty disgusting conditions you have to live in some of the older prisons, slopping out your shit every morning and so on. That's not to say I was entirely comfortable though. You'd have to be mad to get too smug in one of those places, especially if you know what goes on there. As it turned out I was right to keep my wits about me. As I entered the exercise yard on the second morning of my stay with Her Majesty a tubbyish, incongruously posh guy singled me out.

'What you in for?' he asked. Not the most original of conversation openers considering the circumstances!

'Stolen property,' I replied warily. 'You?'

'Oh I'm up for a massive fraud job in Hong Kong. They're trying to extradite me and I'm fighting it, because I don't want to go back there...It's not going to be good for me there...It was worth two or three million!'

With that we carried on strolling around the exercise yard talking about this and that and that was the last I thought of it, until the next day's exercise, when he came up to me again.

'You're on the same landing as me!'

'Oh?' I said without much interest.

'Yes – and Cheeseman's on our landing too!'

The name was obviously meant to provoke a reaction. It meant nothing to me at the time but I subsequently learnt that he was talking about a bloke called Keith Cheeseman who was in for something to do with treasury bills – and that was when alarm bells started ringing in my head. When you're inside you have to be constantly on the lookout for who's trying to pal you up and get information out of you and this was obviously what my new buddy was up to. He'd chatter on about high finance and all sorts of scams and casually drop in the subject of treasury bills in the hope that I'd be convinced that he was in the know and drop my guard. You'd be amazed how many intelligent people fall for that kind of tactic – not me though! I was having none of it. You, I'm gonna swerve, I thought, convinced that this guy had been put in there by the cops to see what I really knew about those treasury bills.

'I've never heard of him,' I replied and swiftly changed the subject. After that I avoided the bloke as much as I could – and it was just as well that I did because a couple of days later, shortly before I was granted bail, they put a young guy in the cell with me. I asked the usual question.

'What you in for mate?'

'Armed robbery,' he replied and because he seemed a pretty hopeless case and had no solicitor I told him to ring mine. That's me – heart of gold!

A couple of days later I was bailed and was talking to my brief in his office.

'By the way, Don,' he said. 'You know that kid you put in touch with me?'

'Yes?' I said, hoping to hear that he'd been able to help the poor little sod out in some way.

'Well he wasn't in for robbing an armoured vehicle...'

'Ah!' I said. 'I thought he wasn't the type. What was it, shoplifting or something?'

'Wish it was Don. Your boy's a rapist! He raped a young girl...A very young girl'

I shouldn't have been surprised. Or shocked – but I was. No one admits to crimes like that inside because of what the other inmates are likely to do to you! In fact if you believed what the average con told you, you'd think the country was overrun with armed robbers!

Martin went on.

'A couple of days after you got out, they got into the cell and he was found later – stabbed in the arse...'

Knowing what this implied in jail culture, he trailed off, leaving me to draw my own conclusions. Stabbing up the arse is a sure sign of a nonce case.

Before I had a chance to digest that unpalatable little nugget, Martin served up another piece of unwelcome news – confirming my suspicions about that chubby posh git who'd tried to get pally with me in the exercise yard. As I'd thought, he was now a witness for the prosecution against him. He'd sucked up to the bloke, gained his trust and extracted some sort of confession from him. Thank God I'd sussed what he was up to or I'd have been seeing him next in the witness box.

Talking of which, it was time to prepare for my trial, which was to be at Knightsbridge Crown Court. Naturally, I passed all my copious notes about that raid and everything that led up to it to my solicitor but I also suggested that he got hold of all the custody records because they'd corroborate a lot of what I had to say about the way I'd been treated by the police. Strangely though, when he received them, he found that they'd been conscientiously filled in at regular intervals right up until about two hours after I'd first arrived in custody – in other words, there was no record of my complaint about the way Mooney and Leader had treated me. Nothing at all in fact.

'So where's the record of the rest of the time I was in custody then?' I demanded, as if Martin could tell me, which of course he couldn't. 'I mean it can't just stop like that because they have to keep a record all the time!'

So it remained to be seen whether the bastards had managed to fit me up – but there was no doubt that they'd already stitched me up!

On the day of the trial at Knightsbridge Crown Court before Justice Collins, the prosecution served up all the relevant papers, as is their obligation, and – you've guessed it – their copy of the custody records was complete, right up to the point at which I walked out of Barnet cop shop! Funny enough, though, there was no mention whatsoever of my complaining to the Custody Sergeant. Around that time, according to them, they had checked on me and found me sleeping peacefully. I suppose that must have been because, according to them, they hadn't put a suicidal Iranian nutter in with me, and therefore no one had tried to strangle himself and therefore I must have imagined banging on the door for help when the guy started losing it! My arse, I did. They'd obviously got hold of the custody records, ripped out what was there and got the same Custody Sergeant to rewrite the history of my stay because the faked records were all in exactly the same handwriting. I don't know why, but I felt quite disappointed in that Custody Sergeant – I'd thought he was a decent copper who did things by the book. After all, the whole point of him is to protect prisoners from being abused. What a two-faced git! And these coppers call people like me dishonest!

Anyway, at least I had a good barrister on my side – Stephen Leslie – and he'd requested what's called a *voir dire*, which is a sort of trial within a trial. Once the jury has been sworn in, it's sent out while the barristers present their legal arguments to the judge alone. As part of this process, Stephen asked to see the notebooks of all police officers involved.

Appropriately, given his name, DS Leader was first in the witness box, cocksure and smug as always.

204

'DS Leader, may I see your book – in which you made your notes at the time of the arrest?'

Reluctantly the snide copper produced it and handed it over. Stephen took the pad from his hands and held it between thumb and forefinger, eyeing it with distaste. And then, suddenly, he chucked it up in the air and across the courtroom like it was a bit of used chewing gum. The judge looked on open-mouthed – as did all the rest of us. Including Leader, who didn't look half as cocky now!

'What the...' Leader began.

Stephen looked him in the eye, then turned and levelled his steady gaze at the rest of the court, pausing just long enough for the dumbstruck silence to sink in...He should have been on the stage that guy. Then again, I suppose, in a way, he was.

The judge regained his composure and reasserted his position.

'And what, Mr Leslie, was the purpose of that piece of playacting?' he boomed.

'Quite simply, my lord, I discarded it because it is rubbish.'

Again silence reigned. This was better than the Royal Shakespeare Company!

Leader began to speak again.

'Why did you...?'

But Stephen silenced him with a glare and then cut him to pieces with a methodical demolition of his notebook's validity – or lack thereof.

'Firstly Detective Sergeant Leader, your notebook is not dated...Nor is it signed by the Superintendent in charge of the case as required by PACE (The Police and Criminal Evidence Act) and furthermore it achieves the impressive feat of omitting almost every procedural requirement in the book, thereby rendering it inadmissible as evidence. It is, Detective Sergeant, rubbish! For all we know you could have written the contents of this work of fiction last night – and I put it to you Detective Sergeant Leader that that is exactly what you did!'

Uproar ensued and while waiting for the babble to die down, Stephen retrieved the notebook and once more held it up for all to see before dropping it onto the desk in front of him and picking up a sheaf of papers and handing it to Leader.

'This is your typed statement. Please would you read it for us – specifically I would like you to read to us this paragraph.'

Leader read the paragraph Stephen indicated.

After another of his tense dramatic silences, Stephen handed Leader his notebook

'This is your written statement. Please would you now read aloud for us the same paragraph,' he said, pointing out the place on the page.

Leader read it out – and it was identical to what he'd read out minutes earlier. You could tell by the faces of the people in court that they were confused – it should be exactly the same shouldn't it? That was the point wasn't it?

Exactly!

'Now Detective Sergeant, I'd like you to read what is written in your original statement – rather than what you think is there.'

That put the cat amongst the pigeons.

'I did,' Leader protested feebly.

'No you did not!' boomed my man – a man who I was growing to respect more by the minute. 'Now, read it again!'

Leader did so. But Stephen wasn't satisfied.

'Now read it slowly please.'

Leader looked sullen, but complied and, on this second re-reading, it was evident that this statement was not identical to the typed version. A couple of words were different. Only a couple of words, you might think, but a couple of words in a court of law can make all the difference.

Stephen homed in on this point.

206

'Clearly two words have been added to the typed statement that were not part of your original statement and that is not as it should be. Would you not agree DS Leader?'

'It's just a typing error,' Leader replied, none too convincingly.

'I see,' Stephen said quietly and then abruptly boosted the pitch of his voice so that we all flinched.

'Right!' he snapped. 'Back to the book!'

He held up the notebook – which I should point out was not your usual copper's little notepad; it was an A4 size one, and that fact was important.

'It's a rather large notebook is it not?'

Leader shrugged.

'Larger than the usual policeman's notepad, I'd say.'

Leader shrugged again.

'And throughout the operation targeting my client's house and premises you were carrying this book and noting every detail of every event and every action?'

Leader nodded.

'And amidst all this activity you were able to make these notes of exactly what you found on the premises?'

'Yes,' Leader replied.

'And no detail of what went on in that house escaped your attention and is missing from your notes?'

'No,' Leader mumbled.

'I see,' said Stephen. 'Now, may I ask, are you a member of Greenpeace?'

'Yes,' Leader replied, 'but what is the...'

'And how do you suppose that Mr Murfet knows that?' Stephen cut in.

Leader was really on his back foot now.

'Well he's got ways of finding things out,' Leader snapped back.

'So you're suggesting that my client has gone to some lengths to find out whether you are a member of Greenpeace?'

Leader nodded, baffled.

'Detective Sergeant, I'd like to offer a more likely explanation of how Mr Murfet came by this knowledge. During your search of his home you came across some documents pertaining to that organisation and asked Mr Murfet what was their significance. When she simply replied that her daughter was a member, you volunteered the information that you and your wife were also members. But strangely, there is no mention whatsoever of that conversation in your notes. If you are saying that no such exchange occurred, I wonder where on Earth Mr Murfet would have formed the impression that you and your wife belong to Greenpeace?'

Leader shrugged.

'I see,' Stephen said in a tone that I'd now come to understand was calculated to communicate his scepticism to the court. 'Now, I'd like to discuss Martin Lee, Mr Murfet's solicitor.'

Leader shrugged again, evidently failing to see where this was going. Stephen pressed his advantage.

'When you announced that you were arresting Mr Murfet and taking him to Barnet Police Station, did not Mr Murfet ask his wife, in your presence, to call Mr Lee to inform him of the arrest and to request that he send a solicitor as soon as possible?'

'I'm not sure,' Leader mumbled.

'Either you know or you don't know. I can assure you that this conversation did take place in your presence – and I have verified this with Mr Lee. Yet there is no mention of it in the notes you claim to have made so conscientiously about every last detail. Why was this rather important conversation not written down?'

There was no response from Leader.

'I can only conclude that, contrary to your claim, you did not make a note of everything that happened and everything that was said that day – far from it.'

208

Another of those dramatic silences followed as Stephen allowed the import of his argument to sink in. And then suddenly he galvanised the court with his next onslaught. And boy was it nice to witness Leader getting a taste of his own medicine. He enjoyed the power he had over the people in his interview room and he abused it. Now he was outclassed, outgunned and overpowered by someone who didn't need to lie and cheat to beat him! Lamb to the slaughter is the phrase that comes to mind – or should I say pig?

'Now, I would like to fast forward to the point at which you have Mr Murfet at Barnet Police Station and are questioning him. At the beginning of the interview according to your written statement, Mr Murfet says – and I quote – "I have committed no criminal offence and I decline to answer any questions." However, the transcript of the tape does not tally with this. In this version there is no mention of the word "criminal" at all. Mr Murfet never uttered the word and it follows that you must have added it to the transcript provided to the defence. Why? I suggest that it was purely to suggest that Mr Murfet was guilty of something, even if you had no proof of any specific criminal offence. By adding that one word, you hoped to suggest that my client was implicitly admitting to another form of offence – an allusion perhaps to the fact that when you failed to find conclusive evidence of criminal activity you decided to contact HM Customs and Excise. In short, Detective Sergeant, you were determined to destroy my client regardless of whether there was evidence to support your case!'

Leader glared back at Stephen defiantly.
'Go on,' he said quietly.
'Certainly. Your first question was about the antiques you found at the house, which you had established were stolen.'

Leader said nothing.

'Now, that said, what would your next question be?'

'I don't know,' Leader replied like a schoolboy getting a telling off.

'Come along Detective Sergeant...what would your next question be? What would the natural line of questioning from that point?'

Leader shrugged ineffectually.

'Let me help you then. I'm referring to your own notes here – the part that mentions that while you were in his house Mr Murfet volunteered the information that he knew that these articles were stolen property. Since my client then opened the interview by saying that he had committed no criminal offence (your words) I find it rather surprising that you did not pick up on the glaringly obvious contradiction. Would not your next question be along the lines of: "How can you sit there and say nothing when you've already admitted to us that you knew they were stolen?" Does that not make sense?'

'I suppose so,' muttered Leader.

'But you didn't did you. What did you ask him next? You asked him about some bearer bonds and treasury bills and then pursued that matter for the next eight minutes without referring to the antiques once despite the fact that you claim that Mr Murfet had admitted that they were stolen. Had he done so, I suggest that you would have interrogated him relentlessly on the matter until you were sure that you could secure a conviction. Instead you let it drop for the entire interview – which suggests to me that Mr Murfet made no such admission!'

Justice Collins interjected.

'Detective Sergeant Leader, did you take your notebook with you into the interview room?'

'No.' Leader grunted.

The judge looked incredulous.

'And why not, may I ask?'

210

'I didn't need it,' Leader countered sulkily. 'I was and am perfectly capable of remembering everything that happened and was said.'

With that Stephen released Leader and Mooney was called to the stand. Now obviously he hadn't been privy to the cross examination of Leader – but everyone else in court had, and the similarity of the line of questioning and the responses to what had just gone before made a very powerful point. I won't go into the full details of Mooney's ordeal in the witness box for that reason – suffice to say he left the court a considerably moodier man!

In essence the prosecution's point was exactly the same as with Leader. The written statement differed from the typed version in precisely the same way and, just like his colleague, Mooney put the discrepancy down to a simple typing error. If that were true, it would have been an incredible (as in unbelievable) coincidence because although more than a week had passed between the typing of Leader's statement and Mooney's the two statements were identical to the extent that the 'typing errors' involved the addition of the same two words in the same places. This was pretty damning and Mooney left the court under a cloud after Stephen had turned to the judge – who'd been visibly unimpressed with the responses to his own interjections - and said, 'I think we've made our point.'

Leader, obviously, had left the courtroom before Mooney was called but was probably still loitering around the building, eager to see me go down. And the judge was clearly aware of this because the moment the doors swung shut behind Mooney he addressed the court.
'I want those two witnesses removed from this court. Not merely from this room but from the building.'

There was a ripple of activity among ushers and court officials and, after a long silence in which we all wondered what the judge had in mind, he called us to attention.

'Now that they have been removed, I should like to instruct the court that I shall not accept anything that those two officers had to say. I found the evidence they provided unconvincing, their answers to my learned friend's questions evasive and their answers to my own even more so. In short, I will not allow their evidence in this case.'

Turning to the counsel for the prosecution, he said, 'Right, what else have you got?'

'Well, that was our case really...' the Pros began.

'So what are you going to do?' demanded the judge, knowing all too well that the complete demolition of their key witnesses had made the prosecution's position untenable. 'I will not have your witnesses in my court, so I repeat, what do you propose?'

The Pros thought about this for a moment or two and then, with a sort of 'hands up' gesture, said, 'I think we have no option but to withdraw our evidence.'

'Very well,' said the judge. 'I'll say again that I am very disappointed with the calibre of these officers – their conduct has been appalling.'

With that, he called the jury back in and instructed them to find me 'Not Guilty' – and by 2pm the whole thing was over and we were outside the court flushed with sheer relief!

Stephen phoned Martin Lee – as well as being a top criminal solicitor, he was also a very good friend of mine.

'Martin,' he said, 'it's all over!'

'What do you mean?' he replied in surprise (obviously, he'd been expecting a protracted trial).

'Well, Don put his hand up to it – and he got six months!'

At that, Martin went completely berserk!

'What the hell do you think you're doing then? I send you down there because you're meant to be the best – to do a proper job and make sure my client's acquitted and now you tell me he's changed his plea and been convicted!!! I don't believe it. There's no way Don would put his hands up to anything...I've got a good mind to...'

Laughing, Stephen put me on the phone.

'Martin, it's Don! He's pulling your plonker mate. It's all over and I'm out!'

An audible sigh of relief was followed by another stream of invective about us winding him up – but I could tell he was pleased!

Well I hardly need to add that I was very pleased with Stephen's performance! In fact, as it happened, my son Bradley was due to face the beak the very next day at Wood Green Crown Court on another trumped up charge of possession and distribution of cocaine. So, once he'd stopped berating me about that admittedly rather cruel wind-up, I asked Martin if he could arrange for Stephen to do the same service for Bradley (you have to do these things through the solicitor, rather than deal directly with the barrister). Stephen turned up as requested at Wood Green Crown Court and proceeded to demolish the prosecution's case and establish that it was a fit-up just as he had with my own and Bradley was duly acquitted.

Although I'd been acquitted myself, I wasn't going to leave it there. Determined to hound Leader and Mooney just as they'd hounded me, Martin and I took the case to the Police Complaints Authority and pursued the matter of the missing and faked custody records. I wanted those two bent coppers off the street for good – but the powers that be, typically, didn't agree. After two or three meetings, at which they appeared to be taking it seriously, things just seemed to fizzle out. Despite the presiding judge's unequivocal condemnation of the two officers as liars whom he would not have in his court, the complaints people said that they could find no evidence that they had acted improperly. No surprises there – they just can't stand it when you beat them at their own game, these coppers. Basically they just very, very bad losers!

And that was the end of that – or almost. It turned out that while I'd been 'away' the Customs & Excise people had been snooping about up in the barns on my land, thanks to Leader tipping them off, malicious git that he was. They discovered that the guy I'd been renting them to hadn't been making wine in there as the cops had suspected – he was making vodka! And quite a lot of it too, considering they found seven stills bubbling away in there. Quite a while later, when Stansted Airport was built, I was reliably informed that the Customs people had the photos of my barns and the actual stills on display in their airside area – because it was the largest illegal distillery they'd ever busted in the UK!

And if they couldn't nail Don Murfet – they'd get his son, purely out of spite! In fact they admitted as much to me after Gregg was charged and successfully prosecuted for illegal possession of some of the firearms they'd found in my loft, despite the fact that they knew damn well that they were deactivated. For example they took away the World War Two Mark VI Webley .455 pistol, which had been given to Gregg by Adam Ant's father, Les Goddard – despite the fact that since the thing had been sliced in two using an oxyacetylene torch it was quite clearly unusable. It couldn't even hold together, although the hinge was still there with which you opened it to eject the cartridges from the barrel.

Next they turned their attention to Gregg's pump action shotgun. Now, after the Hungerford massacre, it had become illegal to own this type of gun, which is why we sent it away to a reputable gunsmiths to have it adapted to comply with the new law, which I believe said that you could only have a

214

shotgun capable of firing two cartridges plus one in reserve. To their great frustration, we had proof of the modification stamped on the barrel and Gregg had an up-to-date licence for the weapon – so they couldn't get him for that! Then there was the rocket launcher, which Gregg had bought perfectly legally from the Quartermasters Stores in Islington. All it consisted of was an empty fibre glass case really, because when you fired it, the trigger mechanism and in fact the whole shooting match, to coin a phrase, went with the rocket and all you had left was the outer casing. And that's what Gregg had bought – a spent case, complete with the army markings as a decorative souvenir. Notwithstanding the fact that there was no rocket in the thing and it couldn't be fired, they informed us that it was now illegal because the barrel wasn't rifled – again following the changes in the law after the Hungerford massacre – and that they'd notified all the firearms dealers of that fact ('Rifling' is the spiralled groove in the gun's barrel or bore, which produces the projectile's rotary motion). They didn't bloody well bother to tell the general public though – and I'm damn sure there are hundreds of kids with these things hanging on their walls completely oblivious to the fact that it's now an offence to own one. So now the police had one up on us. You'd have thought that would be enough. But they were desperate to stitch up someone in my family and they took away the Webley. That didn't bother us much – we knew there was no way it could be used. In fact it hadn't been fired since World War One!

I was underestimating the depths of petty vindictiveness they'd stoop to! Unbelievably, they took the revolver to a laboratory where they went to ludicrous lengths to prove that it could be fired. And they did finally manage to get it to fire – but only by fixing it tightly in a heavy duty clamp first and then taping it together – which made it a firearm in the eyes of the law. This now allowed them to charge Gregg with possession of a firearm without a licence. I wasn't impressed! 'You're mad, the lot of you!' I raged. 'You know full well that gun can't be fired. At least not without it being fixed in a clamp.'

They just laughed it off.

In court, it was pointed out by expert witnesses that the Webley hadn't been fired since the Second World War. And the expert actually said that he wouldn't fire the thing for love nor money – it was just too dangerous.

Gregg just wanted the whole nightmare over with and didn't want to fight the case. I did – but his idiot of a barrister made no effort to persuade him to fight it and completely cocked up the case. Gregg ended up with a criminal record for firearms possession and a £600 fine – and I ended up chasing the terrified barrister up the street out side the court! Among the other odds and sods they'd confiscated was Gregg's World War Two Webley holster and, for no reason at all as far as I could see, they seemed determined not to let us have it back.

Mooney came up to me after the case.

'Look, I'll get that back for him!' he volunteered.

'Oh well that's fucking generous of you! He should never have been charged in the first place – and you bloody well know it!' I spat back.

'Look, it wasn't him we were after – it was you. We were after your legs – not his but unfortunately that's just the way it went...' he said, as if that made it all hunky bleeding dory.

They were absolute pieces of shit, Mooney and Leader. How their superiors justified keeping them on in the police after the judge at my case had so clearly stated that they were corrupt I'll never know. It shows just how bent the whole police system is, the fact that they were happy to keep on two officers who'd been proved to be liars and cheats after their laughable 'Complaints Authority' had done its usual thing of going through the motions and finding in their favour.

Summing all this up, it's blatantly obvious that the police were determined to nick me, whether they had the evidence to or not. OK, they'd got a search warrant on the basis that they suspected that I was in possession of those treasury bills – but when they failed to find them and instead found all those antiques, they made no effort at all to find out whose they really were. Let's face it, to be classed as an antique, an item has to be more than a hundred years old – and it will have passed through countless pairs of hands, some legitimately and some dishonestly. So if you deal in antiques you're more than likely to end up with one or two that are on a stolen list somewhere – but you have no way of telling. As it was, only a couple of items in their haul turned out to be nicked anyway.

Oh well, at least you didn't lose anything, you're probably thinking. If so, I doubt you've ever had a spin by the police and had your property taken away. Because they never gave any of it back. Come to think of it, in all the times I've had things taken away from me by the police, I don't think they've returned anything at all! They even nicked my passport once – one that I treasured because it showed all the places in the world I'd been to and when, memories I could never replace. Not that they cared.

That wasn't the first time I'd been picked on and fitted up by the police – and, depressingly, it wasn't to be the last. Several years later I had a bloke with a tipper truck taking a load of rubbish away from my land. As I opened the gate in the top field to let the lorry out into the lane a bloke was walking past. Now that, in itself, was worthy of note because my nearest neighbours are in a hamlet – not even what you'd call a village – a mile or three down the road. Even further afield

217

there's only the odd village so you don't see a lot of people strolling past. I nodded politely at him, like you do.

'Morning,' I murmured, in the usual English understated style.

'Morning,' he replied in kind.

Something about him didn't seem quite right. He seemed slightly out of place – but I couldn't put my finger on why. Then it dawned on me – it was his highly polished smart brown shoes. Not the kind of footwear you generally see on people rambling through the country lanes. I thought no more about him – until, later that day when I set off driving into town to meet up with some friends and, arriving at the lights where the lane joined the main road, I noticed something odd about the car that had drawn up behind me (you get plenty of time to notice things at those lights because they're five changes of traffic lights quite often mean a five-minute wait!). Although there was apparently only the driver in the car, he seemed to be talking. Bearing in mind that this was before the days of hands-free mobiles, I could only conclude that he was either mad or talking to someone I couldn't see. Surreptitiously monitoring him in the rear view mirror, I at first thought he had a child in the back. But it wasn't – it was a fully-grown adult lying down across the back seat. I didn't like the look of this at all. So I put my foot down and headed off down the country lanes I now knew like the back of my hand. Sure enough, the car followed and I took my new 'friend' on a tour of the local sights and interesting shortcuts and switchbacks until a new tail took over. I took them down to Epping, where I paid a visit to my insurance brokers.

'After I leave,' I said, 'if anyone comes in asking questions about me, could you give me a ring and let me know?'

They did ask questions. And my brokers did phone me as promised. Now I knew for certain someone was on my case – and off I went, once more leading the bastards on a wild goose chase (or should I say a wild Murfet chase, because I was getting pretty pissed off by this time!). I turned round and headed back in the direction I'd come from.

Now I'll have some fun with them, I thought with a grim smile as I took a sudden swerve towards the motorway. And sure enough, we went through the whole rigmarole of a police pursuit and, totally familiar with the way they work, I watched as they overtook and veered up off ramps only to slip down the on-ramp and reappear behind me or as one car slowed and allowed its replacement to take over. Finally, having led them on a grand tour of what must have amounted to a good fifty miles, I was heading back homeward and, when I turned off onto the country lanes three miles from home, the latest pursuer just drove past on the main road.

So, alone at last, I went home, assuming that, for today at least, they'd had enough. But, now I knew they were after me again, I couldn't relax – I'd have been a fool to. And I needed to make a phone call. There was no way I was going to make any calls from home – they were sure to be listening and taping every word. So a few hours later I jumped in the car and set off for Bishop's Stortford, a few miles away.

Standing in a phone box in the middle of the town I clocked a car, cruising towards me at an unnaturally leisurely pace and in the front passenger seat was a familiar face. It was the brown shoed guy I'd met in the lane that morning! I didn't let on that I'd spotted them – but they'd obviously spotted me because the car parked up as soon as it passed the phone box. I cut short the phone call with my friends, explaining the situation and saying that I'd be back in touch once I'd got rid of my 'company'. Just to make sure they couldn't connect me to anyone by checking the last couple of numbers dialled from the phone box I quickly called my daughter and then my son. Hanging up abruptly, I then proceeded to take my new buddies on a little ride around the more awkward back streets of Bishop's Stortford before heading home to round off a completely and utterly wasted day for them!

What you have to bear in mind with these people is that they simply don't have the resources to shadow you 24/7 – that's just for the crime films and novels. What they're forced to do is take a day out of whatever they're up to – let's say once a month – to follow you and see what turns up. It's just an intelligence gathering exercise – they want to know who's who, what you're doing, who you're talking to and so on and on and bloody on until they get something they think they can use. It doesn't necessarily mean they've got anything on you – or even that they've got any good reason to be following you. They're just hoping!

In the end, I've found that, contrary to popular belief, you're not innocent till proven guilty as far as the cops are concerned. In fact there are two areas in which the opposite is definitely the case: firearms and taxes. Oh – make that three: the heinous offence of happening to be related to Don Murfet!

*   *   *

LONGLEAT: MAD MONKEYS, HIPPIES AND HIPPOS

A major open air festival was being planned at Longleat near Warminster in Wiltshire and I was invited to go down and give the venue a once over and discuss the security implications. At the time Lord Bath was still alive, but I was dealing with Christopher Bath (not the current Marquis of Bath, the larger than life hippified toff that you're probably thinking of!). And I must say, being a private visitor to that magnificent old house was really something. Designed and built in the sixteenth century by Sir John Tynne the fabulous country seat is set in a beautifully landscaped park designed by Capability Brown. More than a little overawed, I was shown into the grand old library, where the meeting started off informally – I suppose they wanted to sound me out. Amidst the social chat, they showed me around the incredible collection of antiquities they had stored in there. I was absolutely fascinated. Among the countless treasures was the very first book ever printed, by Caxton himself and famous paintings and much too much more for me to recollect and after a while we were joined by the promoter and some people from the local authorities and went out scouting around the grounds for the best site, referring all the way to a huge map of the estate. Touring the grounds was equally exciting – it being a safari park – and on our travels the Estate Manager told me a story about the Chimpanzee Island (which unsurprisingly is the island they keep the chimps on!).

One day one of the rangers was out on his rounds when he noticed a chimpanzee strolling about on the mainland. Which was strange, because the whole point of keeping them on the island was that they wouldn't (or couldn't) swim across! It turned out that someone had chucked a long pole or bit of tree trunk or something like that over to the island and the clever little ape had used it to vault the water! And although they look cute, an adult chimpanzee is very dangerous. The young ranger radioed for help – but in the meantime he had to try to make the situation safe. He edged his Land Rover closer, hoping to lure the escapee into the cage on the back. Baring its teeth in a cheesy grin, it seemed to be laughing at him – but then they always do, don't they! So he stepped slowly out of the cab and approached, holding out a hand – and, being used to people, the chimp took his hand and allowed the ranger to lead him back to the Land Rover. The plan was that once he'd lured the ape inside, he'd snatch his hand away and quickly lock him in.. What he didn't reckon on was just how clever chimps are – and how strong! He tugged. The chimp tugged back – harder. He was stuck – but not for long. After one final attempt to free his hand, the chimp obligingly did it for him –it opened its powerful jaws, clamped them round the ranger's arm – and bit it off at the elbow!

Incredibly, this young kid had the presence of mind to shut the chimp inside the vehicle before he collapsed in what must have been unbearable agony. The Estate Manager rushed to the rescue, called an ambulance and, having picked up the young ranger's shredded shirtsleeve with the torn-off arm still inside, sent it with its former owner to hospital. Fortunately they saved the lad's life, though sadly not the arm – and the Marquis of Bath generously saved his job and ensured he had employment for life on the estate. There is one bit of good news to end the story – apparently he was quite impressed with the standard of care provided by one nurse in particular. So much so, in fact, that he married her!
  So there's a little PG tip for you – chimps ain't as cuddly as they look on the PG Tips ads but they're just as disarming!

Anyway, after that horror story we continued our tour of the park, eyes now peeled for marauding monkeys as well as likely concert sites. And we settled on an unusual, but quite inspiring set up. The stage would be at the rear of the great house, which would make a fantastic backdrop (much like that featured in Neil Diamond's 1977 concert at Woburn Abbey) – and between the performers and the audience would be The Leat, an open watercourse or canal like the ones that feed a mill. It would be an effective barrier all right – and it would all look very dramatic, I thought. But of course it raised some unusual security scenarios. What if people tried to swim across? But they'd thought of that and asked me to consider having some of my men patrolling in boats. That seemed fair enough to me – a perfectly sensible idea. Until they dropped in the next little nugget of information...

'Is there anything in the Leat?' I enquired, thinking of Koi Carp or other pondlife that might need protection.

'Oh yes,' they said breezily. 'Hippos.'

'Hippos?' I parroted dumbly.

'Yeah man,' one of them replied with a smile.

Well, I was speechless. I mean I've had some pretty intimidating blokes handling security for me over the years but I reckoned a herd of bleeding great hippopotamuses (or is it Hippopotami?) might just do the trick of putting the average punter off taking a dip!

'And you're worried about people swimming across? I should bloody well think you are!' I exclaimed when I regained the power of speech.

'Well it's OK – they're vegetarians!' they explained.

'So was Adolf Hitler,' I said for some reason. 'Can't you round them up and pen them in somewhere, just while the gig's happening?'

'Well they're not the easiest of animals to move about. If they don't want to go they just don't go!' came the expert opinion. I could see their point. I couldn't imagine how you'd make a hippo do anything it didn't want to – and I certainly didn't fancy the idea of trying. I took another tack.

'What, exactly, would a hippo do to someone who decided to jump in the water with it then?' I asked with trepidation.

'Well, he should be all right. At worst he might bite you...He wouldn't eat you though!' this guy said calmly.

'Oh well that's all right then, as long as its just a hippo bite. Nothing serious then!' I retorted, thinking about the damage a chimp can do and multiplying by ten. All in all, as a security professional, I was less than comfortable about the idea. Bloody terrified would be more accurate. And, call me old fashioned, sending my blokes out to control herds of hippies was one thing; herds of hippos (or whatever the collective noun for hippos might be) was quite another!

'Well I think it would be best if your rangers manned the boats because they know what they're doing,' I suggested, trying to be realistic about a job that was looking increasingly surreal. 'You could put signs up everywhere warning the punters about the hippos and my guys will patrol both sides of the Leat to make double sure no one gets in there.'

To my relief, all concerned seemed to accept that this was a more sensible plan. But the relief didn't last long.

'About the lions...' someone piped up.

'Lions?' I repeated incredulously.

'Yes, the lion compound,' he said.

'What about it?' I asked, dreading to think what was coming next. Maybe they wanted us to walk the lions about on dog leads to make sure they didn't eat anyone.

'Well, we'd like some of your men to guard it.'

'Why?' I stammered. Surely they were securely fenced in. Weren't they???

'Well it's what we call a double skin – an outer perimeter fence further out made of Mau Mau fencing. Thing is that it's not impossible for someone to climb over the outer fence and get in...And with a hundred thousand young rock fans there, who knows, someone might just try!'

(Mau Mau fencing is very strong and very high – so named because it was used to protect property in Kenya against the Mau Mau guerrillas in the fifties and sixties. The inner fence was not so substantial – mainly serving to create a safe zone in which the rangers could safely patrol the perimeter.)

'But what about the second fence...the inner fence?' I asked.

'Well, you see that's not quite so substantial...It's just the first line defence really. It just makes a space for our rangers to drive round the enclosure in. So we'd like some of your men to be inside the perimeter.'

'How many lions have you got in there?' I asked, as if it was a casual enquiry.

'Quite a lot!' he smiled.

'Can they get over the fence?' I went on.

'Well I think they could if they really wanted to!'

Oh marvellous! I thought.

224

'Let me get this straight,' I said. 'You're asking me to tell my men that some of them will be inside the perimeter fence of the lion compound – and that they should be all right because the lions will only jump over the fence if they bloody feel like it!'

'Erm, yes...' he said.

'Well I can tell you right now, they ain't gonna like it. I mean my guys are hard – but not that bloody hard!' I laughed. I wasn't laughing on the inside though. This was getting weird. They didn't want a rock 'n' roll security firm, they wanted Tarzan!

Anyway, we left it at that for the time being and continued surveying the site. There were more meetings with more public officials and senior police officers about all sorts of complications – such as the fact that parts of the estate were public rights of way, which meant that anyone could stroll through at any time. I was familiar with those kinds of issues, having worked on similar events at Knebworth, where a public footpath ran right through the arena but I couldn't help thinking that leaping lions, chomping chimps and herds of hippos presented a more serious public health risk. I'm funny like that!

Of course I'm taking the mickey out of the Longleat people's laid back attitude here – mainly because of the contrast with that of a London boy like me. Chris Bath was a lovely chap and he certainly had no intention of being lackadaisical about the potential risk to my men or the punters. It was just that he and all his team of rangers had grown up with all these terrifying wild animals roaming around this vast expanse that was effectively their back garden. There was nothing unusual about it to them – and in retrospect I bet they were wondering what I was making a fuss about! It didn't cross their minds that what they were asking was way beyond the call of duty for even the most experienced rock 'n' roll security guy. I

225

mean, I know the gutter press always describe rock 'n' rollers as 'animals' but in my experience they're actually pussycats! Not bloody lions!

How the hell I was going to convince any of my guys to patrol the lion enclosure I did not know – short of issuing them all with big game rifles. And as for the hippo situation, how could I suggest they go out in a little boat that a hippo could capsize with a casual shrug. Let's face it, none of these dangerous animals would be in their mildest mood when suddenly blasted with thousands of watts of thundering rock and flashing lights. I'm no expert – but I reckon they'd be shocked, then pissed off, then bloody angry!

I hate to say I told them so...But I told them so! The gig never happened. In the end everyone agreed that the problems were too many, too tricky and too dangerous. Mind you it was worth the trip and all the meetings just for the pleasure of meeting Christopher Bath and his people and being privy to the wonders of Longleat.

*   *   *

RUSSIAN GYMNASTS IN THE MID 70'S

Remember Olga Korbut? Well, for the benefit of the under forties, she was a young Russian gymnast who became the darling of the British press and public. At the height of her fame, we were handling the security for a big gymnastic event at Olympia The police warned us to expect some sort of demonstration against Russian treatment of Jews by the non-violent Jewish Defence League and possibly by the more militant Zionist *Haganah* – and they wanted us to make sure that things didn't get out of hand.

So we were keeping our eyes peeled for trouble – and when we saw anyone acting strangely we confiscated all of their material, banners and stuff and Special Branch would take them off our hands.

Special Branch approached us to inform us that they'd spotted a car belonging to a member of this group – and that they wanted our help. If we spotted these guys, we were to apprehend them and escort them to an area away from the venue from where Special Branch would discreetly take them away. And sure enough, on the first night of the show some of these protesters burst out with their banners as soon as the cameras started rolling. Anyway, it turned out that the Women's Jewish Defence League merely wanted to hand in letters of protest, which wasn't a problem at all. Other, more militant organisations were obviously hoping to stage some more dramatic protests and get some publicity but overall even their protests were peaceful and it wasn't difficult to control them as requested. Funny to be working with Special Branch instead of trying to out smart, and out run them as we usually did!

We used to go everywhere with these Russian gymnasts, taking them out sightseeing, shopping and socialising – and it amused me to see the contrast between Olga Korbut, who was about the size and weight of your little finger, alongside the seventeen stone bruiser known as 'Fat Fred' who I'd assigned to her – not to mention the huge great Russian weightlifters. They were quite a handful to look after, I can tell you! Mind you, we generally assumed that they could take care of themselves! And in the background, always a few yards away like sinister shadows were the secret security men – probably Special Branch and their Russian counterparts, watching in case any of them tried to defect (this was of course long before the fall of the Soviet Union).

CHAPTER SEVEN

1973/4

DAVID CASSIDY, AUSTRALIAN TOUR

NEW CROSS HOTEL, SYDNEY

'Don!! My room's on fire!!' came the panicked voice on the phone. It was David Cassidy, phoning from his penthouse suite. Three floors below in rather more humble accommodation, I shook myself awake and glanced at the clock as I hopped around the room feverishly struggling to get my trousers and pants on, literally getting my knickers in a twist! It was 6 am. Once trousered I raced barefoot up three flights of stairs, arriving breathless and banging at David's door. It opened and WOOF! Out billowed an impenetrable cloud of inky black smoke, through which the slight form of David Cassidy emerged choking and gagging. I lunged for him, caught his arm and dragged him outside, a black and white minstrel figure, naked but for his underpants and a thick coat of soot – in fact the only bare white skin visible was the two white lines traced by the air entering his nostrils. Shutting the door on the black pall, I rushed him down two floors to Gerry Slater's room, where I kicked, police raid style, on the door, my arms being occupied in trying to support the dead weight of David's slumping form. Having instructed Gerry to take care of David, I rushed up to the floor below the penthouse with Billy Francis and a couple of the others and we sprinted up and down the corridors banging on doors yelling 'FIRE!!!' and telling everyone to get out of there sharpish. As the hotel's befuddled and blinking guests peeped mole-like from their doors and were suddenly

228

galvanised by the look of urgency on our faces, I called down to alert Reception and the emergency services.

We went back down to check on David, my heart pumping with a sickening mix of adrenalin and the awareness that his safety was my responsibility alone – this was a personal security man's worst nightmare! But he was reasonably OK, thank God, although he'd inhaled an awful lot of smoke and had to go to hospital to be cleaned up and given oxygen and what have you. The fire department, on investigation, found that there hadn't in fact been a fire at all. The swimming pool pump had somehow gone into reverse and started pumping noxious fumes directly into David's room – and only David's room. In hindsight it all suddenly made sense. There'd been no sense of heat when he'd opened the door – and I'd seen no sign of flames. Nevertheless, who knew what the fumes could have done to him! He might have died in his sleep from carbon monoxide poisoning, not to mention the hundreds of other guests, many of whom were families with young kids.

The firemen escorted us back to the penthouse. It was like walking into a black hellhole – drifts upon drifts of soot like a negative shot of a white Christmas. Everything in there was coated in soot – including every last thread of David's stage clothes. That morning the big question was whether or not to cancel the day's show. In an ideal world you wouldn't do a major concert after inhaling a chimney's worth of soot – but the schedule of a major international tour's incredibly tight. If we cancelled the gig, it couldn't just be slotted in – it would be ages and thousands and thousands of fans would be disappointed. So in the end the old showbiz adage prevailed: the show must go on! Now there was the problem of stage clothes. I suppose if he'd been The Damned or someone a bit on the Goth side, we could have got away with him going on in clothes covered in pitch black soot – but it wouldn't exactly sit well with David's whiter than white image! We did somehow manage to salvage some of his costumes and get everything cleaned in time for the evening's show. David somehow managed to turn in a decent performance – though understandably a tad under par, but the audience, mostly aware of the previous night's near tragedy were even more than usually on his side and they buoyed him up and carried him through it. Nevertheless, that was one long, horrible, stressful day for all concerned.

When the press got hold of the story there was quite a furore – and I was lauded as a hero for saving the star's life and perhaps those of the hotel's other guests! But it's not false modesty when I say that I was only doing my job – keeping my priorities straight and making sure my artist didn't come to harm.

I first met David Cassidy when David Bridger, the Artist Promotion guy at Dick Leahy's Bell Records, rang me up to ask us to look after David – because his first promotional tour of the UK a short time earlier had been fraught with problems. I think they'd based him on a boat on the Thames and they had hordes of kids turning up and trying to get out to the boat. Anyway, they didn't want a repeat of those sorts of shenanigans so they asked the best in the business to handle David's security (though I say it myself!) on what was to be his first proper British and European tour!

Of course I agreed like a shot – after the success of the Partridge Family (a popular TV programme at the time, David was hot property – and as soon as he arrived we went to meet him and his crew, including, of course, his manager Ruth Aarons who, incidentally was the former American table tennis World Champion. Ruth didn't join the tour though – she delegated all that sort of thing to her fresh-faced bunch of preppy types who worked in her office, two young

230

guys and a girl called Teri Geckler. They'd hired a plane for the tour from a Dutch company called Transavia, which the Osmonds also used – which was a very good idea because it meant they could take all of the band and crew and, crucially, the press, including all the broadsheets as well as the tabloids and the pop papers.

A couple of days into the tour – in Spain I think – a couple of the press guys came up to Gerry Slater, my business partner and Tour Manager, who was also helping me with security, and me with a bit of a gripe.

'Look Don,' they said, 'this is all very nice being flown around Europe and seeing all the concerts – but they're keeping us away from David!'

Now that didn't seem like a very clever move. This was David's first tour outside the US and if the journalists felt shut out and weren't getting any interviews they were bound to get the hump. And since their editors would expect them to come back with something, they'd end up making the whole thing up in a way that was unlikely to show David in a very sympathetic light! Then, the very same day, all the press were assembled for a pre-arranged photo call. They waited patiently as the appointed time came and went. Then they waited impatiently a little longer until finally Teri Geckler appeared to make an announcement and this supposedly professional manager proceeded to make one of the most inept and downright damaging press statements I've ever witnessed in all my years in the business. No pictures today, she was saying to the disbelief of the bored and frustrated press posse, who were just dying for something juicy to get their teeth into.

'David's broken out!'

Well we all knew the security was tight – but surely that didn't mean Cassidy himself was under lock and key! No, it turned out that his celebrated baby face had 'broken out' in –

horror of horrors – a few zits because he was understandably out of sorts after all the travelling.

Not the greatest disaster to befall the career of a teen pop idol. But it could be if you blurt it out to every hack in the notoriously vicious British press! I couldn't believe it! Of course they reported this little nugget – but someone had to do something about this before they got hold of something really damaging so, the first chance I got, I tackled David about it on the plane.

'Look David, you've got to start cooperating with these guys. Talk to them – otherwise all you'll get is bad press. Don't worry about photos. Leave it with us. If we say they can't take any shots of you, they won't do it.'

Of course this was naughty of us – we were taking advantage of the close proximity to the star that security work afforded us to go behind the back of his real manager and her assistants. But after all, it was for his own good! Once we explained the total inadequacy of the people he'd surrounded himself with, David took everything we had to say on board and the atmosphere of the tour was transformed. From that moment on he was happy to sit down and chat with the press at almost any time they liked – and since he was undoubtedly an extremely charming person, he put them completely at ease and he soon had them eating out of his hand.

The remainder of the tour went off without another hitch and as soon as the show arrived back for the English leg, David called a meeting with Ruth Aarons and almost immediately the entire original crew and tour management staff was gone. On David's recommendation and with the cooperation of Bell Records, Ruth put David's entire world tour in the hands of Gerry and me. I never saw Teri Geckler again – or her two sidekicks. Hardly surprising when you consider that their utter lack of experience nearly caused one of the biggest PR disasters in pop history. From day one it was evident that none of them had ever been on a rock 'n' roll tour before –

232

they were running things the way they ran their office in LA – and it just doesn't work like that!

Gerry and I became very close to David during the course of that tour and became his confidants as well as his security and tour management advisers. The world tour, and by extension his career, went from strength to strength, helped in no small part, I'm proud to say, by our company's guidance and careful management. Of course the guy's a major talent – but he was no ingénue. On the contrary that baby faced young star had a very old and wise head firmly on his shoulders; one of the people that manage to combine being a 'personality' with real strength of character. Because he'd first achieved fame in the Partridge Family, it was easy to be misled into thinking of him as a kid – but you have to remember that he was already in his mid-to-late-twenties when he was playing the sixteen-year-old Keith Partridge! An essential part of David's character was his unfailing ability and willingness to turn on the charm when it was called for – and that talent and cooperative attitude came to our rescue on many occasions when the shit was about to hit the PR fan.

The next great test of our security prowess was a set of four concerts, two of which were matinee shows, over two days at Wembley in March 1973. Since matinees are, by definition, in the afternoon, the kids were able to turn out in force – so as well as all the thousands on the inside, we had thousands upon thousands more milling about outside the venue, which made getting David safely in and out a complete nightmare. And this was where, though I say it myself, my unique skills came to the fore: the kind of ability to plan a quick getaway you don't tend to develop in completely legitimate careers, shall we say! Call it escapology, if you will (I will!) – I know that I was the best man in Britain, maybe even the world, for spiriting famous faces in and out of places undetected by the thousands of fans or the press. I could put anyone –

absolutely anyone – through a crowd without even the most rabidly desperate fans finding out!

I remember one time we got the Osmonds – all of them – out of the Churchill hotel without the world's press and mobs of fans noticing, only to have the group's management demand that we sneak them back in and bring them out of the front doors again. It was the only way they could get rid of this mob that was verging on a full scale riot and, thanks to the cameras they had set up in front to capture everything, it made good viewing on CBS news in the US! Incidentally, The Jackson 5 were staying in the same hotel at the time – but no one made a fuss because they weren't yet quite in the Osmonds' league and the two groups' famous friendly rivalry had yet to come into play.

Anyway, I got David in and out for all the four shows without a single fan sussing what we were up to – until the very last show. We'd parked an unmarked transit van outside the back of the stage and left it there all day – that way it would have been there so long without moving that no one would give it a second look. A TV crew from either the BBC or ITV was filming the show and as David left the stage they filmed his rapid escape, running backward with their cameras as he dashed down the corridors towards a discreet side exit right beside the waiting van. Incidentally, unlike some artists, who stick around for a bit of a 'meet and greet', David was always out of the venue, into a vehicle and gone like a shot. His fans were so insistent that, if he didn't get away the instant he closed the show, he'd be stuck in there for hours before there was any hope of the hysterical mob dispersing.

Anyway, on this occasion, we bundled David into the van and the camera crew bundled in behind him with all their lights and equipment and we pulled the roller shutter down behind them. The driver, deliberately, was a fairly old gent –

far from the big muscle-bound security guy they'd be expecting and anyway, we arranged for some noise to kick off at the main stage doors to create a diversion while we made our getaway. But something went wrong. Suddenly there was a deafening banging on the van's flimsy metal panels and the frenzied wailing of hysterical fans crying, 'David!! David!!! We know you're in there!!!'

It was actually quite terrifying – and it's all dramatically documented in footage shot for the programme that the TV crew were making. Oh shit, I thought, wondering how the hell they could possibly have found out. Maybe they're just taking a long shot and banging on every vehicle in sight on the off chance he's in it, I mused, completely baffled.

Then I sussed it. They had a pretty good idea all right – because the van had a fibreglass top and the camera crew's fiercely intense lights were shining out of it, lighting the whole thing up like a Christmas tree! We might as well have had a giant flashing neon sign saying DAVID'S IN HERE GIRLS – COME AND GET HIM!!!

Anyway, it wasn't a major disaster – after all, the doors were locked, so we and our star were perfectly safe and the poor girls never even got a look at him. Hindsight being 20:20, of course, it was the fact that we'd taken the TV crew with us that was the flaw in the plan. On another night, I'd slipped in with David crouching unnoticed under a coat in the footwell of an old VW. My guys were so well-rehearsed that they were expert at looking in the other direction, thereby diverting the fans' eagle eyes while we rolled casually past with the window open and I slowed down so that David could slip out and enter the venue through a side door while I drove on a little way to a separate door. The next night I used the same tactics with Gerry's little mini and cruised through with the sunroof open and no one paid me any attention whatsoever.

It has to be said though that none of this would have worked if David hadn't been so impressively fit and limber. He could squeeze himself into what seemed to be the most impossibly small and awkward spaces – which made my job a lot easier. Just as helpfully, he wasn't one of these stars that insists on making a grand entrance regardless of the risk to the kids created by the inevitable hysteria or the vast public expense involved in policing his appearance. And the danger wasn't only to the kids themselves – if they actually got hold of the object of their adulation, he or she was in very real danger. They might not mean to harm their hero or heroine but hundreds of flailing, frantic teenage fingernails can cause a frightening amount of injury! The great thing about David was that he never questioned my judgement or my instructions – however bizarre they might sound...And sometimes the plan could be quite elaborate. A not untypical Don Murfet briefing to David was: 'Wait here in complete darkness for precisely three minutes and, on my signal, the door will open. Then you run across the corridor, down the stairs, round the back, over a wall and into the open top of the getaway vehicle'

David would listen carefully – and then he'd just do it! It was the same with the Osmonds – because I had a reputation for getting people in and out unnoticed, even the biggest stars would comply with the strangest instructions.

The only trouble was that my success in this department inevitably dropped the problem of the fans in the laps of my people handling the security at the venue. Surrounded by thousands of screaming girls who were utterly convinced that the star was still in the building, they hadn't a hope in hell of convincing them otherwise. They used to try all sorts of angles to get rid of them. They'd point out that no one had seen them come in – so how could they know that their hero/ine hadn't left the same way they'd arrived? They used to try and convince them that there was a secret tunnel through which the stars escaped, presumably Colditz style from under their teenage sentries' noses. Some – not my boys I hasten to add, even negotiated with the fans and allowed a small party back inside to search the place for the star, see for themselves and then let the others know that he or she really had left the building! Of course that never worked. They'd emerge to declare that the star wasn't there and their cohorts would accuse them of making a deal, just so that they could meet them alone. They had my sympathy, those beleaguered security guys – but that part wasn't my problem, thank God! I gave my guys standing orders that if the fans were still around once they'd secured what needed to be secured they should say goodnight to the fans and walk away to their transport. That's what they always did – and the fans didn't usually hang around for long.

Actually, over the years this constant game of cat and mouse with the fans became a normal part of the job – and we had quite a lot of good-humoured fun with them. The girls would actually come up to us before a show.
'We're gonna beat you this time!' they'd say playfully.
'Great – give it your best shot,' I'd reply, because it was all part of the game.

But they never did beat us, I'm proud to say.

There's one very important point about David's concerts – and those of acts like The Osmonds and The Monkees. And it's one that, refreshingly, David understood completely. That is that the audiences are much, much younger than those for a rock 'n' roll concert – in their early teens, or even younger – which means they're more hysterical and generally are less able to look after themselves – and you have to plan everything accordingly and build that awareness into every move you make. Handling these events the way you'd handle a rock gig is a big – possibly fatal – mistake and it was for their own safety as well as his own that we made sure they never got close to David. With other acts, the Bay City Rollers, for example, you'd go through the same process but for different reasons – but that's another story!

I know about the dangers involved with concerts involving very young girls through bitter experience – David's ill-fated show at the White City Stadium (now long gone) on May 26th 1974, at which a fourteen-year-old fan called Bernadette Whelan, despite our best efforts to protect the kids from their own hysteria, collapsed into a coma from which, tragically, she never awoke. A few days after the event, when her doctors were forced to make that awful decision to switch off the machines that were all that kept her body, if not brain, alive, there were two inquests on the agenda. One was the legal inquiry into the precise cause of her death. The other was our own painstaking investigation into what could have been done to prevent the tragedy, if anything, and what could be done at concerts in future to ensure that it wasn't repeated.

With hindsight, of course, I can see some of the underlying conditions that contributed to a situation that got out of control – but I can say with all honesty that they have little to do with the security operation itself and a lot to do with the physical and emotional state of the kids by the time the show started. As I've said countless times in this book, pop concerts for younger kids are incredibly fraught with emotion and there's not much you can do about that. All you can do is your utmost to provide a safe environment in which the kids can work themselves up into a frenzy of adulation without doing themselves any damage. A good thirty years on, today's promoters have learnt lessons from past events and the industry as a whole has come up with innumerable measures to keep crowds under control – but back in the early seventies a vast open air pop concert for young kids was pretty much unprecedented. With very few prior examples to model it on, the design of the crowd control operation had to come from our own experience and ingenuity and it was very effective at meeting the demands we expected to be placed on it. What we hadn't counted on – and I don't think anyone could have expected us to – was the fact that a stadium show almost by definition, means there are no allocated seats.

That last point may sound trivial – but it's absolutely crucial to a teenybopper whose life revolves around getting a glimpse of her idol! In a normal venue you buy your ticket with a seat number on it – and there's no rush to get in there because your seat's your seat and that's that and it was easy to marshal what little space was left between the front seats and the stage. In a stadium, you might have a ticket – but there's no guarantee you'll get a good view. You have to fight your way to the front. Which is why we were faced with hundreds, probably thousands, of little girls queuing up right through the night before the gig, which incidentally was in the daytime. I briefed all my men very carefully so as to do everything possible to keep them safe and relatively comfortable throughout their wait. We arranged for Portaloos to be provided nearby and maintained patrols throughout the night in case any of the 'nonce cases' I'd become so depressingly familiar with on the inside put in an appearance and tried to interfere with any of the kids.

As you can imagine, by the time the gates opened and the fans poured into the stadium like the charge of the light brigade, we had thousands of utterly exhausted, unfed and probably dehydrated kids on our hands: a combination that would be enough to make anyone light-headed. Add the arrival on stage of David Cassidy and you've got one giant hysteria bomb. The sheer volume and pitch of the screaming was unbelievable, even to a tour-hardened pro like myself and my crew – and it made David's job near impossible, almost completely drowning the foldback (the wedge-shaped on-stage monitors by which performers hear each other on stage). Straining valiantly to make out the band's music above this cacophony, David did a top job as usual – as did my men in the front line against the waves of frantic teenagers vying for position at the front.

We'd deliberately designed and built a curved barrier (as opposed to the usual straight line) between the arena and the stage, thereby controlling the pressure against it. My men faced the crowd, spotting girls (and it was almost all girls) who seemed to be in trouble, plucking them from the crowd and taking them out to the wings of the stage. This was standard practice – and one that's always worked very well. The trouble was that the kids caught on that if they appeared to faint the security staff'd rescue them – and that just might mean getting a bit closer to David, or even meeting him. In fact, all it meant was that they'd get treatment from the St John Ambulance people if they needed it and then be sent back into the arena nearer the back. But that didn't stop a massive epidemic of feigned fainting – to which we had to react just in case they weren't acting. In fact the crowd (I think they numbered something like ten thousand) can't have been too compressed because time and time again we'd rescue a girl who was fainting at the front and send her out at the back only to find that she'd worked her way to the front again a few minutes later. And of course she'd be doing an Oscar-worthy job of acting again!

You could never assume that they were faking it of course – and, sadly, among the hundreds of kids we extracted from that dog eat dog mob, was poor Bernadette Whelan. She didn't look good. I could see those dedicated St John Ambulance people carrying out the chest compressions and mouth to mouth resuscitation with urgent determination –

240

and then she was carried away to an ambulance to hospital, where, as I said, she slipped into a coma and died about three days later. But of course, we weren't to know that she would later die. The show, as they say, must go on – especially since all these kids had paid what was to them a fortune and stayed up all night for this. But I had to do something to reduce the feverish intensity. I took David offstage. Not a popular move, as you can imagine. Mel Bush, the promoter, tried to speak to the crowd but to no avail. So I had a word with Tony Blackburn, who was the compere, and asked him to appeal to them for some calm. He did his best and some sort of order was restored – but not for long. As soon as David reappeared the hysteria was amplified to its former level. So I took him off again and bundled him backstage before walking back to the front to face the hordes of frantic girls and address them myself.

'Look,' I appealed, 'everyone must take at least two steps back to relieve the pressure at the front. OK? Two steps back is all we need. If you don't we won't be allowed to carry on with the show again. I repeat: David won't be coming back unless you all take two steps back.'

It worked. For the rest of the show they were a bit more controlled, if you can use the word control for that kind of adulation. David completed a triumphant show and, as usual, we whisked him away double quick – in fact he was out of the building almost before anyone realised he'd left the stage. It was then, when checking on Bernadette's condition, that we were informed that she was still in a coma. Not the best news. And the start of a very sad and testing time for all concerned, not least because of the inquests, legal, formal and otherwise, that I mentioned at the beginning of this sad episode. Much as you wish you could, you can't just put something like that behind you and forget about it. The Health and Safety people, the local council and the press were all looking into the matter, along with the official coroner's inquest and out of all this came the beginnings of what came to be known as 'The Pop Code' – a set of guidelines for safety at concerts, which I believe Lord Melchett was instrumental in drawing up. It was a document full of good intentions, which unfortunately were countervailed by some impractically idealistic ideas – but more of that elsewhere.

Before long, David was being relentlessly hounded about the whole tragic affair. Utterly and completely distraught, he just went to ground. No interviews, no appearances and certainly no shows – we buried him, kept him out of the way for as long as it would take for him to get his head together again. The press, circling like vultures round poor Bernadette's death, laid the lies on thick and laid the blame at David's door – and mine. There were reports of her having broken legs and of others injured in the crush. They were lies. There were accusations that the security had been wholly inadequate – and they were lies too. Of all the vast number of people seen by the St John Ambulance teams, I think four had to go to hospital, three of whom were diabetics suffering from hypoglycaemia as a result of having stayed out all night without food and water before going through a bout of complete and utter hysteria. There were no broken bones and, in fact, the only person detained at hospital that day was Bernadette.

The worst thing about that kind of allegation is that you can't really answer back. The part that hurt me most, obviously, was when they claimed that we hadn't provided proper security. In fact that couldn't have been further from the truth. As Mel Bush testified at the official inquest, not only did we comply with the current GLC regulations stipulating the levels of staffing and security measures required – we doubled them! Yes doubled!! So you can see why I resented the suggestion so deeply that we'd cut corners in any way. The bastards were suggesting that I'd been gambling with little girls' lives – I'd only have been doing that if I'd just fulfilled the legal requirements and ignored what my experience and conscience told me was needed – which was a lot more.

At one point I was confronted by a surveyor, employed to look into whether any structural problems had contributed to the situation. Of course there weren't.

'What do you know about crowd control?' I demanded of him. 'And how much experience have you had of dealing with thousands of hysterical teenage girls?'

None was the answer. And there's the problem – there have been similar incidents since and now we recognise the state people can get themselves into and just how dangerous it can be. I still maintain that the root cause of tragedies like this is the fact that these kids stand in a queue for 36, even 48, hours and will not leave it for food or water or to get out of the sun or the cold because that means losing their position and their one chance of getting to the front at the show. Once you take that fact on board, it's not surprising that they're often in a desperately weakened condition long before the concert even starts. Then, having fought their way to the front of the stage, nothing on earth is going to make them relinquish their prime position – not the need to eat or drink or go to the toilet. And that's something that the people in charge of security can do nothing about. In effect, the kids are made ill and their bodies in a distressed condition before they even get in – to an environment in which you'd never dream of placing anyone in less than totally rude health!

The inquest concluded that Bernadette's trunk had been compressed for some short period – I don't know how long, something like a minute maybe...But anyway whatever the cause, it certainly wasn't the barrier because she wasn't tall enough for it to have compressed her midriff and chest area. And anyway, according to her friends' testimony she wasn't

243

anywhere near it. Even if there had been the enormous pressure of thousands of bodies thrusting her up against it, it would have been her ribs or perhaps her shoulders that took the brunt of it. Interestingly, her friends reported that Bernadette was holding her bag in front of herself so it seems much more likely that the pressure of the bag against her trunk area was part of the problem. Maybe the crowd pushed it up against her; maybe a friend was squeezing her too tightly in the euphoria of seeing their idol...Maybe...Well there are so many maybes that it was downright irresponsible of the press to claim that she was simply crushed to death. All we know for sure, thanks to the coroner, is there were no bruises on her body (as surely there would have been had she been crushed against the barrier or trodden upon) but the red flecks of blood in her eyes showed that pressure on her trunk had prevented breathing and deprived her brain of oxygen, resulting in the coma from which she never awoke.

And then, of course, came poor Bernadette's funeral. And the press showed their usual degree of respect – bugger all, that is. They put it about that David would attend and, as much as he wanted to, it simply wasn't on. It would have turned it into a circus, a feeding frenzy for media vultures and fans alike, which was the last thing David wanted. So staying away and allowing her a reasonably dignified ceremony was the best thing he could do for Bernadette. Paying our respects by not attending the service itself, we arranged for a very nice wreath to be sent to the family and David personally took a lot of trouble to get the words right that went with it. The media, of course, don't have any such scruples and Bernadette's family had to run a gauntlet of insensitive hacks and a gaggle of fans that had gathered in the hope that David would turn up. I doubt very much that any of them were there to pay their respects! Just to make sure it all went without incident – and to pay my respects privately – I went along

244

and watched the funeral from a respectful and discreet distance.

The press may have insinuated that David was somehow to blame – which was ridiculous – but in later reports it was some consolation to him that Bernadette's family made it quite clear that they didn't blame him at all. Anyway, I personally, and everyone I worked with in the security business learned a lot of lessons from that awful day's events and kept them in mind in our concert security plans from then on.

Depressingly, not everyone in the business took the lessons of Bernadette Whelan's death to heart – as The Who later found out when several people were crushed to death in the scramble as the doors opened on their gig somewhere in Cincinnati. Yet again the fans had been queuing all night in freezing cold conditions and those at the front were at the most pressure not to relinquish their prime positions. So they hadn't eaten or been to the toilet – they hadn't even moved. They were weak, numb and possibly verging on hypothermia – so when the doors finally opened and the hordes behind them started charging in, their legs and bodies couldn't get moving fast enough. The people at the back hadn't been there as long – and if they had, they'd at least had some exercise, eaten and drunk. So they surged forward, those at the front just crumpled and the rest trampled over them. No one had learnt – and people died.

I'm happy to say, though, that we did take those lessons on board – and that's why there were no tragedies at Queen's massive NEC concert in Birmingham that Autumn, which I believe was the biggest standing indoor gig ever with an attendance of some 12,000. Again thousands of fans had queued all night - and we gave a lot of thought to planning things to take account of their weakened and distressed condition by the time the band came on. For one thing we'd arranged the barriers outside in a sort of zigzagged chicane, which meant that they couldn't charge straight through. Inside the hall, that measure was backed up my guys, whom I'd briefed very carefully. They lined the entrances to slow the fans down; if anyone tried to run through, they were stopped and told to slow down. That way, those who'd waited all night got the prime positions they deserved without a stampede and once the first thousand or two were safely in place the fans that followed were easier to keep calm because they knew the best places had already been taken. With no pressure, they just ambled in, in a civilised fashion with no trouble at all. You see it's all about recognising where the crisis points occur – and we knew that the riskiest of the lot is the moment the doors open. That's why, on many occasions, we'd get the doors opened quite a while before the advertised time.

DAVID AT THE RACES

When the chance came up to play a huge outdoor show at the Sydney racetrack, David jumped at the chance, being an avid racehorse aficionado and breeder and David, Gerry and I all went for an enjoyable day out combining a pre-gig recce with a bit of a flutter a couple of days before the day of the show.

Since it was a daytime gig in the height of the Australian Summer, there was no need (or any point) for the vast (and hugely expensive) banks of high-tech lighting you see at concerts these days. So the stage was a lot less elaborate than the purpose-designed show stages you see at places like Glastonbury these days. Come to that it was a lot less elaborate than the kind of thing you'd get at Wembley or White City in those days. Basically, it was just scaffolding – and I'm damn sure it wouldn't have met the safety requirements for a London gig. But I was still gobsmacked when, halfway through David's show, the stage seemed to join in the frenzied dancing and the whole thing began, visibly, to move as the sheer weight of the crowd pressed against it. Swaying sickeningly backwards and sideways like a building in an earthquake, it was downright bloody terrifying. But of course the fans were oblivious to the peril they were in, surging and crashing against the front in rolling waves that threatened to sweep the whole ramshackle construction off its shaky foundations. Heroically – but stupidly – some of the security guys were trying to get under the stage, trying pointlessly to prop it up. Suddenly envisioning another rock 'n' roll tragedy, I tried to stop them. 'If it's gonna go, let it go,' I roared, while at the same time wondering how the hell I could get David, his band and the full-on orchestra off the thing before it fell apart...But maybe there was another way. Stop the cause of the problem!! I rapidly gathered together as many guys as I could get hold of and positioned them in front – a human dam, to hold back the teenage tide. Somehow, they succeeded and we got through the show and the accident that had been waiting to happen wasn't allowed to happen.

David's Adelaide Stadium show proved to be just as hairy. It wasn't looking too good from the start – we arrived to find that the whole area had been severely flooded and the waters were still receding, leaving the entire ground floor of our hotel about a foot deep in water so that we had to wade through Reception to reach dry land at the stairs! But we'd obviously missed the worst of it because when we got to the stadium for the dress rehearsal, we found a massive tidemark right the way round – and it was a full eighteen feet up from where we stood. Now that's one hell of a flood! Otherwise, though, everything seemed OK and the show went ahead as planned...for a while.

As David emerged from the tunnel, through which the sportsmen would usually reach the pitch, my blokes and I surrounded him, protecting him from all sides as usual and setting a swift pace towards the stage. But suddenly David came to a halt, panic stricken, and tried to turn and dash back into the tunnel. Confused, we attempted to steer him forward...And then we realised. A mob of fans was hanging down from the seats over the top of the tunnel and some had got hold of him by the hair! With his hair being wrenched upwards, us pushing him forwards and himself fighting his way backwards he was lucky to get on stage with a hair left on his head – and I bet a few of those girls went home happy with a clump of those precious Cassidy auburn locks!

Halfway through the show, I was watching the audience from my usual position at the side of the stage when I saw a sight I'd hoped never to see again, one that sent cold shivers right down my spine. At the back of the stadium was a cantilevered stand, mobbed out with screaming kids. And, unbelievably, the whole thing was moving; it was swaying like a bush in a breeze! The consequences of it collapsing didn't bear thinking about and, with Bernadette Whelan's fate foremost in my mind I dashed frantically off the stage and got hold of the promoter and the police.
'Look at it!' I shouted at them. 'That stand's alive! The whole bloody thing's swaying about all over the shop!'
Amazingly they didn't seem very bothered.
'Oh, that's OK, no problem,' they breezed.
'Well it might be OK for us standing here,' I stormed back at them. 'But it's bloody well not OK for those kids on the stand. Call me old fashioned but I'm not really in the mood for watching a whole stand collapse at a David Cassidy concert and seeing hundreds of teenagers get crushed to death...I don't really fancy being part of that kind of thing – I'm funny like that!'

248

They muttered some rubbish about how they knew their stand and how much strain it could take – but I wasn't reassured.

'That's all very well,' I replied angrily, 'but it's designed for cricket fans, who all sit there quietly and clap politely. It ain't the same thing as thousands of hysterical little girls all jumping up and down in unison, believe you me! I think I'm going to have to take David off stage,' I went on, knowing that was the only way to get the kids to calm down. All I knew was that at least if I could get the kids to stop rocking, so would the stand!

At least that made the complacent promoters and plods respond – and they said they'd send some of their people over to check it out. But when they came back, it was with the same blasé attitude: 'We know our stand; it'll be fine!'

I wasn't happy, but I allowed the show to go on against my better judgement and, thank God, the stand stood up to the punishment as they'd said it would. Nevertheless I couldn't breathe easily until the show was over.

Scarier still was David's show at the Bellevue in Manchester. I was looking on as BBC TV presented Martyn Lewis was doing a piece to camera about the concert as he walked along an elevated walkway, when suddenly dirty great lumps of roof started raining down around him. Wondering what the bloody hell was going on, I looked up and – to my absolute horror – saw that the roof was straining under the weight of hordes of teenage girls! Never underestimate the superhuman ability of a star struck teenager! They'll do anything to get a bit closer to their idol – and this lot were risking their lives with gay abandon as they crawled across this rooftop to get into a section of the venue that was closer to David. With visions of horrendous carnage making me shudder I went charging up staircases, out of a fire escape and out onto the rooftop. It was only as I was standing there hauling the kids one by one back from the brink of disaster that it occurred to me that the appropriate response to this situation was to be downright bloody terrified!

Hang on a minute, I thought. If this roof goes I'm going down with it, and with all these kids on top of me!

Not a pleasant prospect. I've never been so terrified in my life. But somehow, with the help of some of my men, I managed to get them – and myself - off there and down to safety. It wasn't easy though. Trembling with fear as we were, we knew there wasn't any point in just telling these girls that the roof was going to collapse any second. In that hysterical state, all that mattered to them was David Cassidy. Death meant nothing whatsoever – and nor did injury. If these kids saw David on the other side of a busy main road they'd be off across it like bullets out of a gun. And they wouldn't care if there were a sixteen-ton truck bearing down on them. To them, at that time, it was totally irrelevant. So we had to physically grab them and manhandle them kicking and screaming off the roof – all the time struggling to stop hordes more of them climbing up there.

The moral of the story is that there's a lot more to security than having a few blokes standing about near the doors – which is all some of these half-arsed outfits used to do. It wouldn't surprise me if they're still as lax today. You've got to get a grip on the psychology of the crowd you're dealing with – and if you're not on top of that, you'll lose control, very probably with tragic consequences. That's why throughout my security career I made damn sure that the teeny bop idols such as Cassidy, The Bay City Rollers and the like were never seen by the fans in a situation where the kids could come to harm if they tried to get closer.

That's another thing people get arse about tit – they make the assumption that security's mainly for the artists' benefit. It's not! It's relatively easy to keep the artist safe – because he or she's surrounded by experienced, expert bodyguards. It's the kids you're really looking out for – or at least you should be!

With all that experience I thought I knew pretty much everything there is to know about security – but when we arrived in Japan with David, the way the police handled things was a real eye opener. At the airport I was horrified to see a sea of expectant faces waiting for David – there must have been three thousand of them, identical in their school uniforms and clutching pens and paper. That in itself was weird – all Japanese schools have the same uniform apparently, making them look like an army of clones! Well I could see no way of getting David through.

'There's no way I'm allowing David to go through there. There must be another way out of here!'

No there wasn't, they said. I was having none of it.

'Well what happened when The Beatles came through here then?' I demanded to know.

'They come through this way – no other way,' said one of the cops.

'Oh come off it,' I persisted. 'There's got to be. Are you going to risk the safety of all these kids by trying to get David through that lot? You can't just pile through three thousand screaming girls. Someone's gonna get hurt!'

But they were unmoved.

'We show you,' the cop said confidently.

'No you bloody well won't mate!' I chipped back at him indignantly. 'I'm not risking David's life – let alone all these kids!'

'No, we'll have no problem,' the guy insisted again. 'We have what we call "the truncheon,"' he added with a smile.

'Hold up a minute – did I hear you right? You're not thinking of beating your way through with a bloody truncheon are you? Are you bloody mad?'

'No, no, no,' he repeated. 'We show you.'

Well, I had no choice but to cooperate – against my better judgement. And I've never seen anything like it in my life! With the kind of efficiency that only the Japanese could muster, they formed up about thirty policemen into two parallel lines either side of Billy Francis, David and me. The ranks met at one end, making a sort of pencil shape. This, evidently, was what they called 'the truncheon'. Then, with Billy and I holding on to David at either side, the whole 'truncheon' started marching briskly forward, their thirty pairs of boots pounding the ground in unison with utter precision, sounding like a train. I couldn't believe it; in this 'truncheon' formation we cut through that crowd like a knife through butter. No one got near us and in minutes we were in the car and gone, the 'truncheon' now re-formed into a wall of cops between the car and the kids until we were safely out of sight. The organisation, the discipline, the machine-like regimentation...It was all absolutely amazing. I've never been so impressed before or since! They could teach our police a lesson or two about crowd control – and they prove that there's absolutely no need for the hysterical scenes you see at the airports in the UK when some star or other arrives.

Of course, when you're looking after a major star it's not just at the concert itself or the airport that security's an issue – you have to keep a constant eye on them, which is why I would usually take a room adjoining David's. As usual, I'd got a room with a communicating door to David's and Billy Francis had a similar arrangement on the other side – so our man was as safe as houses. Or at least so we thought until I heard this almighty banging on David's door and some bloke ranting and raving outside in the corridor.
'Come out! I know you're in there!' he was shouting. He was not a happy bunny.
Then it dawned on me what must have happened. Earlier, down in the hotel lobby a very attractive young woman was hanging about, evidently not with anyone, and even more

evidently with the serious hots for David. Nothing unusual about that – it would have caused more fuss to have found a bird that wasn't mad about David to be honest. So we thought nothing of it when she disappeared with David and went to his room. Now it seemed that she wasn't alone – and her husband was understandably upset that she'd buggered off with this international pop idol and was presumably doing what millions of other young women would have given their right arms (and probably their left arms and both legs and all the tea in China too) to do! I looked out of my door – and sure enough there was this guy, banging away on David's door like there was no tomorrow.

'What's up mate?' I asked innocently. As if I didn't know.

'I know my wife's in there!' he wailed. The poor bloke was absolutely gutted – and I can't say I blamed him. Bit of a tough one to live up to really, your wife getting off with one of the most sought after stars in the world! God knows how he'd found out she was in there – it wouldn't surprise me if she'd phoned him from David's room to taunt him with it. I've seen that happen and worse besides.

'No! You're mad mate! There's no one in there with him,' I said, all pally and soothing. 'Wait here a sec mate. I'll go and have a word with him,' I went on, tipping the wink

to Gerry, who'd appeared behind me. While I placated the bloke, who was now beside himself with jealousy, Gerry alerted David on the phone, nipped through the communicating door, plucked the bewildered babe from David's arms and, hushing her protests, hustled her through the communicating door into my room just in time for my entrance to David's room accompanied by the frenzied husband. 'Look, mate,' I was saying breezily, waving my hand at a suite inhabited only by a slightly dishevelled and bemused pop star, 'there's no one in here with him!'

Of course, while her husband was searching the wardrobes and the bathroom for his errant other half, she was off and out of my room like a shot, no doubt to get up to more mischief elsewhere. The husband never twigged. And, I must admit, we added to his humiliation by giving him a right old coating off for crashing the hotel, banging about the place and accusing us and our artist of all sorts of rubbish. He looked like a broken man by the time we let him get away. Poor mug!

When you're dealing with a man in as much demand as David was, you're bound to be party to all sorts of sexual shenanigans – and of all the incidents, one in particular springs to mind. On that same Japanese tour yet another gorgeous girl was making her intentions towards David more than clear – and Mr Cassidy was evidently in a playful mood. 'Let's have a bit of fun,' he said to me with a wink as he whisked her, hardly believing her luck, off to his room, along with Henry Diltz – a lovely and charming man – who was David's official photographer and who started taking a few shots of her and David.

Meanwhile, Gerry, Billy and I were in my adjoining room, looking on through the crack of the door that we'd unlocked and left just slightly open. We must have looked like a bunch of horny but oversized schoolboys, peering avidly through the tiny gap with me, the smallest at the bottom, Gerry leaning over me and Billy gaping over the top of Gerry. David and the girl were sitting on the bed, chatting and beginning to engage in a bit of gentle petting – nothing too naughty. Yet. Henry, permitted to remain there by virtue of his status as 'court photographer' and snapping happily away, said lightly, 'Hasn't she got a lovely figure David!'
'Yeah, she sure has,' murmured the appreciative Cassidy.
With that it took little persuasion to get her to expose her breasts, which were very nice, as all us onlookers agreed. Henry wasn't displaying a lot of the professional detachment you might normally expect of a seasoned photographer. Far

254

from it – he was ogling this pert pair and snapping away like his life depended on it, getting closer and closer...then closer still until his lens was virtually prodding the girl's boobs. We weren't that surprised – Henry was famously a 'tit man'. But we were surprised when he suddenly dropped all pretence of being interested in photographing her, leant forward and BIT HER NIPPLE!!!

Well, we fell apart, laughing till we cried. How we avoided being discovered I'll never know! I don't know if David could hear our stifled giggles but anyway he shouted loudly enough to drown us out.
' Henry! What the hell are you doing? You're mad! Get out of here!'
And with that Henry came to his senses – or at least he seemed to.
'I'm sorry, I'm sorry...' he burbled in the unusually gentle version of an American accent I'd come to love him for and that made him so forgivable, 'I got carried away.'
And the lovely thing about Henry, with his laid-back attitude and ponytail to match, was that you knew he meant it. Well, I say that, but as he retreated humbly he was still snapping away – almost compulsively, now I think about it. He just couldn't help himself. A tit man to the last and a photographer too, what else could the poor bugger do? Anyway, he kept backing away – towards the door...Well, you'd have thought so. But no. While David and the girl were otherwise engaged, shall we say, he slipped behind the luxuriant curtains that draped from ceiling to floor and, incredibly, kept right on snapping feverishly away.

In the adjacent room the three of us collapsed in spasms of suppressed laughter. We were writhing about on the floor in side-splitting agony – which only got worse as things hotted up in David's room when the poor girl proceeded on the mistaken assumption that Henry had shuffled out of the door.

She resumed the level of intimacy she'd reached before Henry's *faux pas* with considerable enthusiasm – but David was understandably distracted, knowing that Henry hadn't been the only voyeur and assuming that there were still three pairs of eager eyes out on stalks behind that door. It was clear that things couldn't go any further. He needed rescuing – and, wiping tears of laughter from my eyes I stumbled out of my room into the soberingly cold corridor lights. I rapped smartly on David's door – and he answered, clearly marshalling the acting talent that made him such a hit in 'The Partridge Family' to create an aura of total innocence and comply humbly with some spurious demand about some fake interview I'd come up with on the spur of the moment.

Politely and apologetically, David explained to the girl that this was an unavoidable commitment that his dutiful manager had brought to his attention and that there was no alternative to her leaving. Left with no choice she complied. And the second the door closed behind her and the three of us plus a humble Henry entered his room, David exploded into the laughter he'd been holding back for what had seemed like hours. He was streaming with tears.
'Henry! Henry!' he spluttered. 'I could not believe it – you bit her tit!!!'

Of course there was more than that – and worse. On David's tours and on all the others but most, I'm afraid, has to stay under wraps to protect the innocent – and the not so innocent. The fun and games pop and rock stars famously get up to when they're on tour may look outrageous, even a bit pervy, to the uninitiated. But what it comes down to is the fact that these people can't just go out for a drink like the rest of us – people like David were literally trapped in their hotel rooms by the fans outside. And that's why people make their own entertainment, push the limits of what they can get away with and generally piss about. And whatever you read in the press, I can tell you that there's almost never any malicious intent.

David had a serious side though. I've already mentioned how mature he was in outlook – and he was also just as caring and romantically inclined as his countless fans would have imagined him to be. One day I received a phone call. It was David.

'Don, I'm flying in from LA. Landing at six am. You've got to meet me!'

It sounded urgent, whatever the problem was.

'Sure,' I said and in the morning I picked him up at Heathrow, bursting to know what the mystery was. But even when he got into my motor Mr Cassidy wasn't giving much away.

'OK Don, we're going to the Westbury Hotel,' he said as if he was briefing me on a military operation. I put my foot down and headed back into the smoke and, as we sped along the Westway he finally smiled and turned to me.

'We're going to meet my future wife!' he stated.

Blimey I thought, he's a fast worker. I didn't even know he had a girlfriend. And I was a hell of a lot more impressed when he told me the name of his intended. It was only the fabulously gorgeous film star Kay Lenz!

'Bloody hell!' I said with feeling.

'But, Don, here's the thing. She's not expecting me...But it's her birthday and I've bought her a real special present. I want to surprise her – but I don't even know what room she's in...'

'Leave it to me,' I said, just for a change.

Now I began to see why he needed me with him so desperately. If you've ever tried to contact a major international celeb in a snooty hotel you'll know that you get short shrift if you don't have the room and probably the fake name they've registered under. Mind you, if you've got David Cassidy in tow it gets a lot easier – and anyway we'd stayed at the Westbury many times, so I knew the manager. Apologising for the ungodly hour of the morning I explained the situation, pointing out that David had just flown in from LA specially to surprise Miss Lenz. The manager thought for a moment and then gave me the room number.

I knocked on the door.
'Who is it?' a sleepy, muffled but familiar voice called out.
'Telegram Madame!' I chirped in my best mockney accent.
'Leave it outside will you...'
'Sorry Maam, I need a signature,' I replied officiously.
'One second,' came her reply.
The door opened, revealing to her the sight of David holding out a resplendent silver fox fur.
'Happy Birthday!' he beamed as she gazed, amazed and adoring, at him through tear-filled eyes.
With that I took my leave of the happy couple. It was the end of my little good deed for the day – and the beginning of a very happy chapter in David's life.

*   *   *

LOCH LOMOND FESTIVAL

When I was asked to go and recce the site for the Loch Lomond rock festival I turned up secure in the knowledge that I'd already been confronted with the worst security nightmare imaginable – and that I'd been right in thinking that was a non-starter. And the first thing I saw when I got there was an enclosure full of dirty great brown bears! I couldn't believe it. Here we go again, I thought.

Then I was told that the compound full of bears was to be used as the arena for the concert. The idea was that they'd move

258

the bears to another compound – but of course, if we wanted to give the site the once-over and check out the other compound we had to drive through the bears' area. Marvellous, I thought.

I should explain that the bear compound was (and presumably still is) secured by a double gate system – not that this gives you much comfort when you're looking at these huge great beasts through the fence! As you drive through the huge electrically operated gates at either end of the compound they quickly close behind you, leaving you in a sort of holding area behind another set of gates. Only when the big outer gates are secured will the inner ones let you through.

'Just go through this gate,' some bright spark said, 'and they'll let you through and you follow the road through the bear compound till you get to the gate at the other end. They'll let you out there, and that's where the arena's going to be.'
'Oh great. Fine. OK,' I muttered. This job seemed to be getting more dangerous the older I got. I'd survived dangerous criminals and gangsters, hysterical hordes of teenyboppers and drug-crazed rock stars and now it seemed I had to learn to be Lord of the bleedin' Jungle! I wasn't exactly comforted by the fact that the compound was disturbingly similar to a prison compound with its double gates at either side. Anyway, I could hardly refuse and soon, Gerry Slater, Mick Upham, Robbie Wilson (I believe) and I were driving through past the bears, two of which were copulating like, well like wild bears! I couldn't believe the frenzied way the male was going at it and how long it went on – like a pneumatic drill he was! I won't repeat the jokes we made on the subject – suffice to say that it was agreed that if he turned his amorous attentions our way one of us was going to have to be sacrificed to save the others!

259

Before long we pulled up at the gate at the compound's far end. But our exit was barred by about a dozen great big bears, casually laying around and relaxing on the road in front of us.

'How we going to get out?' I asked, not at all alarmed. Not a bit. Honest.

'Well someone's going to have to move them,' said the promoter calmly.

I didn't like the sound of that. I'd already seen how incredibly fast they could run! Well, guess who got the job of moving them. Yes, it was muggins Murfet!

Gingerly, I stepped out of the car. Immediately Mick, or one of the others pulled the door shut behind me. I opened it like a shot – that was my escape route! I took a few shaky steps towards the huddle of beasts. No reaction. Looking back towards the car for guidance I saw the promoter nodding in encouragement...Another few steps closer. One or two giant hairy heads turned in my direction, then turned back, unimpressed. Bloody hell, I thought. Here goes! And with that I started shouting my head off and waving my arms around like a teenybopper at a David Cassidy concert. And, would you believe it, the bears all legged it, lumbering away as placidly as a herd of cows! It was a proud Murfet the bear-tamer that climbed back into the car – and we drove through the two gates and got to the other side without incident.

Tickets weren't selling as well as they might be, and the promoter needed to give sales a boost. The night before the gig, there was to be an event in Glasgow that gave him the perfect opportunity: Celtic were playing Rangers – always a very big match - so he had the bright idea of getting hold of a couple of bear suits, for his people to wear to promote the concert at the football match. Meanwhile, all the roadies and lighting and sound technicians would carry on preparing the arena. Now, the site/organisers' office was a large Portacabin type hut and very late that night they were all in there having a drink after a very hairy day, unaware that it was about to get hairier, when suddenly the door was flung open. They all looked up expectantly to see who'd just turned up – to be horrified by the sight of a bleedin' great brown bear rearing up and roaring in the doorway! Well, you can imagine the response! The poor sods, drunk and knackered nearly crapped themselves and absolute mayhem erupted through that cabin, which got a lot worse when it dawned on them that that door was the only way out!. How none of them died of a heart attack I'll never know! Obviously, some bright spark had decided to put one of the bear suits on and give them all a fright – and I think it was a lot more effective than he thought it would be! That hut was full of a lot of very unhappy people – and the bear impersonator wasn't the most popular man on the site that week.

One of the problems with using an arena designed to keep dangerous animals in, was that it wasn't so good at keeping people out. First of all we had to get rid of a load of local kids who were camping on the hillside overlooking the arena so they could see the show for nothing. Working with a very tough and highly efficient Scottish security company, my guys went up into the hills and told them to sling their hooks without much trouble. But it was closer to home that the real difficulties arose. The fences were incredibly strong, being designed to stop bears getting out, like the steel mesh they use in reinforcing concrete floors and so on is the best way I can describe it. The top of the fence, about ten feet high I suppose, was rounded off by sheets of corrugated iron so that even if a bear scaled the inside of the fence, it could go no further. But the opposite was true for fans trying to sneak in over the fence. The wire was easy to climb up and the iron supports to which the corrugated iron was attached were just like the rungs of a very large ladder from the outside. Anyone could clamber up, dangle from the curved iron and drop down the other side. This was irresistible to anyone desperate to see the show – so we had the rangers patrolling the arena's perimeter throughout the eve of the concert.

Unfortunately, they weren't patrolling another identical-looking enclosure in which the bears had been placed for the duration. And that was the compound that a drunken fan mistakenly climbed into that evening! He broke an ankle dropping down from the top of the fence and lay there helpless among scores of dirty great brown bears. If the rangers hadn't heard his cries for help and come to the rescue I dread to think what would have happened to him.

You'd think everyone involved would have learnt their lesson about the danger of these bears – but no! The day before the gig, the promoter and a couple of guys were hanging around talking next to the bears' compound when one of the beasts charged at the fence and stuck its huge hairy, razor-clawed paws right through. Well, I've never seen a human face go so white so suddenly. Another near heart attack!

At one point, while I was having a walk round the site checking on things, my stomach turned over when my nostrils were assaulted by the most awful stench I've ever smelt. It didn't take long to track down its source: the rotting, fly-ridden carcass of a horse and a few other smaller corpses scattered around nearby. Rotting flesh has got to be the most nauseatingly hideous stink known to man and I couldn't take it for long. It turned out that this was how they fed the bears. They'd get whole horse carcasses from the knackers yard and dump them in the compound for the bears to tuck into when they felt like it. Well, of course you've got to feed the bears – but how they expected the punters to stand downwind of that all day I don't know. I mean the stench of festival toilets is generally hard enough to bear, especially back in those days, but rotting horses was beyond the pale!

All in all the promoters and their people were nice enough and very well-intentioned, but what with all the dangers it was a bit of a Mickey Mouse operation – possibly the worst-run festival site I've had the misfortune to work on. It was only by luck that no one got killed.

*   *   *

Talking of animals, we were doing a reggae gig at The Rainbow in Finsbury Park, which as I've mentioned before, is a beautifully ornate art deco theatre in North London where I'd worked with many famous acts at various times n (I think it's used by some sort of cultish religion these days – although you wouldn't know it to look at it because it's a listed building and they can't change its character, thank God. Or thank the local council, to be more accurate!). On the night in question though, I think it was Bob Marley. Anyway, in those days we used guard dogs – we had a pack of highly trained Alsatians.

Outside the main doors that led into the grand foyer was a heaving crowd – mostly Rastafarian, almost all black, reggae fans (this was before many white people caught onto the reggae thing) – pressing urgently up against the doors as my men and I stood guard on the inside, bracing ourselves for the moment they opened, dogs held securely on their leads. Well, at least most of them were! Just as we were about to unleash the crowds and let them in, I went over to have a word with one of the dog handlers whose dog wasn't on a sufficiently tight leash. Unfortunately for me, I was right to be concerned because the lead stretched just far enough for the animal to sink his teeth into yours truly! And guess where! In the worst place imaginable, that's where. Into the crown jewels of yours truly, that's where! Talk about agony! My excruciating pain was a pleasure for the hundreds mobbed outside. I think it excited them more than the show they'd come to see. If I could have sold tickets for the dog on bollocks incident I'd have made more than the promoter that day – they were laughing heartily and gesticulating at me through the doors. Call me old fashioned but I wasn't seeing the funny side. I was in absolute agony. Luckily the dog had missed my most vital bits – but even a quick sharp snap of an Alsatian's choppers in that general area is no picnic I can tell you!

But my agony aside, there was another reason for my being royally pissed off by the incident.
'What would have happened,' I said through gritted teeth to the evil mutt's handler, 'if that had been a punter?'
'Well I'd have had him on a tighter lead,' he had the balls to reply.
I was not impressed with that!
'You should have him on a tight lead the whole bloody time!' I rasped, hoping that I still had any balls at all. 'God forbid a punter walks past you when your concentration lapses for a second and that vicious mutt sinks his teeth into them!'

I should point out that we didn't use dogs all the time. Certainly not at kids' shows. Just ones attended by adults – say eighteen to early or mid-twenties – where we expected trouble. And to be honest we did break the rules at gigs like that. All fire exits, by law, had to be unobstructed – but we padlocked some of them because time and time again, people would work bits of wire or coat hangers through the gaps from the outside, hook the panic bars and open the doors and we'd be faced with thirty, forty, fifty uncontrollable punters, often armed with sharpened afro combs. And we didn't enjoy having to deal with that very much – we were funny like that!

264

We weren't blasé about safety though – when exits had to be locked we always stationed a man there just in case we had to get the audience out in a hurry. And of course we always kept a weather eye open in case the fire officer turned up – because he'd have stopped the show on the spot and revoked the venue's licence if he'd caught us!

It wasn't that the predominantly black gigs were necessarily worse than others – but it did make sense to make sure we had a lot of black guys and girls on the team for those shows. And we'd get them to do the rub-downs on everyone that came in. We weren't after their dope – although that's generally what they thought. We just didn't want people in there carrying lethal combs and knives with which other punters – and of course my blokes – might get stabbed! The trouble was that the black kids were the greatest objectors in the world – they complained about everything. I'm not being racist – that's just the way they were. I guess it was a cultural thing, but they were so determined to get round things and blag something somehow. For example, they'd show you their ticket and make some sort of a fuss in the process while another load of people snuck in elsewhere. So that one ticket could end up getting about twenty people in if you weren't careful. If you weren't aware of the scams they pulled, they'd show you that ticket and as soon as your eyes turned away, it would be palmed back to the next person. Actually it was absolutely fascinating to watch some of their moves – the sheer cheek was staggering. Even as we escorted Bob Marley and his crew into the venue through the stage door about fifty people tried to blag their way in with him, creating a crush outside the door. One of my men was waving at the crowd, trying to get them to move back, when a hand shot out of the mob, snatched his watch straight off his wrist and disappeared in a flash! We never even saw the culprit's face – just a fleeting glimpse of his arm and he was gone!

CHAPTER EIGHT

VARIOUS TIMES

PAYOLA AND OTHER SCANDALS

When you're dealing with hard men, gangsters, villains or just powerful people on the legal side of the fence, you have to remember one thing. Not every single last one of them, but certainly most people, however big and hard they are, have someone for whom they have total respect, or who they're scared of, or who's their guvnor! So when a situation like that crops up – where someone's getting very heavy – I always get in touch with people from the area they come from and find out who they are, what their true strength is and, most importantly, what are their weaknesses – and they always have at least one, I assure you!

Almost always, I find someone who knows the person concerned and who's much heavier than they are – and of whom they're scared. Once you've found the one they're scared of you phone them up and say I need you to have a word with so and so.

It was like that in the case of Don Black's brother and the BBC scandals back in the late sixties.

Before I launch into this particular story, I should probably explain the music business triumvirate that was the Black Brothers! Cyril Black worked for ScreenGems Columbia Music, which was one of the biggest music publishers at the time with the likes of The Monkees on their books. Now Cyril was just an ordinary guy, working as a music publishing executive and his rather more famous brother Don was renowned as the UK's top lyricists thanks to massive global hits such as 'Born Free', 'True Grit', 'To Sir with Love' and various James Bond lyrics written with John Barry among many others. Michael Black, the third Black brother, was a well-known promoter whose speciality was supplying clubs with cabaret artistes and who made the phrase 'Hello Son!' his personal trademark.

Anyway, when you're working with some of the top acts in the country, whether in a record company, publisher, management or agency, you can't help flaunting it a bit. And you do tend to attract a lot of attention - some of it from people you really shouldn't get mixed up with.

Cyril definitely had got the top stars. And he was definitely flaunting that fact! But you have to understand that he was getting calls from people like the BBC, ITV and all sorts of powerful media people, all of whom wanted some sort of favour from him.
...Can you get the Monkees for such and such show?
...Can you get us an interview with so and so?
...Can you get the Monkees to make an appearance at my party?
Those were the kind of requests a guy like that was getting - and often fulfilling - on an hourly basis. Talk about being in demand! So you can understand it, really, when he gets a bit carried away and perhaps gets a little bit above his station...And that, I think, marked him out as a potential victim for the vultures who circled the rich pickings of the music business. Namely the News of the World, on this occasion.

The News of the Screws, somewhat hypocritically, I might add, had decided that they were going to expose corruption in the music business. Now I don't know about you, but that particular exposé was hardly news to me!

Here's what the bastards did. They rented a very sumptuous flat just off Park Lane – probably the most expensive part of London's West End – and fitted it out with hidden cameras and state of the art recording and surveillance equipment. In this little Park Lane palace they ensconced two guys purporting to be extremely rich men (farmers, or something like that, I think) who had discovered an incredibly beautiful and talented girl singer.

They would invite likely targets from the music business to their apartment to hear their 'discovery's' demo tapes and see her photographs. And, to a man, they were impressed. She was an absolute stunner – the kind that made your eyes pop out. And then they'd hear the recordings, which were awesome, leaving no doubt in their minds that here was a real star – not so much in the making as already made. All they would have to do, it seemed, was sell her! What they didn't know, of course, was that the photos of this goddess were of a model they'd hired specially, that the voice on the demos was that of a top session vocalist they'd recorded earlier and that the whole thing was one big scam!

Of course, you can imagine how they approached someone like Cyril to approach in turn a couple of unfortunate BBC producers. They simply lured Cyril to the flat with the (amply fulfilled) promise of unstinting quantities of Champagne and caviar and, I'm sure, less respectable indulgences. Once he'd seen the voluptuous photos and heard the demos of the putative star Cyril was quickly convinced that here was a girl who could make it – with or without their help. The two fake rich boys went on to say that they had more money than they knew what to do with and that they effectively wanted to 'buy her a hit'.

268

You can imagine what went through the victims' heads: She's going to make it anyway. And if these guys insist on giving us money to make her a star, who are we to turn it down? It would almost be rude not to help them. So, yeah, we'll have some of this!

Having agreed to ensure that this girl got a hit record, Cyril, the producers and the top DJs they needed to involve to guarantee the airplay the record would need to succeed, found themselves being entertained in a style that was decadent even by the heady, hedonistic standards of the 'swinging sixties'. They partied with the likes of Janie Jones, the notorious high class call girl, and at those parties they were plied with plentiful booze and sex (and the rest!) in a determined attempt to loosen their tongues along with their morals.

Of course the record sounded so good and the photos looked so good that the DJs would have happily played the girl's record if they'd been asked to do so merely as a favour without any of that rigmarole. But that wasn't the point. The aim of this nasty little game was to stitch up Cyril and co and all the DJs. And it succeeded! The single was played – in fact it got quite an impressive amount of airplay. And then, inevitably, the News of the World blew the whistle and exposed everyone they'd embroiled in their plot.

An enormous hue and cry broke out, and the ensuing 'Payola' scandal pumped out by the press implicated BBC producers and DJs in taking bribes and sexual favours in return for airplay and other services. Of course there was a court case. Jack Dabbs was sacked – but it was Cyril who took the worst of the flak because he'd been up at that Park Lane penthouse apartment so much, giving it the big one, inadvertently mentioning names on tape and implicating God only knows how many people in the scandal. One name I do know he mentioned was that of Johnny Walker, the disgraced Radio One DJ (who's now back at the Beeb!).

'Oh yeah, I'll just bung Johnny a few quid and he'll do it all right – he'll do anything for me!'

That was the kind of thing they taped him saying – and much more besides. Poor sod was only showing off. But that didn't help him much when it all came out. When the integrity of half the music business was called into question, it didn't take long for the victims to look for someone to blame. All these DJs had managers and agents and other associates – and they were all now in the frame for high level corruption, buying singles into the charts and worse. So they were steaming! They were livid! And someone was going to pay. Of course they all went for the bloke they thought had set them up - and that was poor old Cyril, whose name had been liberally sprinkled over the News of the World's tawdry stories, more because of his naïve bragging than because he'd been instrumental in causing the shit to hit the fan. He was utterly and completely lambasted!

Guess who got a call from Don Black about that particular nightmare? Yes, it was good old Don Murfet!

'Look Don,' he said, 'I've got this BIG problem.'

And he went on to tell me the whole story and the names of the people involved.

'They're going to hurt Cyril. I just know they are. He's my brother and I don't want anything to happen to him...Can you help me Don?'

I made a few calls and found out what their game plan was and who was the guv'nor of whom. And, as luck would have it, I knew one of them quite well – so I arranged to meet him.

'You can't hurt Cyril,' I said.

'What d'you mean I can't fucking hurt him. Of course we're gonna hurt him. He's ruined a lot of people's lives,' he fumed at me.

270

He had a point, I suppose – but I had mitigating circumstances to offer.

'Yes – but look, just because he's got diarrhoea of the mouth it doesn't mean it's all his fault. The poor sod was set up. You should have seen the way they set him up – it wasn't an amateur job! Who's to say you wouldn't have fallen for it? If they'd filled you full of alcohol and God knows what else, you'd probably have shot your mouth off to microphones you didn't know were there!'

He muttered and grumbled, unconvinced. I went on with my defence.

'Come on, put yourself in his place. He's all pissed up, high and completely relaxed and – yes – he was bullshitting, inventing things...Everyone does it sometimes. He was boasting his little head off because he couldn't have known he was dropping anyone in the shit!'

Still he was unconvinced.

'No, no, no. That's not good enough. We're under a spotlight and it's all coming on top. We've lost valuable contacts; we've been squeezed out of all the action...Nope. It's just not got enough,' he repeated, as if I hadn't already got the message.

'Look it's happened. None of us can change that,' I said, quietly but very firmly. 'And I'm very sorry mate, but you can't just make Cyril your scapegoat. For a start, it's not all down to him by any means. And anyway, Cyril's under my protection. We're going to be minding him, so whoever you send after Cyril will have to go through my people. And you know what that means...'

He nodded and muttered something unintelligible again. I took it to mean he was beginning to see my point.

'It means a war!' I continued, emphatically and with what I hoped was a certain amount of menace. 'And over what? Fuck all – that's what!'

There was a long, weighty silence. I held his stare, literally open handed now that my cards were on the table.

'All right. All right,' he grated resentfully. 'We'll leave him alone. I don't like it. In fact I hate it. I wish we could get to the little git and hurt him but we won't do it because – yeah, you're right – we don't want to have a war with you and your boys. There's been enough damage done,' he added with a resigned sigh.

And he was as good as his word.

I got onto Don Black the first chance I got.

'It's all right Don – Cyril's going to be OK. He's protected. But for Christ's sake make sure he doesn't do anything silly. Tell him not to talk to anyone else at all about any of it – nobody! Tell him to just keep his head down and keep his mouth shut! As long as he does that he's not going to get damaged – I can promise you that,' I lectured, quite sternly to make sure that Don would communicate the seriousness of the situation to his brother.

'Thanks a lot Don,' the great songwriter Don breathed with relief.

'But anyway, although as far as I'm concerned it won't happen, I suggest that both of you make sure you watch your backs from now on!' I added, just to drum into him the real risk that if Cyril opened his big mouth again, my protection would go out of the window – and, very probably, so would Cyril.

And nothing did happen to Cyril – at least nothing violent. I had a few words with a few other people and gradually the whole thing just seemed to melt away.

Of course it wasn't in my power to intervene where Cyril's career was concerned. Basically he was finished in the music business – and any other for all I know. I'm sure having your name plastered all over the gutter press as the perpetrator of major fraud and the receiver of sexual favours from a renowned prostitute doesn't look all that good on one's

272

executive curriculum vitae! So, inevitably, I suppose, Cyril got out of the country – he didn't have much choice. And that was a shame because he was, and still is, I expect, a lovely guy – as were all three Black brothers.

It was also a terrible shame that this nice bloke had to be the victim of those conniving bastards who set up the whole vindictive scam. It was a classic 'honey trap' – and I'd challenge almost anyone to resist what was on offer. I mean, it's one thing catching someone with their pants down, as it were. But it's a very different thing spending vast amounts of money and effort seducing people into compromising situations and then having the gall to vilify them for falling for it. As far as I'm concerned the name that came out of that whole scandal deserving the most shame was that of the perpetrator: the News of the World.

*   *   *

A similar scenario happened with a very senior executive from Bell Records who began an affair with a young lady who, unbeknown to him, was already involved with some gangster. The cuckolded mobster, of course, found out and, of course again, issued this Bell executive with some seriously scary threats. And guess who he called. Yep – me again!

I got a secretive, panicky call asking if I could get right down to the Bell offices – which I did. On arriving, I was ushered with quiet urgency into this executive's office. He stuck his head out of the door, scanning the reception area to make sure no-one suspicious was in sight, and closed the door behind me with a rapidity that told me just how scared he was.

'What am I going to do Don?' he asked me, the strain shifting his voice up by about an octave. 'I'm married for Christ's sake...I haven't got a way out...'

'Slow down. Calm down,' I interrupted. 'Give me the name of the guy that's threatened you and I'll find out just how strong he is and I'll see what I can do.'

Sure enough it was another bully. No-one I thought was much of a problem – just some bloke who was trying to throw his weight about because he'd found out that his bird was playing around. You can probably guess the next sentence. Yes, I made a call to another very good friend of mine – in this instance, Harry Hayward who was a very well-known character in South London.
'Do know this guy, Harry?' I said.
'What that fucking mug? Yeah I know him all right!' he said with more than a touch of venom.
'Well, Harry, he's giving a friend of mine a very hard time and I'm not happy about it...' I started. But Harry cut in like a shot.
'He's just an idiot Don...He's full of shit – you don't want to worry about the likes of him!'
The thing was, of course, that it wasn't me who was worried.
'Yeah, if you say so Harry. But it's not me. He's frightened my mate – and I don't know him from Adam (no pun intended – this was long before Mr Goddard came on the scene!) So will you make a little call for me?'
Harry was more than enthusiastic. He obviously wasn't keen on the little toe rag. So much for him being this big gangster! I thought.
'Yeah, yeah, yeah – I'd love to give the little git a coating!' he said with relish.

And that's exactly what happened. Not long afterwards, Harry called, his voice still crackling with sheer satisfaction at whatever it was he'd said or done to the offending wannabe gangster.

274

'It's sorted Don. Don't even give it another thought. He won't be making any threats to your mate again. That's history now. Done. Finished. Put to bed.'

'Thanks very much mate. I appreciate it. I owe you.'
'No you don't you silly sod,' he said – bless him. 'It's just a little favour I've done for you, that's all. No problem. You can do me a favour sometime in return!'

In fact, that's how business was done – in my world at least – most of the time. Mind you, I'm not saying that every nightmare scenario could be sorted out as quickly and easily as that – far from it. Of course there are times, and there have been many in my personal experience, when someone's about to be physically hurt for some reason, or is about to have his marriage or career ruined for some reason and no-one can do a thing about it. It's nothing to do with whether the person on the receiving end deserves to be threatened – it's just that sometimes nobody has the power with the right people or in the right place to help. I have to say, though, that nine times out of ten, when friends and friends of friends have come to me for help, I've found someone with the strength and the will to come to the rescue. When the shit hits the fan, you just can't put a value on the friends and contacts you've made over years and years in the business: they're priceless.

I often thank my lucky stars for those contacts – because few other people have that kind of help when something really nasty happens. Once, while David Cassidy was at his peak as the undisputed god of teenybopper pop he found himself being blackmailed. Now, the obvious response to blackmail, which is after all a serious, and very nasty, crime, would be to go to the police. But the trouble with blackmail is that, by definition, it means that the victim has something to hide. In the case of an international superstar the implications are

275

multiplied a hundredfold – even if they're being blackmailed for something everyone else would find fairly innocuous. Having an affair with a woman, for example. When you're not even married! It's no scandal – but when you're supposed to be squeaky clean, as all the new boy bands have found out, the slightest hint that you're a normal guy with normal urges is enough for the press to slaughter you!

Unfortunately for the girl concerned, my company, Artistes Services, was looking after David at the time and when he asked for help I shot straight over to Richmond, where he was staying, and got him to give me the low-down. I dug up a bit of history about the girl – and the fact that there was a history worth unearthing says a lot about the spuriousness of her blackmail claims. A couple of us paid her a visit and told her the facts of life in our world – as opposed to hers. And that was the end of it!

That kind of thing has happened to me on numerous occasions with many, many people. People share their problem with you and, to them, it's utterly insurmountable. They simply can't see a way out of it.

But, more often than not, it isn't insurmountable and I've found a way to deal with it. And usually, I've managed to convince the person threatening or blackmailing a friend or a friend of a friend that they'd be better off forgetting their nasty little scheme and finding some other mark.

There's all sorts of corruption in the music business – even today, I'm sure. But in those days it wasn't run by accountants and financiers as it is these days. It was creative people who were in charge and made things happen, whether they were managers, A&R people or producers – people whose background was in music and the business of music. Unlike the hard-nosed accountants today who look at top

276

talent and only see the bottom line and keep everything on a tight financial rein, the 'Artist Liaison' people were let loose on London with their own credit cards and expense accounts. And they used them to the full! They just loved taking the artists out to dinner, lavishing them with anything their hearts desired and introducing them to so and so who could do them a great video or such and such who'd be great to produce the next album and so on and so on. In short, there were more kickbacks going on than in a rugby match. For example, you'd get someone to direct a video for so much money and you'd add a few quid (and by that I mean more than a few!) on top for everyone who put the director and the band together – and the band and the director, come to that! In fact, I have to admit, I've done it myself with my car company. The Osmonds were staying at a house in Surrey that we'd found for the record company – which was a nice little earner for my company because, in addition to charging them for scouting for suitable and secure locations, we were contracted to handle their security. I might add that security for the Osmonds at the height of their fame was not a trivial job!

Anyway, I submitted the outline costs for the whole project to the guy at the record company. He didn't seem startled by the amount. But I was startled by his response!

'Can you stick another couple of grand on for me?' he enquired as if it was the most reasonable request in the world. 'Because I want to buy a boat.'

'Oh I see,' I said, trying to look unperturbed. 'Fine. Well it's up to you isn't it. I'll tell you what our price is - you tell me what you want me to invoice!'

And that's how it went on. I'd invoice him what we wanted for the job plus his outrageous kickback. He'd sign it off and smooth the invoice's way through accounts and get a cheque paid to us pronto and we'd give him his rake-off in cash. It became a regular, quite normal way of doing things from the top executives copping that kind of backhander from the likes of us to the lowly A&R boys taking their families or the latest bird they'd pulled out for a no expense spared slap-up dinner at somewhere chic and far from cheap like the White Elephant (more of which soon), after which the beneficiaries of the record company's generosity were miraculously transformed on the expenses sheet from the humble mister and missus A&R man's mum and dad to David Cassidy or Donny Osmond or whoever else was flavour of the month!

Talking of the White Elephant...I became quite well-acquainted with the owner, whose daughter, incidentally, was married to the famously gravel-voiced, rock with a capital 'R', Radio One DJ Tommy Vance. Her son, it transpired, was not so settled – and was more than a bit wayward in fact. He had got himself in trouble with some drug dealers. She was very worried and, as people tend to do, she asked me for help. I met her at her Curzon Street restaurant. And, over dinner, she told me the story, which wasn't an entirely new one to me, although it was very clearly a great shock to her.

Her understandably naïve version of events was this.

He'd got involved in drugs and had been coerced by a so-called friend into going to meet these dealers to score a very serious amount of gear (in this case I believe it was hash or grass). So far so good. But the moment he pulled out his frighteningly large wad of cash and the dope was banged down on the table, the place was raided by some mob that snatched the money and all their stash! The dealers then turned very nasty, accusing the boy of having brought in these people to rob them and demanding that he paid them for all the lost drugs. Of course, he'd lost every penny he had in the 'raid' he didn't have the money to pay them – and they were threatening him with all sorts of terrible damage if he didn't cough up!

278

Of course I knew what was really going on.

It had to have been the dealers who'd set him up – and the 'friend' who'd convinced him to get involved in the deal had to be working with them. The 'raid' was a put-up job by their own people so that they could screw this little rich kid for the price of their entire stash and keep all the gear to sell elsewhere – or to run the same scam again and again.
Because if he couldn't pay, they knew Mummy and Daddy would cough up once they knew what might happen to him. At least he had had the sense to own up to his mother – God alone knows what they'd have done to him if he hadn't! His mother was no fool though and, having made some attempts to resolve the situation, quickly realised that she was out of her depth and came to me for help. Understandably, she didn't want to get the police involved because, obviously, her son would get nicked. But she felt she had little alternative and she was ready to call the cops if that would save her son from God-knew-what at the hands of these extremely nasty people. I assured her that it wasn't only the police that could save him. I interrogated her, as gently as I could, to get as much information out of her as possible. And then, using the facts I'd gleaned, I did my usual thing and made a series of calls in which I pieced together a better picture of these guys. It transpired that they operated out of a squat off the Finchley Road just north of the station.

So I went down there with some of my men and staked it out. We checked out every aspect and every detail of the building and established exactly how many people were in there. And it turned out that it was a nicely run outfit, with lookouts posted at strategic points and a steel reinforced door and so on. Credit where credit's due, these guys knew what they were about.

Unfortunately for them, though, it just happened that just upstairs from my office at the NOMIS complex in Sinclair Road, W14 was an outfit called Short Associates, which had strong ties to the SAS and many former SAS men on their payroll – all of whom were happy to work freelance for me because I didn't do things by the book! As far as they – and I – were concerned, the end justifies the means – and if that means working outside the law then so be it. You got quicker and more permanent results that way!

Even worse for our opponents, money wasn't a problem for the owner of a restaurant as exclusive and prohibitively expensive as the White Elephant. In effect I had *carte blanche* as long as the outcome was that we saved her son.

'Here's the problem,' I said to my team, 'and here's what we have to do...'

I went on to explain the job in detail and it was one they were happy to get their teeth into – and not just for the money!

With the best trained, most professional and, frankly hardest, blokes in the world on your team you don't go charging in like a bunch of thugs – that would be a shocking waste of talent. No – we watched that squat patiently for about a day and a half to establish the patterns of their day and found out the time when most of the gang would be inside. At the appointed time we walked brazenly up to the front door and knocked loudly.

'What d'you want,' said a voice through the letterbox.

'I need to speak to Tony,' I said calmly.

'Errrr...Why?' came the response, suddenly a touch less cocksure.

'Because you've made a serious error. You've set up and stitched up someone that we're looking after. I'm just telling you now that it's all over.'

'Nah...You've got nothing,' the voice sneered.

'Tell you what I have got, son,' I said, momentarily reminded for some reason of Michael Black's signature phrase. 'I've got some seriously professional men out here and quite a lot of cans full of petrol. We've got the whole building covered and if you don't agree to leave my friend alone we're going to torch the place and sit outside and watch you burn.'

No response this time. All I could hear through that letterbox was the owner of that cocky voice and his cohorts scrambling like their lives depended on it (and they did) for an escape route. Of course they didn't get far. That Shakespearian phrase 'Hoist by his own petard' comes to mind – because they'd fortified the place quite impressively against the police raiding them and busting in. Which of course made it quite hard to get out. When they did get out of the back doors, they were confronted by several shadowy figures emerging from cover and striding purposefully towards them. What's that slogan they put on the T shirts? Don't mess with the SAS! Well these guys didn't. They scurried back into that squat even more rapidly than they'd scuttled out. So now they were caught like the proverbial rats in a trap – or should I say prats in a trap?

They were utterly terrified – as well they might be.

'Let me see the petrol can,' the letterbox man said.

'Hello again – you've come back. How nice to talk to you again!' I said.

No answer.

'That was only one can – we've got plenty more out here...' I continued.

Silence.

And we know you've got no phones in there. No-one's gonna help you...' I persevered.

I could hear movement in there – a bit of scrabbling. Then silence. And then there was a rustling sound. What are they doing in there? I thought. Then I realised – it was the sound of feverish, fervent, frightened whispering. A hurried and

281

hushed conference was in progress. I turned and winked at any of my hidden colleagues who might be able to see. It's working, the wink said. And I hoped it was true. I decided to push my point home and pressed my mouth against the letterbox.

'If you think,' I hissed, 'that you can rip off someone we know and then try and threaten them, beat them up, torture them or blackmail them to get money out of them, you've picked on the wrong people. Go and find some other mugs to fuck around because you're out of your league.'

Letterbox man made some vague attempt at retaliating but I shouted him down.

'You thought you were picking on some little rich boy who'd stump up some dosh the moment you got heavy – but you don't know the meaning of heavy. I'm here because his mother's way too loaded to give money to little wasters like you lot. She doesn't have to because she's very, very rich and she can afford to pay me and my team for as long as it takes to put a stop to the likes of you.'

Silence. So I carried on.

'And she wants this stopped tonight. So we are going to stop it. Either you're going to leave him alone and promise us that's the end of it, right now, or we're going to torch the place. Or we could just come in and beat you up – but that would be letting you off lightly wouldn't it!'

No comment – other than what I'd swear was a whimper.

'So I think, on balance, we'd rather just burn you to the ground – we haven't got a problem with that. I mean, it's just a squat isn't it. And you've had an accident. Oh dear, they'll all say...Never mind...No-one will give a toss!'

To say they were terrified would be a massive understatement. There was nothing they could do. They couldn't get out because we had the place surrounded – and anyway, their defence measures made it as hard to get out as

282

it was to get in! We could literally smell their fear – and I'm not exaggerating.

It was a very strange experience, conducting a conversation with a letterbox in the middle of London at the dead of night – but it worked, and that was the end of it.

Again, this episode illustrates how my way of doing things can be quite a good idea. I'm not saying I can solve anything – but at least in cases like this we could ensure that the bloke who'd got himself in trouble was made safe and his mother's mind put at ease without either of them getting in any bother with the police, who, I might point out, would certainly not have provided the bloke with any protection even if he had gone to them!

Let's face it, people like those drug dealers are outside the law in the first place. They don't even believe in the law. So the threat of the law means next to nothing to them. They're only vulnerable to their own kind – to people who work to the same code of ethics as they do. When they single out someone and intimidate them – someone who's not of their world; someone whose only source of protection is the police, they know that whatever happens the police aren't going to watch over their victim twenty-four hours a day. And they know that the police aren't going to come after them and smash them to pieces. But when they find they've picked on someone whose mother has real power (for power, read money) – then, they get scared. Because she was in a position to show them a level of power that was way out of their league – and it frightened them. And it worked. Because we would do whatever was necessary to stop them – and they knew it!

Some might say that kind of power's not big or clever – but any time you need that kind of back-up, I can assure you, you will think it's big, clever and wonderfully effective! Let's just say, by way of example, that someone very rich and powerful is about to sue you for a large sum of money – money you haven't got. One hundred, two hundred grand or maybe a lot more. It doesn't matter what the scale is – let's assume it's a fortune as far as you're concerned and that they've got you by the balls. And then they start squeezing. Well that's the position several people I've known have found themselves in – and what I've said to them every single time is this:

'Look, if these people are threatening you and are going to ruin you financially and they're doing it with malicious intent, knowing they've got you by the balls...Or at least you think so and so do they, there is another way. Don't let them drive you mad – for about ten grand you can have them put down. You might make them stop – but even if you can't and you're going to lose your money anyway, why not spend a few quid and inflict some severe punishment on them. After all, if you're going down, you might as well get some fun out if it – at least you get the last laugh knowing it hurt them very badly to hurt you! And as long as it's done professionally there'll be nothing to link you with what happens – no-one can prove that you had anything to do with it.'

BOOK SIGNINGS AND OTHER STRANGE HAPPENINGS

We also used to provide security for book signing events too – and some very unusual ones at that. At Chappell's of Bond Street we handled security and crowd control for Margaret Thatcher's book signing and Ted Heath's too (the former Prime Minister, not the band leader). A particularly weird one was President Archbishop Makarios's appearance at the Rainbow Theatre, where we were on very familiar ground but extremely unfamiliar territory – Makarios was a very hot political potato in the uproar about the Turkish invasion of

284

Northern Cyprus at the time. He was appearing in Finsbury Park because there's such a large Greek population in North London and it was a very different kettle of fish managing crowd control of a politically motivated mob rather than teenyboppers or rock fans – and again we were working closely with Special Branch. In essence, the brief was the same as if we were working for someone like David Cassidy. We had to make sure Makarios got into and out of the venue unscathed – and as I've mentioned before, I'm a bit of a whiz in that department. The big difference was that we were used to protecting people from people that loved them – this time the threat was people who hated him! It didn't help matters that Makarios wasn't young and agile like most of our charges – on the contrary his altogether more sedate pace and dignified demeanour meant that we had to re-think our timings completely to effect a safe exit. We were doubly aware that while it had to be 100% effective, our security operation couldn't look oppressive – so we compensated by doubling the layers of protection. This, I reckoned would buy us vital time should anything unpleasant occur. Luckily, and I believe partly thanks to our security strategy, the whole event passed off without incident.

CHAPTER NINE

A LITTLE ABOUT VOLUME TWO

I hope you enjoyed the stories here in the first volume, if you did then I thought you might like to know a little bit about the next book. Having lived and worked as I did throughout these eras, then it's a surprise if I don't mention my time with bands like the Beatles, the Osmonds, and the Bay City rollers.

Truth is that for a lot the artistes I worked with it was a day to day routine and often without a chance to get to know each other properly. I don't want to be judged as a name dropper like the authors of some recent autobiographies who claim to have been here and there and done this and that with such and such a legend. All I can say is whom I worked with and how I found them.

Several years working with The Beatles and the NEMS Organisation (or Disorganisation) were the source of many stories, which will be in the next volume along with further adventures with Peter Grant, whom I knew for thirty years, and with Led Zeppelin and Peter's other groups. I'll also talk about the times I met Michael Jackson and the phone call from America one evening that led to my setting up the world's biggest security company, specialising in show business and mainly, but not exclusively, the music business.

I will tell how my current battle is one that I can't win – for I have Multiple Myeloma, which is cancer of the bone marrow. It is an ongoing to keep it under control while still trying to lead a normal life.

Coming from a family of four brothers and five sisters and being the second eldest was I suppose always saying 'leave it to me' even in the early years during which I remember doodle bugs and V1 rockets rearranging the local scenery. Because I didn't have what the business calls 'good ears', the reliance I placed on my wife and children's ears proved fortuitous on many occasions in judging the merits of groups; my own technique was based on carefully studying crowd reactions and keeping up with inside knowledge

286

from the business. When working at concerts I was more at home backstage, front-of-house, in the VIP enclosure and sometimes side-of-stage – not to watch the act but as a vantage point from which to watch for crowd trouble, check that my men were working and not watching the show and, of course, to see if I could pick up any business.

Despite going on many guided tours that your average tourist would sell their mother for including a tour of the Kennedy homes and many other famous places I was always working so when there was a story to be remembered it was itself very special as it was all work

I was, and probably continue to be, an opportunist at heart, and from that crime was a natural progression. At first this was out of necessity because when I was very young we were a very poor and large family (ten children and no father) but as life and work developed crime became a challenge in itself because I had been framed by the police very early on and wanted too show them what a good learner I was. I never got involved in armed robberies, any form of housebreaking or violence. My activities were well-organised and planned and very little was left to chance. The thrill of the challenge was my prize; the money was the reward for all the planning involved.

All I can say is I hope you had a chuckle and the occasional more serious thought while you have read volume 1.

Wishing you all the best

Don Murfet

Acknowledgements

First and foremost to my wife June and my children Bradley, Gregg and Lyndsey for all their support, encouragement and assistance.

To Kevin Saunders for making sense of my manuscripts and tapes and producing this finished copy and Jonathan Miller for putting it all together and making it happen.

To Allan Ballard for his wonderful photos and input.

To Dr Oxley and Dr Al-Refaie and their fantastic team, who treat me and their other patients with dignity and care and keep my cancer under control.

To all my close friends, who kept pushing me to write a book of my life – I hope you're happy now because there will be three, possibly four, more volumes and even then I'm sure some events will be lost in the clouds of time!

To all the stars and their associates, record companies, lawyers, press, security staff, fans, the police, the villains, the nice people and the horrible people in the music business, because they all contributed something to making it a memorable life. And it's a life in which I can honestly say I've never been bored, even for a day.

Special thanks to Dave Payne, Sid Sofos, Linda and Ben Hatherall, Mick Upham, Gerry Slater and Roxanne Cahill.

And there's more! The following is a list, with no sense or order or importance, of people I've worked with over the last forty-odd years, many of whom were involved in some way in some of the stories. I will do my best to give them all credit throughout this and the coming volumes where possible but I want them all to know that I haven't forgotten them. They were all part of my life – mostly good; a few bad.

At the time of going to the printers these names were the ones I could remember but as I research my notes and files for the other volumes I'm sure that many more will come to mind and I'll add them to this list in the forthcoming books. I haven't mentioned artistes and VIPs because they'll all get a mention somewhere, however brief, but only if I have something to say about them that will interest the reader!

Barry Dickens, Harvey Goldsmith, Dee Birchmore, John Curd, Richard Cole, Rex King, Benjy Le Fevre, Rick Hobbs, Matthew, Roger Holt, Andy Wishart, Matthew Freud, Billy McKilroy, Ian Wright, Patsy Collins (deceased), Alexis Grower, Mick Upham, Gerry Slater, Sid Sofos, Mick Jackson, Paddy 'The Plank' Callaghan, Wally Gore, Jim Callaghan, Fred 'Fat Fred' Basset, Danny Fielding, Ray Washbourne, Brendan Cahill, Linda Irons, Ben Hatherall, Dave Payne, K.C., Dave Moulder, Barry Murfet, George Murfet, Bob Maxey, John, Ron and Terry Franklin, Billy and Danny Francis, Paul Morreta, Harry Haywood, Annette Kay, Ray Robinson, Norman Slater, Terry McLellan, Roy, Randy Bentwick and Kris, Alfie Weaver, Michael Jackson (deceased), Bernie McKenzie, John Charles (deceased), Derek Kozlowski, Peter Gerrard, John and Paul Bettie, John Ferguson, Peter Abbey, Dave Beeching, Maurice Oberstein, Vic Lewis, Don Black, Lenny McLean, Stuart and Lorraine Page, Laz, Chris Iyocoumi, Tim Poulton, Eddie Faulkner, Jay Cooper, Sparky Tavares, Alistair Taylor, Peter Davis, Mike Rutt, Dave Barry, Arthur Edwards, Vince, Robbie Wilson, Ted Cheek (deceased), Ron and John Wise, Frank Westall, Alan Chandler, Stephen Chandler, Barry Clark, Jerome and Roy, Ken Wall, Ron the Dog, Shaun Jacobs and Steve, Carl Isaacs, Eddie Ramsey, Martin Lee, Ralph Haemns, Michael Kyriacou, Roy Lewendowski, Jimmy Wise, Pete the Meat, Ted Studman, Jack Clark, David Tomlinson, Byron Lake, Bobby Onions, Philip Neophytou, Brian Harding, John White, Cecilia, Theresa Vickery, Peter Chant, Carol Caplin, Stephanie Gluck, Mike Mansfield, Hilary Tipping, Hilary Stewart, Derek Witt, David Bridger, John, Pat and Bill Harley, Dee Murray (deceased), Paul Staples, Dave Whiting (deceased), Michael Bradshaw, Anita and John Bly (deceased), Mike Ranger, Cosmo, John Hoy, Christine and David Cobbold, Mike Goode.

Cover design & internal layout by David Stockman –
www.irreality.biz